RITES OF JUSTICE

The Sacraments and Liturgy
as Ethical Imperatives

Megan McKenna

ORBIS BOOKS

Maryknoll, New York 10545

The Catholic Foreign Mission Society of America (Maryknoll) recruits and trains people for overseas missionary service. Through Orbis Books, Maryknoll aims to foster the international dialogue that is essential to mission. The books published, however, reflect the opinions of their authors and are not meant to represent the official position of the society.

Bible quotations, unless otherwise noted, are from the *Christian Community Bible* (Catholic Pastoral Edition), 10th ed., 1993. Excerpts from "The Transformation of Silence into Language and Action," by Audre Lorde as published in *Sister Outsider: Essays and Speeches*. Copyright ©1984. Published by **The Crossing Press**, Freedom, California. Used by Permission. Excerpts from *Conjectures of a Guilty Bystander* by Thomas Merton. Copyright ©1966 by The Abbey of Gethsemani. Used by permission of **Doubleday**, a division of Bantam Doubleday Dell Publishing Group, Inc. Excerpts from *Holy the Firm* by Annie Dillard. Copyright ©1988. Reprinted by permission of **HarperCollins Publishers**. Excerpts from *The Peaceable Kingdom: A Primer in Christian Ethics* by Stanley Hauerwas. Copyright ©1983 by the University of Notre Dame Press. Reprinted by permission of **University of Notre Dame Press**. Excerpts from *An Interrupted Life: The Diaries of Etty Hillesum 1941-1943* by Etty Hillesum. English translation copyright © 1983 by Jonathan Cape Ltd. Copyright ©1981 by De Haan/Uniboek b.v., Bussum. Reprinted by permission of **Pantheon Books**, a division of Random House, Inc. and Uitgeverij **Balans**, Amsterdam. Excerpts from *Magisterium: Teaching Authority in the Catholic Church* by Francis A. Sullivan, S.J. Copyright ©1983 by Francis A. Sullivan, S.J. Reprinted by permission of **Paulist Press**. Excerpts from *Report of Greco* by Nikos Kazantzakis reprinted with the permission of **Simon & Schuster**. Copyright ©1961 by Helen N, Kazantazkis, copyright renewed ©1993 by Helen N. Kazantazkis. English translation copyright © by Simon & Schuster. Excerpts from *The Christian Disciple* by John F. Skinner, published by **University Press of America**, 1984. Material derived from *The Cross in Christian Experience* by W. M. Clow, published by **Hodder and Stoughton**, 1908.

Queries regarding rights and permissions should be addressed to: Orbis Books, P. O. Box 308, Maryknoll, New York 10545-0308.

Published by Orbis Books, Maryknoll, NY 10545-0308
Manufactured in the United States of America
Manuscript editing and typesetting by Joan Marie Laflamme

ORBIS/ISBN 1-57075-108-0

For Henry Francis O'Loughlin
From the west coast of Ireland to the east coast of Florida
priest, prophet, poet, immigrant, migrant,
worker for the kingdom that endures with justice.
One word reveals what sticks in the farmworkers'
and cane-cutters' minds:
VERDICT: ver/dict: the truth uttered aloud for all to hear.
In deep gratitude for the truth of your life in words,
in service and devotion,
and in prayer with the least of our brothers and sisters.
You teach me that the Truth will be told, the Truth will set us free,
the Truth will win out. It will!
For "La verdad padece pero no perece":
Truth suffers but never perishes.
May justice go before you and peace follow along your path.
And glory dwell in our land (Ps 85).

Contents

Introduction

We begin with a story to set the framework for what we want to look at and come to understand with our minds and hearts. It is a story about liturgy, sacrament, and repairing the world with justice and redemption. "The Shell Story" is ancient yet ever new, universal yet singular to all human beings.

☥ Once upon a time there was an island that lived on ancient ways. Its most prized possession was a conch shell that was sounded ritually to still the winds, ease the storms, and placate the rain and thunder beings. It was a way to sing to the gods. It was a great whorled shell the color of the moon, patterned and perfect, well worn. It was entrusted to one family, whose youngest member, male or female, guarded it and knew the times to sound the note. It was that one who went out to meet the sea and storms and save the people and the island from destruction as the tempests approached.

While it was in the care of one young man it was lost, carelessly. He was desperate and fearful, and so he sought to cover his failure. He found another shell, almost identical. After all, he thought, no one will notice, no one will know. Eventually a storm approached and he went to the appointed place and sounded the note, singing to the forces of the elements, standing high on a crag overlooking the sea. He blew hard on the conch shell, but the rain and thunder beings knew the difference and were not calmed.

The shell was a sacramental storm wall, made by the elements, by the gods themselves. It had power only as long as the covenant was honored. Without due veneration, respect, and care the covenant was shattered. The rites alone were not enough—and the storm came in.

The winds and torrents swept the young man off the cliff, dragging him down against the rocks and spitting him into an underground cave. Gasping for air and in pain from his wounds, he dragged himself onto a ledge. He was alive, but barely. The cave started filling up with water and was alive with the crash of waves and the moaning of the winds, ancient sounds singing and thundering around him. Deep in the cavern the elements came together and spoke to him, revealing that because of his deception and his fraudulent behavior all the people would perish and the island would be destroyed.

The man begged for his people to be spared. It was *his* sin, not theirs. His prayer was answered, but there was a penance, a price. His life was forfeit in order to restore the balance. And he submitted.

The waters continued rising in the cave, forcing him toward the ceiling. He knew that he would die. But the forces promised him that there would be a new covenant. Even as he died, he was not lost. The people had seen him swept from the cliff into the sea. At that instant the storm had subsided. They realized that he had given his life to save them. So he was not forgotten. He lives on in the peoples' memory.

Time passes and the man's body is broken down to bones, sand, shards, pieces. After a long, long time a young boy, out fishing in a boat, hauls in a net of fish and brings up a bone, moon-white, smooth as silk. He fingers it in awe, lifts it to his lips, and blows into it. One note, pure and lasting, is loosed into the air, and at that moment the man's long-imprisoned spirit is freed. The rites of justice are complete (with thanks to Chris McCoy and Tony Cowan).

We stake our lives—and at times our deaths and our very souls—on such stories. Stories lay the basis for our rituals, our ways of worshiping the Holy and making sense of our world, especially the ravages of evil and injustice and the hope that goodness will prevail. In the liturgy we first tell the story and then we enact the story to make it come true in our lives, communities, and the world. This is dangerous and exhilarating, of life and death import to all who participate, for it either saves us and repairs the damage sin does to the world or it convicts us and judges us everlastingly.

This book is entitled *Rites of Justice*, with the subtitle *The Sacraments and Liturgy as Ethical Imperatives*. Looking at our contemporary rituals, our worship, and our participation in the sacraments will be a reminder that the stories we tell and the dramas of the liturgy extend into our lives, relationships, and world history. Our rites and beliefs expose the world of reality for what it is, too often devoid of spirit, of hope, of submission to the Holy. This is what the world becomes when we do not worship, do justice, and honor the Truth.

The cover of this book bears an icon, The Black Madonna, whose lap has become the holy table. The symbols are startlingly simple: a table, a chalice, a fully grown child in the position of teacher and leader, as well as sacrifice within a house, a sanctuary, on the lap of the woman Mary, in the womb of the church. Mary is in the position of prayer, of offering, as priest overshadowed by the Spirit. The color of red for power and authority by blood and sacrifice predominates with the blue of peace as the basis for security showing in the color of her sleeves, her vestment. Both their arms are outstretched in the sign of the cross, open-hearted, an invitation. The ritual that is literally the heart of our lives, our worship, and the base of all other rites is eucharist: the thanksgiving of table offering, of eating and drinking together, and of being offered as holy to God the Father with Jesus in the power of the Spirit. It is done as church, as the children of God together, a holy people, priests with the authority of holiness and justice. Mary, as the mother who holds her child on her lap in the cup of wine and blood, holds us as children are held, firmly and yet without grasping, freely. The icon is mysterious, confusing; it invites us to look again and again for meaning, to submit to the gaze of the icon and its symbols, to understand by contemplating and listening to its unworded meanings.

The icon is a statement of belief, hope, and love. It is also a question directed at us: where are we in the icon? Do we position ourselves at the table, in the sanctuary, the cup of blessing, on her lap, with the grown child? Do we stand beside her, together as church? Do we stand with upraised hands in supplication, offering, or salutation? Do we stand at a safe distance, separate from the figures and symbols, as the women stood watching at a safe distance from the cross and tomb when Jesus was buried?

In a sense Mary is standing as a weather vane, an indicator of what is all around her. There are people, individuals or communities, that are weather vanes in our society and church. They are traditionally termed prophets. They reveal pain, sin, evil, and injustice that have reached obscene levels among the poor and the outcast, those whom society seeks to ignore or destroy. These prophets show our level of faithfulness, our concrete worship of God, and they testify to our belief or lack of belief in the Holy. These people manifest the degree of real spirituality that is operative in us, as believers, as church. They cry out for those whose very existence shames us and reveals the lie inherent in our prayer and protestations before God, convicts us and separates us from God (in separating ourselves from them, for God in Jesus has steadfastly joined them, bonded himself to their bodies and hearts). God is, in Jesus, the sacrificial victim, embracing all those we sacrifice to idols and other gods, whether military, economic, national, or other. In their cherished position with God they save or condemn us forever. In the presence of Jesus as their fellow victim and brother, they are favored children of God.

St. John Chrysostom's Eucharistic Prayer—"Send down thy Holy Spirit upon us and upon these gifts here set forth"—contains a strong emphasis on the Holy Spirit changing the people who celebrate as well as changing the gifts themselves. That is what this book is all about: conversion and transformation of our rites, sacraments, and liturgy, but also of those of us who celebrate them together.

In the hills of Appalachia there was a tradition of miners taking canaries into mine shafts. The men sang, kept them company like children, named them, fed them tidbits. The men who carried their cages were honored to bring them down or carry them up. The canaries were an early warning system—the canaries died quickly when there was too much carbon monoxide, and then the men knew they had to get out fast. There are such people—early warning systems in any culture or country or religion who signal with their quick deaths the extent of death among us—always. Surprisingly, our rites and sacraments reveal the inherent values of these people and their presence among us and remind us most intimately of our calling as children of God to honor them, live in solidarity with them, and be their voices—and their friends.

In a sense our sacraments and liturgy themselves are such weather vanes, signaling what lies in our immediate presence if only we have eyes to see and senses that are acute. We will look to Jesus, weather vane of God, and his ethic of life handed on to us, his friends, to see how we are to be weather vanes in the world. We will see if the church expresses warnings and gives solace and sanctuary to all those in need and looking for a place to dwell, the kingdom of unending justice and everlasting peace. We will examine whether we too live as the Black Madonna, whose lap has become a table that feeds the hungry and gives drink to the thirsty, that instills in us a hunger for justice and truth and gathers us from all the corners of the earth into the intimacy of one family in the Trinity. For this is in essence what our liturgy and sacraments seek to accomplish in us: to make us the cup that God loves to drink from, the bread broken and shared, the food that is sufficient for everyone's needs, and the gathering place for all those called to live in the kingdom. Are we the blessing cup, people who are a source of blessing for those in need, for sinners and sinned against alike? Are we welcoming, large-hearted, and open-handed as we worship our God and draw others into God's family? Are we the lap that becomes the table?

A Pastoral Reminder

All of the situations and sacramental rituals and the liturgy discussed in these pages are steeped in laws, customs, theological language, and spiritual symbols deeply embedded in real peoples' lives and relationships. Any of them can be rendered lifeless when those who use it fail to understand the pastoral purposes that root it in reality. For Jesus, all human laws, even the Sabbath laws, were intended to be interpreted in the light of their basic pastoral purpose of serving the good of the sheep. At the time of Jesus, and in our time as well, many of the laws and rites are far from serving the good of the flock. In fact, the mass of human regulations leaves most people feeling excluded and lost, like sheep without a shepherd.

Laws at best have only general validity. We need to develop the ability to discern when the good intent of a law would be vitiated by keeping to the strict letter of the law in a particular instance. The traditional name for this ability is *epikeia*. Aquinas insists that this ability is a virtue and not a way of evading the law; in fact, its aim is to make sure that the deepest purpose of the law is achieved. And the deepest purpose of the law will always be the pastoral good of persons. What some have called "the gap virtue" is particularly important for priests and those in pastoral ministries, and it becomes increasingly important the greater the gap grows between the official regulations of the church and the demands of pastoral practice. *Salus animarum suprema lex* ("the good of the individual is the essential component of the common good"). It is the common good itself that calls for the virtue of *epikeia*.

Perhaps Jesus was making a similar point in his pastoral story about a shepherd leaving the ninety-nine and going to search for the one lost sheep. Where there is a gap between the official regulations of the church and the demands of pastoral practice, the latter must always take priority. Obedience is to be alert to the cries of the sheep and listen to their deepest needs and hear and obey the voice of God. This is the gap virtue. People are not just the first priority in liturgy and sacraments and rites; they are in a real sense the *only* priority, the primary symbol and the place of transformation is their person and the communities that embrace them. (My thanks to the folks in Liverpool for these insights.)

A Note on Quotations, Poems, and Stories

Since I was about ten, I have collected phrases, stories, words, and descriptions that have touched me and catapulted me into levels of imagination and spirit and nudged my ideas into writing. I recorded them into my "Quote Books," and usually wrote down the author and the title of the poem or book. However, I seldom included page references, publishing houses, years of publication, and so on. Many pieces from my "Quote Books" find their way into my writing, pieces that cannot be duplicated or improved upon for their elegance, insight, clarity, and voice. They are in this book in large numbers. While I have searched diligently to find specific references, many, alas, are tagged with just the author's name and the title of the book or poem. I have decided to include them in this form because of their appropriateness to the issues at hand and because of the beauty of their voices.

1

Jesus, the Ethic of Christians

✠ Once upon a time there was a tiger cub. When it was very young it lost its mother to a hunter and wandered far and wide, looking for a way to live. It soon found a herd of goats on a mountainside and fell in with them. It ate grass, chewed on plants, and played with the goats, butting and bumping heads. It thought it was a goat and was treated as one of the flock by the others. Then one day a tiger came up on the ridge looking for prey and all the goats fled in panic and terror. But the tiger cub stayed, wondering why the flight. It soon saw the tiger coming down the hill and started to play, trying to butt it with its head, rolling on the ground in front of it. The tiger looked at the cub strangely and then batted it with its paw, its claws safely withdrawn—and the cub went rolling head over paws on the grass. It got to its feet and looked at the tiger.

Again it moved, wanting to play and wondering why it had been cuffed. This time the tiger cuffed it harder, with claws out, scraping its face as it sent it flying across the grass. The cub got up gingerly and began to back off in fear. But the tiger moved quickly, grabbed the cub in its mouth and carried it off, over the hill, its gait growing stronger and wilder. The cub was entranced and yet a bit afraid. The journey continued until the tiger came to a lake and dropped the cub unceremoniously into the water. As the cub shook the water from its fur and stood up, it noticed its own reflection in the water. It looked at its reflection and then at the tiger above it again and again. And then it knew what it was and let out a tremendous roar! The compassionate scratch of a tiger paw released the tiger within. Now the cub looks at life through its own tiger eyes!

Thomas Merton tells a variation of this story in one of his earlier journals and says: "I met a tiger in myself who is not familiar, who says, Choose! and knocks me halfway across the jungle. I met a tiger in the church who is not familiar, who says, Choose! and knocks me halfway across the jungle. Why do I get the feeling this is going to happen again . . . and again . . . and again?"

These reflections are about choosing; but they are not about options. They are about imperatives. They are about the imperatives of the gospel, the liturgy, and the sacraments that are core to our natures, though we might be unfamiliar with them. They are about the tiger who is the Christ. When we meet him in the liturgy and the sacraments, he might be unfamiliar, but he says "Choose!" and knocks us halfway across the landscape of our present lives. This is going to happen again and again in our lives as Christians.

In the writings of Micah, the prophet, we hear the words: "You have been told, O man (and woman), what is good, and what Yahweh requires of you: To do justice, to love mercy, and to walk humbly with your God" (Mic 6:8). It sounds simple and straightforward enough. Justice and mercy and the reality of walking with God are required of those who wish to do good. Justice and mercy are the domain of ethics. Walking with God is liturgy, ritual, sacraments. The command is given in the plural, to a *community* that walks with its God and learns to do good in imitation of God. Ethics and liturgy are bound together in people. Ethics and liturgy are the contemporary expressions of faith, combining past, present, and future in the continuing story and history of the people that belongs to God. It is in the people that the connections between being human beings and religious beings are made, nurtured, and matured. It is in the people that religious beliefs are manifested in values, ethics, and a way of being in the world, especially in the larger world that does not believe in the shared history, traditions, and experience of God. The ethics and liturgy of a people become the manifestation of the glory of God to the earth.

"You have been told" echoes ancient ways, tradition, and memory. It is part of the ritual itself. For Christians this refrain is heard again in the earliest statements of belief in the eucharist and how it is to be celebrated within the community. Paul speaks formally to the church in Corinth:

> This is the tradition of the Lord that I received and that in my turn I have handed on to you; the Lord Jesus, on the night that he was delivered up, took bread and, after giving thanks, broke it, saying, "This is my body which is broken for you; do this in memory of me." In the same manner, taking the cup after the supper, he said, "This cup is the new Covenant in my blood. Whenever you drink it, do it in memory of me."

So, then, whenever you eat of this bread and drink from this cup, you are proclaiming the death of the Lord until he comes (1 Cor 11:23-27).

Here is the ritual, the sacrament, and the liturgy of the church. And the following words connect sacrament to life ethic. "Therefore, if anyone eats of the bread or drinks from the cup of the Lord unworthily, he sins against the body and blood of the Lord. Let each one, then, examine himself before eating of the bread and drinking from the cup. Otherwise, he eats and drinks his own condemnation in not recognizing the Body" (1 Cor 11:27-29). Paul's words are blunt. To participate in the ritual and not to live its reality in life is to call down a judgment on ourselves. Ethics and sacraments in a Christian's life are intimately bound up together.

The tie that binds believers in both sacrament and ethic is the person of Jesus Christ. It is he who breaks the bread and shares the cup. It is he who is the bread and wine. It is he who takes the lead, gives the command, and renews the old ways of "doing justice, loving tenderly and walking humbly with our God." It is he who is *the* sacrament; it is his life that is *the* ethic. The word *religion* means "to tie or bind together." It is derived from a word that means connective tissue, like a sinew attached to bone and muscle. A Christian, a follower of Jesus' way to God, is to be "bound together" with Christ in his way home to God, to be bound in the sacrament and ethic of Jesus, the Christ of God.

A later account of the eucharist is found in Luke 22:14-19. Here Jesus gives the ritual to his friends and followers: take, give thanks, break, pass it around. "Do this in remembrance of me." Thus has the formula for the ritual, the celebration of eucharist—our way of giving thanks to God in Jesus, for Jesus, with Jesus—come down to us. It is simple: take, give thanks, break, pass it around. The ritual celebrates the life of Jesus, who took all of creation as a gift from God, blessed and gave thanks to his Father for it, broke it, shared it, gave it away to anyone who wanted it, anyone who was willing to take it.

Jesus takes words and makes them into an announcement of the kingdom of God. He dares to call Yahweh God his Father and exhorts his friends to call God by this new name of Father. In so doing, they accept a new relationship as sons and daughters of God, no longer servants but brothers and sisters to Jesus, Lord in the kingdom of God. It is Jesus who takes any gift, whether a few loaves and fishes from a young boy, or the desire of a Pharisee who climbs a tree because he wants to see Jesus so badly, or a hand reaching out in trust for the edge of his cloak. He takes all these gifts and breaks them open, makes them new, and passes them around. In these gifts is a new covenant, a new testament, a new promise, a new tie that binds together. Jesus takes hearts and finds love; he takes fields and finds treasure hidden within; he finds trees and nests of safety in the tiny mustard seed. He uncovers the kingdom of God, his Father, everywhere in creation. And he says to his followers: do *this* and you'll remember me.

Jesus takes the law and breaks it open to expose its spirit and life. Then he takes the hearts of men and women and breaks them open to see whether they are true or not. He takes weakness, sin, and disease and breaks them open to find health, strength, peace, and hope. Finally, he takes death and finds within it everlasting life. Whatever he takes and breaks apart and blesses God for, he shares with his friends and gives them the command: "Do *this* and you will remember me."

To remember does not mean merely to bring to mind; it means to "re-member," to put back together again, to make present again. An old saying puts it well: "To remember is to meet again" (Martin Buber). When we want to feel Jesus' presence with us again, when we want to proclaim his kingdom, then we do the ritual: take, bless, break and share, not just the bread and the wine, but our lives. And it happens again. All the things that he did happen again. We do them. The ritual makes possible forgiveness, life given abundantly with more than enough to go around, power and strength in nonviolence, hope in the face of despair, and grace in every moment and part of creation. Those who celebrate the sacrament of Jesus, do *this*: walk humbly with the Father as Jesus walked, act justly, and love tenderly. The story continues, the history unfolds, the mystery grows, the manifestation to the world is announced again and again. God is with the people still. Our religion is our reality.

This is the bare outline of the beginnings of a theology of ethics and sacraments—doing justice and celebrating mercy, loving tenderly, remembering what our God has done for us in Jesus and doing *this* for all the world to see and take to heart and believe in again. But theology isn't neat, pat, and clean, or always experienced as a living, breathing reality. This book seeks to look at the theology of the sacraments and liturgy specifically as they demand an ethic of justice. When a believer in a community celebrates eucharist or baptism or confirmation or any of the other sacraments, what is he or she saying about belief, values, and the demands of Christian life? Using Paul's words to the Corinthians, we will examine ourselves and call down judgment upon ourselves to see if we eat and drink the sacrament of the Lord worthily or stand in jeopardy of our lives. We will call ourselves, the church, to accountability as believers and see if we are revealing to the world our belief in the way of Jesus, the ethic of Jesus, as well as celebrating and borrowing his words, gestures, and intent in the rituals of his life, death, and resurrection.

In the past it has often been the experience of the church to receive and celebrate the sacraments (and often liturgy as well) on a primarily individual and personal level rather than on a communal and interpersonal level. The command "Do this in remembrance of me" is spoken to the community of those who believe, the church of Jesus Christ, not only to his individual disciples and friends. So we will examine our shared heritage and tradition, not just our individual chosen ethic or value judgment. This will, of course, reveal that the church stands on a teaching and prophetic ethic and transmits that call to conversion prophetically first and then pastorally deals with individual and collective failures to realize that ethic in public.

One conclusion that will immediately become apparent is that at present the church does *not* connect ethics and sacraments on either a personal or a communal level for the most part, and the church holds very few persons accountable for their ethical behavior, except in selected instances dealing primarily with the sacrament of marriage. There seems to be a lopsided accountability in this sacrament and accordingly more pastoral problems with the practice and the celebration of it in connection with liturgy and eucharist than with any of the others. But if the other sacraments were dealt with as consistently and as demandingly, the sacrament of marriage might look very different indeed to Christians and might proclaim something quite different indeed to the world.

What also will become immediately apparent is the dichotomy between proclaiming an ethic connected with a sacramental structure and then allowing children with very little understanding of the ethical demands to participate in the reception of the sacrament. The sacrament quickly becomes something personal in meaning, devoid of consequences, free from demands for conversion in the child's life. This, of course, continues in the adult who still approaches the sacraments and liturgy (and often ethical demands) as a child in mind and heart and practice.

Perhaps what is most destructive in the long run is that community cannot develop in such a situation. Ethics, the shared behavior and value system of the believers, and the ritual enactment and experience of power extended into the lives of the believers in sacrament and ritual don't just happen. We don't "do *this*" and most often we don't "*remember* Jesus." We don't come together, bound in ties of expression, behavior, and tradition, and witness to the world around us. Instead, we individually approach the God of Jesus and individually select from among the traditions of the church. Instead of gathering the church, the believers in Jesus, we often separate believers in the presence of one another and under the noses of the world that watches us.

In each chapter of this book on the sacraments we will deal with the theological bases of a tradition from scripture and history. This will be a prophetic challenge to reconnect the ethic of Jesus in his announcement of the kingdom of peace and justice here on earth with the sacramental structure and the symbol base of the particular sacrament in the community. Then we will look pastorally at the practice of the sacrament today to see where gaps in belief and practice are the greatest and suggest possibilities for change. We will look at the ritual of liturgy, in word and in bread and wine, in the same way.

It will surprise many that the church, especially in the United States, has based its criteria for celebration of the sacraments and the liturgy on the retention of knowledge and information; this is a teaching base rather than a conversional base that can be witnessed to and attested to in behavior. We have primarily associated readiness with information rather than with change of heart, mind, and practice—or even the desire to change.

In addition, there is a decided reluctance and hesitancy on the part of ministers and catechists to demand public assent to the values of the church prior to participation in the sacraments and liturgy. It seems that individuality and a personal understanding of belief are sacrosanct, and that it is not appropriate to ask others publicly to commit themselves to accepting and defending the ethical demands and values of the gospel and the church. We would rather keep to our private beliefs and personal conscience as indicators of commitment instead of committing to any sort of communal accountability. This is quite different from the practice of the early church, which kept the sacraments in abeyance as steps on a road that was both personally and publicly acknowledged and celebrated in community.

Since the Second Vatican Council, over thirty-five years ago, the church—its essence, definition, and experience—has been much discussed among Catholics. Today the church is seen as the people of God, the new Exodus, the New Jerusalem, the body of Christ or, as in earlier definitions, the mystical body. It is the sacrament of the risen Lord, the herald of the good news, and the gathering of base Christian communities. It is a collegial and hierarchical structure and body, and it can operate as a professional business corporation and national body. It is a pilgrim people, an immigrant church, a sanctuary. According to the definition of Martin Luther King, Jr., it is "the place we go forth from" or "the gathering of sinners." It is the conscience of the world that seeks to find modern, practical, and pluralistic yet unified ways of transforming economics, converting nuclear missiles, abolishing the death penalty, and protecting the unborn and aging. It is loving our neighbors in an age where neighbors are starving in Africa, persecuted in Latin America, and numbering in the billions in Asia. It is the place where Christians should most easily find the presence of the risen Lord in word, sacrament, and relationships. It is a sacrament in the midst of a world intent on technology, nationalism, racism, ever-new ways of defending and destroying itself, conquering space, and teaching people to appreciate democracy and law while living with torture, illiteracy, poverty, starvation, and the lack of basic human rights—all in the name of law or religion or government or individual rights.

Doing justice, loving tenderly, and walking humbly with our God in the face of all this doesn't appear to be so straightforward or easy after all. The reality of the Incarnation, our God becoming human and dwelling among us, is most often old news, old history that is useful to state and local governments and that is ritualized as much in contemporary national holidays as it is in churches.

The child who was to be the cause of the rise and the fall of many is still such a portent. This child was born of an unwed mother who would have been stoned to death according to the law if a just man had not intervened and taken her in, along with her child. This child was one of thousands of poor people in bondage to another nation, which sought to count him as a slave. This child found no room in an inn, no hospitality on the road; he was born in a cave like the child of any drifter. Immediately after his birth, he became a problem to the authorities, who heard rumors of his birth. He was seen as a potential usurper to the order of the day, and it was decreed that he die. In the first months after his birth, he became, along with his parents, an alien in Egypt. The family eventually returned to its native land and settled in Nazareth, a place from where "nothing good comes forth," a place the rich and the mighty would never think to look for the child they earlier attempted to kill by slaughtering innocents. Nazareth was a place on the way to somewhere, filled with people who didn't make it, a place of deferred dreams and discontents. And so the child disappeared, became an ordinary carpenter, for nearly thirty years.

Then he surfaces in the company of a religious fanatic, at a time when there were many. When John the Baptist is murdered, he takes his place and chooses disciples, to whom he teaches a kingdom of mercy, peace, and justice—whether they understand or not. His taste seems a bit odd. He picks fishermen who aren't all that good at fishing, tax collectors, retired Zealots who once espoused a violent insurrection against the Roman government, brothers who are nicknamed the Sons of Thunder and who argue over places in the kingdom, and one man who will betray him publicly for a price. He attracts riffraff, prostitutes, rich women, young men, public sinners, detested Pharisees, and makes enemies in both his own religious hierarchy and in the nation at large. He upsets the balance of power, sides with those who have no voice, and tells them that his God, his Father, loves them and that they will get into his kingdom ahead of the others if they repent and believe in the good news.

His good news is surprising: "He is to bring glad tidings to the poor, to proclaim liberty to captives, recovery of sight to the blind and release to prisoners and to announce a year of favor from the Lord" (Lk 4:18-19, *NAB*). It is a message of hope: "Ask and you shall receive, seek and you will find, knock and the door will be opened to you . . . your Father in heaven will give good things to those who ask him!" (Mt 7:7-11, *NAB*). It is an announcement of life everlasting! "I am the resurrection; whoever believes in me, though he die, shall live. Whoever is alive by believing in me will never die!" (Jn 11:25-26). The message at times seems unbelievable or impossible: "Offer no resistance to injury. When a person strikes you on one cheek, turn and offer him the other. If anyone wants to go to law over your shirt, hand him your coat as well. Should anyone press you into service for one mile, go with him two miles. Give to the man who begs from you" (Mt 5:38-42, *NAB*).

The demands and exhortations far exceed the old law, which was precise and sometimes harsh, but binding only on fellow Jews. Now it's different:

> "You have heard the commandment, 'you shall love your countrymen and hate your enemy.' My command to you is: 'love your enemies and pray for your persecutors.' This will prove that you are sons and daughters of your heavenly Father, for his sun rises on the bad and the good, he rains on the just and the unjust. If you love those who love you, what merit is there in that? Do not tax collectors do as much? And if you greet your brothers only, what is so praiseworthy about that? Do not pagans do as much? In a

word, you must be made perfect as your heavenly Father is perfect" (Mt 5:43-48, *NAB*).

The good news sounds more and more like an impossible, ever more stringent demand for ethical behavior that is unreasonable. Sometimes it is maddeningly precise: "Put up your sword, those who live by the sword, perish by it. If I wanted to I could call on power from on high, but this is the way the scriptures are fulfilled, this is the way my Father does things" (Mt 26:52-54, *NAB*). At other times the good news is maddeningly vague, couched in parables, stories, and sayings that are intricate, detailed, and laden with hidden meanings and surprise endings. It seems to say: Be careful, my God is full of surprises. He will come when you least expect him, and you probably won't recognize him when he does appear.

But then more clues, precise commands, and pointblank statements flesh out the old laws. Love your neighbor! How? By giving food to the hungry, drink to the thirsty, welcoming the stranger and alien, clothing the naked, visiting and comforting the sick and imprisoned (Mt 25:35-36). The last explanation of why one should do all *this* is startling: "For I assure you as often as you neglected to do it to one of these least ones, you neglected to do it to me" (Mt 25:40, *NAB*). Life or death forever depends on how we treat our neighbor—anybody, including enemies—for the neighbor is the privileged place where one can respond to God's invitation and good news. It is here in all these stories and sayings of Jesus that the ethic, the fleshing out of the command to "do *this* and remember me" is found.

James Gaffney in *Newness of Life* reminds us:

Practically speaking, Christian ethical tradition has looked back, at every stage, to the Gospels as to an ultimate reference point. . . . It is because the Gospels seem to bring the reader closer than does anything else to Jesus Christ. And it is to Jesus as presented in the Gospels that most people have responded, over the past twenty centuries, with the faith that makes Christians and leads them to adopt a way of life that includes a distinctive ethical orientation. Thus in our earliest post-biblical Christian literature we find ethical teachings referred most frequently to the Gospels—because of their concrete presentation of Jesus—and especially to that Gospel material in which Jesus is presented most conspicuously as a moral teacher. We find a primary preference in this regard for the Gospel of Matthew, and a secondary one for the Gospel of Luke,

both of whom add a great deal of ethical material to Mark. With
the Gospel according to Matthew, the Sermon on the Mount was
esteemed from very early Christian times as a unique distillation
of distinctively Christian ethics.[1]

Jesus' message can be summed up in his first recorded words: "Repent [reform your lives]." This is a demand for radical personal conversion, transformation that is freeing, demanding, ongoing, and distinctive. It assumes that people know something about what they should be
doing as believers in God but are remiss, halfhearted, or too personalis-
tic in their interpretation of what the law, the old ethic, could mean.
Jesus begins by reminding the people that they had to start living up to
the ethical demands of the covenant and, in fact, because more was being given to them if they accepted the good news, more would be demanded of them. This was basically an ethic of "pass it on." What they
had received from God as gift in Jesus, they should now celebrate in
ritual and behavior and show forth the glory of God as Jesus did while
he was with us. Why? Because the kingdom of heaven, the reign of God
in peace and justice, in people and times so mercifully full of content-
ment, love, and just deeds was present in Jesus' life and would continue
in his followers' lives. The beginning, the middle, and the last moment
and experience of the coming of the kingdom and its expression in ethical behavior, community, and ritual would be the moment of conversion.
As God was faithful, so God's people would learn to turn faithfully to
Jesus' way and move further along the road to the kingdom. More and
more they would be ruled by God, see as God sees, judge as God judges,
accept and love their neighbors as God does, become perfect in compassion and justice as God is perfect. It was good news that God looks and
acts like us, dwells with us, trusts us, loves us. It is good news that we
can imitate God more and more, become more and more his children, his
friends, his word of hope and freedom to the world.

The word of Jesus Christ, or better the Word of God that is Jesus
Christ, is the new law, the new demand, the new ethic, the new norm for
behavior and belief. What God has done for us in Jesus, we his followers
now do for others in his name. The reality of Jesus as he is portrayed in
the gospels is the belief of the early church, the understanding of the
ethic he called his followers to, of how they were to continue to bring the
reign of God upon earth until the return of Jesus. It is this understanding
of Jesus, this christology of the gospels, that provides the basis and norm
for teaching and preaching ethics in the Christian community. Ethics for
Christians is a conversion of life that is based on the life of Jesus. Dis-

cipleship is a life turned around, focused on the kingdom and expressed in love and ritual.

In the first chapter of *What Are They Saying about Moral Norms?* Richard Gula lays the foundation for looking at all moral theology by looking at Jesus' teaching and life:

> The most unambiguous demand Jesus makes of his disciples is to respond wholeheartedly to his commandment of love (Matt. 22:34-40; Mark 12:28-34; Luke 10:25-28). In laying down the double commandment of love, Jesus linked and put into mutual relation the love of God and the love of neighbor. The love of God finds expression in the love of neighbor, and the love of neighbor receives its foundation and energy in the love of God.[2]

Gula goes on to quote Rudolf Schnackenburg on what Jesus did by linking these two commandments of love:

> He revealed the indissoluble interior bond between these two commandments; he showed clearly that the whole law could be reduced to this and only this chief and double commandment, and he reinterpreted "neighborly love" as "love of the nearest person," that is, he interpreted it in an absolutely universal sense.[3]

It is the life and especially the death of Jesus that reveal definitively what loving God and neighbor can mean in concrete, historical terms. To accept discipleship under Jesus is to adhere to this impossible, graceful ethic of unbounded love. It is always the "one thing more you must do" (Mk 10:21, *NAB*) that Jesus lovingly asks of the rich young man. The general orientation of our lives in imitation of Jesus is difficult enough, but the more specific responses in our time and history, both individually and communally, are even more compelling and hard to fulfill.

It is Jesus, one among us, who has received all from God and returned it all lovingly to him, including his own life and person in trust. Jesus the Christ expresses for all time and places, for all believers, the fullness of what the Christian moral life, ethical behavior, and life lived as eucharist, as thanksgiving, ought to be. We must be guided by his person, words, and actions, not only in response to God, but to each other in community and to our neighbor in that universal sense that Jesus sought to introduce us to as the way God loves and cherishes us. The extent to which Jesus forms us and gives meaning to our life is far beyond anything in Jewish law.

James Gustafson says it superbly:

> What he means and symbolizes has authority for me, for example,
> . . . I am obliged to consider him both when there is a conformity
> of my own desire and preference with what he represents, and when
> he is abrasive to my "natural" tendency on a particular occasion.
> . . . He is a standard by which my purposes are judged, he is an
> authority that ought to direct and inform my activity, if I acknowl-
> edge him to be my Lord.[4]

Christ is a norm, a prophetic challenge, a parable, a vision of life, a
sacrament, the Word of God, an insight into the workings and the mind
of God, a source of freedom and contradiction, a power for transformation and conversion, and a wellspring of unity for those who remember
him and what he did and why. Jesus' message and life are dominated by
the urgency to proclaim the kingdom of mercy, peace, justice, forgiveness, and abundant life for all. If we call ourselves believers, we take life
as a gift from our Father, bless it, break it open, and pass it around,
finding in the sacrament and ritual of Jesus, as well as his words and life,
the source for our own witness to the glory of God and God's presence
still with us. The potential for discipleship is never ending. Like Jesus,
we are encouraged to grow in wisdom, age, and grace before God and
the earth until the kingdom comes in its fullness (Lk 2:52). We are to
progress steadily within the community, celebrating the sacraments and
liturgy and manifesting with our lives the reality of the kingdom that is
with us even now. Ethics—the ethic of Jesus—is the imperative that
follows upon our belief in Jesus as Lord.

This Jesus reveals not only a specificity and a universality of ethical
behavior but he demonstrates an integrity, a wholeness to living, worshiping and loving. His wholeheartedness—being at one with himself,
creation, and God—is expressed in his relationship with all others. As
Paul describes him, he is consistent. He is always *yes*, not yes sometimes
and no at others (2 Cor 1:18ff.). This wholeness is an integration of body
and soul, personal and communal, private and public, individual and
political, word and deed. It is a communion of religious, political, economic, and social life. He is true to himself, to God who is faithful in
relationships, in material possessions, in public affiliations, in political
decisions and actions, and in religious assertions.

Jesus reveals in this truthfulness a willingness to suffer, endure, and
proclaim his belief in God with passion, even unto death. This is more
than generalized good will; it is a confrontational style of witnessing to

the power of God loving God's people in history. The cross is the obvious symbol of that willingness to suffer for and with us in our struggle to be good, to act justly, to love tenderly, and to walk humbly with our God. Jesus' ethic can break us through to other people as much as it can be a source of breaking down hostility, anger, injustice and lack of love. Jesus "was despised and rejected, a man of sorrows familiar with grief" (Is 53:3).

The essence of this ethic is experienced in forgiveness that gives more, lets go more, loves more, dies more, and empowers more, restoring and repairing relationships and the world. Christ is the way to understand God's ways with us. If we accept it, as did Peter, who thus obtained the chance to say "I love you" three times on the beach after the resurrection, then the only demand we are asked to commit ourselves to is to return the favor of forgiveness to all others. This is the feeding of the sheep. The ethic is first revealed and experienced, and then celebrated in the community, the church at ritual.

If Christ is the sacrament of God, the place where we meet God more surely and distinctly, then the church—Christ's brothers and sisters—is a sacrament too, the sacrament of the presence of the risen Lord in the world. It is here, among his own, that believers and those who watch us should most easily see his kingdom, his reign of justice and mercy, at work, even now. It is here in the church, with his own, that the experience of resurrection, good, hope, and unbounded love is most assuredly expressed. When two or three who acknowledge him as Lord gather, he is present, recognizable, powerful, especially when his church obeys his commands: do *this*, in ritual and in lifestyle and in proclamation. It is here that he is *re-membered*, celebrated, and shared. The church is the peaceable kingdom, the place where the ethic of Jesus is available to the world to see and take heart from, to be challenged by and confronted with as a reality. In the words of the Second Vatican Council's *Dogmatic Constitution on the Church*:

> By her relationship with Christ, the Church is a kind of sacrament of intimate union with God, and of the unity of all mankind, that is, she is a sign and an instrument of such union and unity. . . .
>
> Just as Christ carried out the work of redemption in poverty and under oppression, so the Church is called to follow the same path in communicating . . . the fruits of salvation. Christ Jesus, "though he was by nature God . . . emptied himself, taking the nature of a slave" (Phil. 2:6), and "being rich, he become poor" (2 Cor. 8:9) for our sakes.[5]

It is not just the disciple of Jesus, the individual believer, who continues the work of Christ. It is the church, the body of believers, that reveals the presence of God most clearly. Through the Trinity, God is expressed theologically as community, and it is the church, the community of the breaking and sharing, gathered, thanks-giving people, that witnesses to the good news of God's presence in the world.

For American Catholics the emphasis is often on the individual rather than the communal. The response to the American bishops' pastorals on peace and economics, as well as disagreements on moral issues such as abortion, capital punishment, euthanasia, nationalistic trade agreements, national policies (such as immigration and basic health care) that do not take the poor as normative, the building up and continued threat to use nuclear weapons, and so on, manifest this acutely, painfully, and publicly to all, believers and nonbelievers alike. American Catholics, by and large, ascribe to an individual Christian ethic that is separated from the tradition and teaching of the larger church in both history and connection to the rest of the universal church. Many American Catholics are better defined in their ethical values as independents, as though they voted on individual issues rather than a "straight ticket." It is a pick-and-choose ethic rather than an overall commitment to the ethical standard of Jesus as revealed in the gospels or in the tradition of the universal church, which calls all Christians to a prophetic ethic of more love, more forgiveness, more life, more commitment.

Jacques Maritain's description of the practical atheism of many Christians, quoted by Thomas Merton in 1968, still stands today:

> They keep in their minds the settings of religion for the sake of appearances or outward show . . . but they deny the Gospel and despise the poor, pass through the tragedy of their time only with resentment against anything that endangers their interests and fear for their own prestige and possessions, contemplate without flinching every kind of injustice if it does not threaten their own way of life. Only concerned with power and success, they are either anxious to have means of external coercion enforce what they term the "moral order" or else they turn with the wind and are ready to comply with any requirement of so-called historical necessity. They await the deceivers. They are famished for deception because first they themselves are trying to deceive God.[6]

Merton's commentary follows: "These are terrible and prophetic words, and their light picks out with relentless truth and detail the true face of what passes for 'Christianity,' and too often tries to justify itself by an appeal to the 'Christian past.'"

These words might seem harsh to some, but perhaps two other sections from Merton's *Conjectures of a Guilty Bystander* will flesh out the extent to which Americans consider themselves believers yet dissociate themselves from the reality of the ethical demands of the person of Jesus and the tradition of the church. Earlier in his book, Merton describes the basic sin of Christians this way:

> The basic sin, for Christianity, is rejecting others in order to choose oneself, deciding against others and deciding for oneself. Why is this sin so basic? Because the idea that you can choose yourself, approve yourself, and then offer yourself (fully "chosen" and "approved") to God, implies the assertion of yourself over against God. From this root of error comes all the sour leafage and fruitage of a life of self-examination, interminable problems and unending decisions, always making right choices, walking on the razor edge of an impossibly subtle ethic (with an equally subtle psychology to take care of the unconscious). All this implies the frenzied conviction that one can be his own light and his own justification, and that God is there for a purpose: to issue the stamp of confirmation upon my own righteousness. In such a religion the Cross becomes meaningless except as the (blasphemous) certification that because you suffer, because you are misunderstood, you are justified twice over—you are a martyr. Martyr means witness. You are then a witness? To what? To your own infallible light and your own justice, which you have chosen. This is the exact opposite of everything Jesus ever did or taught.[7]

This individuality, this egoism, sounds and looks a great deal like American individualism. A popular book in the seventies was titled *I'm OK, You're OK*. For a Christian, the book title should read: *I'm Not OK, You're Not OK, But That's OK*. Why? Because it is the gift of redemption that Jesus gives to us, shares with us in resurrection, scripture, liturgy, sacrament, and community, in forgiveness and conversion to new life that makes us OK. What does this look like in reality, in church? Merton tells a story from the late sixties.

> A young priest was sent to preach one Sunday in a "white" Catholic parish in New Orleans. He based his sermon on the Gospel of the Sunday, in which Christ spoke of the twofold commandment,

love of God and love of one's brother, which is the essence of Christian morality.

The priest, in his sermon, took occasion to point out that this commandment applied to the problem of racial segregation, and that white people and Negroes ought certainly to love one another to the extent of accepting one another in an integrated society.

He was halfway through the sermon, and the gist of his remarks was becoming abundantly clear, when a man stood up in the middle of the congregation and shouted angrily: "I didn't come here to listen to this kind of junk, I came to hear Mass."

The priest stopped and waited. This exasperated the man even more, and he demanded that the sermon be brought to an end at once, otherwise he would leave.

The priest continued to wait in silence, and another man in the congregation, amid the murmuring support of many voices, got up and protested against this doctrine, which he saw fit to refer to as "crap."

As the priest still said nothing, the two men left the church followed by about fifty other solid Christians in the congregation. As he went out, the first of them shouted over his shoulder at the priest: "If I miss Mass today it's your fault." Incidents like this have a meaning.

This meaning is simple and objective. Quite apart from the subjective dispositions, the probable sincerity of the warped consciences of the people involved, there is an objective fact manifested here. The fact is that one can think himself a "good Catholic" and be thought one by his neighbors, and be, in effect, an apostate from the Christian faith.

Not only do we see in these men a flat refusal to listen to the plain meaning of the word of God as preached by a minister of the church, speaking in the name of God, but also there is a complete moral and spiritual insensitivity to the meaning of the Mass as the Christian *agape*, the union of brothers in Christ, a union from which no believer is to be excluded. To exclude a brother in Christ from this union is to fail to "judge the Body of Christ" and hence to "eat and drink judgment to oneself" (1 Cor 11).

Doubtless not one of the men who left church that morning would subscribe formally to such propositions. Doubtless they believe that they have in their hearts what they think can pass muster as "charity" for all men. But is it not an abstract and legalistic charity? Is not their attendance at mass a legal formality? Formalities, abstractions, are not enough. Gestures of conformity do not make a man a Christian, and when one's actual conduct obviously belies the whole meaning of the gesture, it is an objective statement that one's Christianity has lost its meaning. . . .The sin of these men must be pointed out quite clearly for what it is.[8]

When Christians listen to a story like this, thirty years later, what do they feel, knowing that racial segregation had been tackled both legally in the courts and religiously in the church? Could we change the details just a bit and come up with a more contemporary example—for instance, the issue of immigration and all peoples' rights to basic health care, shelter, education, and freedom? Or single mothers on welfare as those of the "least among us" who will be the criterion for our love or lack of love, our being sheep or goats? Or the gospel warning of not being able to serve two masters, God and money, and a few pertinent remarks from the bishops' economic pastoral or the words of Jesus in the garden "to put up your sword, or perish by it"? Or not to "resist evil and violence with retaliatory violence in kind" and a teaching on the ethical demands for making peace in the modern world before giving the sign of peace and receiving the Lamb of God? The reaction is about the same in intensity, self-assuredness, and church attendance and its relationship to life's realities—and all this, thirty years after the Civil Rights Movement and the Second Vatican Council. Perhaps the only difference would be that now they would not leave. They would still go to eucharist and ignore the words of the gospel and later complain to those higher in the church structure.

Someone once paraphrased the gospel and said, "By their rites you shall know them." I think that is very true. One of the strongest decrees of the Vatican Council was the reorganization and the restructuring of the rites of liturgy and the sacraments so that they more clearly reveal the saving mysteries and powers of the symbols and the presence of Jesus in our communities. How do we gauge the effectiveness of these changes in our sacramental rituals, and the quality of life in our communities? Another contemporary author, Annie Dillard, pokes fun at our rituals and tells the truth about much of our worship in her short novel *Holy the Firm*. She is struggling in agony over the reality of suffering and the presence of God. She writes:

The higher Christian churches—where, if anywhere, I belong—come at God with an unwarranted air of professionalism, with authority and pomp, as though they knew what they were doing, as though people in themselves were an appropriate set of creatures to have dealings with God. I often think of the set pieces of liturgy as certain words which people have successfully addressed to God without their getting killed. In the high churches they saunter through liturgy like Mohawks along a strand of scaffolding who have long since forgotten their danger. If God were to blast such a service to bits, the congregation would be, I believe, genuinely shocked. But in the low churches you expect it any minute. This is the beginning of wisdom.[9]

Although her writing can remind us of the "old church" and its mystery and rites, its sense of fear and trembling, it really isn't that far from Paul's words to his wayward Christian community in Corinth:

What I now have to say is not said in praise, because your meetings are not profitable but harmful. First of all, I hear that when you gather for a meeting there are divisions among you, and I am inclined to believe it. There may even have to be factions among you for the tried and the true to stand out clearly. . . . Would you show contempt for the church of God, and embarrass those who have nothing? What can I say to you? Shall I praise you? Certainly not in this matter! . . . When you assemble for the meal, wait for one another. If anyone is hungry, let him eat at home, so that your assembly may not deserve condemnation (1 Cor 11:17-22, 33-34, *NAB*).

This too, is the beginning of wisdom, the critique of a ritual.
But Annie Dillard can also describe the church in more tender terms, and we can find comfort in her words:

A blur of romance clings to our notions of "publicans," "sinners," "the poor," "the people in the marketplace," "our neighbors," as though of course God should reveal himself, if at all, to these simple people, these Sunday school watercolor figures, who are so purely themselves in their tattered robes, who are single in themselves, while we now are various, complex and full at heart. We are busy. So, I see now, were they. Who shall ascend into the hill of the Lord? or who shall stand in his holy place? There is no one but us. There is no one to send, nor a clean hand, nor a pure heart on the face of the earth, nor in the earth but only us, a generation of comforting ourselves with the notion that we have come at an awk-

ward time, that our innocent fathers are all dead—as if innocence
had ever been—and our children busy and troubled, and we ourselves unfit, not yet ready, having each of us chosen wrongly, made
a false start, failed, yielded to impulse and the tangled comfort of
pleasures, and grown exhausted, unable to seek the thread, weak,
and involved. But there is no one but us. There never has been.
There have been generations which remembered, and generations
which forgot; there has never been a generation of whole men and
women who lived well for even one day. Yet some have imagined
well, with honesty and art, the detail of such a life, and have described it with such grace, that we mistake vision for history, dream
for description, and fancy that life has devolved. So. You learn this
studying any history at all, especially the lives of artists and vi-
sionaries; you learn it from Emerson, who noticed that the mean-
ness of our days is itself worth our thought; and you learn it, fitful
in your pew, at church.[10]

It is interesting to note that since writing both these pieces, Annie Dillard
has become a Roman Catholic, about as "high church" as one can get.

Our rituals, our sacraments, like Jesus Christ, are more than words in
a language we now understand and manipulate more easily. They are
more than the perceived meanings of certain words and phrases, acceptable or unacceptable to certain groups in the assembly. Sacrament is
symbol, mystery, an icon, a doorway where God comes in. And we cannot escape God's coming. The sacraments and liturgy provide us with
endless opportunities to encounter God, to respond to the Spirit, to convert our lives, to deepen our realization of the ethic we have bound ourselves to as believers and disciples. The sacraments and liturgy allow us
entry into the lives of our friends and neighbors, brothers and sisters in
faith, where we practice that ethic with accountability and maturity, nurturing and nourishment, vision and harsh reality.

We have a tendency to be overly verbal but the symbols and the actions are more powerful in these rites. We learn to relive the stories, let
them speak for themselves, concentrate on the gestures, the song and
dance, the objects, the symbols of bread, wine, water, oil, breath, book,
person, table, altar, space, and even the one that threatens us most, touch.
The ritual gives the model, as Jesus gives the norm, the ethic in flesh and
blood. But rituals must celebrate the reality in our day-to-day lives and
relationships in the community and the world or, no matter how much
we adapt and alter the structure, we will not be transformed and converted. Knowledge of the ritual and its meaning is not enough. We need

to act justly, love tenderly, and walk humbly with our God, so that we can celebrate what is happening in our lives. More than information and correct liturgy we need accountability in our behavior and our relationships with one another.

Rather than require six weeks of baptismal preparation for the parents of children or six months of confirmation classes or a weekend of pre-Cana and six months of conferences, we have to start demanding more. We have to ask questions, hard ones, and demand commitments, promises in public, accountability for our life choices, lifestyles, and behavior both as individuals and as communities. If we profess to be adult Christians, then confirmation must be associated with promises to witness publicly in imitation of the Spirit to the values of Christianity: nonviolence, truth-telling, care for the poor, respect for the holiness of all life and the dignity of persons. These need to be upheld not just as vague generalizations of good will toward humanity but as choices in personal morality, law and government, lifestyle and community.

If baptism is truly to be the initiation into the new life of Jesus, then there must be public evidence of change, of conversion, of altered lifestyles, not just the desire to be baptized. If baptism is to be a public acceptance of the person of Jesus Christ, a beginning on the road to Jerusalem, then our baptismal promises need to be more specific in regard to life, life ever more abundantly within our own communities and in the world.

If eucharist is to be truly thanksgiving for the Bread of Life and the Wine of Hope, then we must commit ourselves to easing hunger and poverty in our churches, nation, and world, hungering and thirsting for justice in reality before we take communion. If eucharist is a sign of our union in God with one another, then we must make sure that divisions are seen for what they are, tears in the garment of the church.

The sacrament of reconciliation needs to confront both individually and collectively those who pick and choose among values. It needs to ask, teach, call to accountability, and seek to repair the destruction to which our choices have contributed as well as encourage us to live non-violent lives of resistance to evil.

The sacrament of anointing and pastoral care for the sick must become a positive reminder that certain people and persons reveal to us the suffering-servant face of our God and that they are to be treated with reverence and special care.

And the sacraments of marriage and orders must be seen as undeveloped and presently more exclusive than inclusive of the people of God and their needs as adult believers. These sacraments attest to the adult values of a Christian. Why are they not available to all Christians? All believers, men and women, need a sacrament to proclaim and celebrate their faithful love and service to the community. Baptism initiates us into the life of Christ, into the life of the church. This life needs to be extended to those who are excluded now. All the sacraments need to be examined carefully, deeply and honestly, along with the ethical behavior and belief of Christians in conjunction with their expression. Both must be adapted and changed, be converted so that each reveals more truly the proclamation of the good news, resurrection, Jesus, and community in the Trinity.

Before we look at the liturgy and the sacraments individually, we will look at the reality of the world, the kingdom of God in the world, and the church; the church's relationship to the world in the light of the Vatican Council; and the bridge that Christians are between the world and the church. The sacraments belong to Christians, to the church, and it is in the behavior, life choices, and lifestyles of Christians, in their relationships and ways of living in the world, that the ethic of Jesus and the sacraments of Jesus find their meaning and power.

We end as we began, with a story.

✟   Once upon a time, a group of disciples gathered around the master to listen to him describe the life of the Spirit, a life of ethical holiness. He told his followers that they needed daily reflection, meditation, and examination of conscience; that they were not to be ruled by their emotions but to act willfully; and that their manner of life must be habitual, consistent, and ever more conscious.

They sought to put his advice into practice. Weeks later the master came for another visit and repeated exactly what he had said before. They asked him questions, seeking more depth and specifics about these rules. He smiled at them and said: "The spiritual life, the moral life, the holy life is like a sieve!" They looked at each other and wondered what he meant by that statement. They discussed his words for many more weeks.

One man said: "I think I understand what he is saying. I do a good deed, and then I feel good about it, but eventually it passes—like a sieve? Or someone does not treat me kindly or justly and immediately all my previous attempts at virtue seem ridiculous and I react poorly—it all washes through me like a sieve?" But later he did not think that he was correct in his interpretation. Another thought he was making fun of them or that he was alluding to a referrence to a sieve in the tradition. Most forgot his exact words.

Later, one woman sought out the master and begged for insight, for the meaning of his words.

The master said: "Let's walk."

Then he took her to a high rock that was near the ocean's edge. He handed her a cup and asked her to fill a sieve. She filled it, watching it run out.

Then he spoke to her kindly and patiently: "While you stand on the rock of yourself, your own consciousness and knowledge and experience, you cannot grow or fill anything up."

"But," she pleaded, "how can I do it then?"

His reply was swift and full of laughter. "Easy!" He seized her sieve and flung it far out into the ocean. She could see it floating on the waves, the tide carrying it for a while, and then it sank out of sight. She looked at him, and he smiled and said: "You must be immersed, disappear! You, your ego must disappear into the Divine. Do it! I command you to be holy, to belong only to God, to be holy as God is holy! That is all that is needed, only that: obey!"

As believers in Jesus, we are reminded in our baptisms that "we live no longer for ourselves alone, but now we live, hidden with Christ in God!" This is the proclamation at the Easter Vigil at the conclusion of the rite of making new Christians and welcoming them into the community. This and only this is what is needed: to be made in the image and likeness of Jesus Christ, our crucified and risen Lord.

Let us pray this ancient prayer of the church:

Glory to you, Lord, whose grace has done so much for us. You became our brother to make us God's daughters and sons; you raised us from the lowly condition of servants to the lofty rank of children and heirs; you made us beloved to you that we, through the Spirit given to us, might appeal to God on behalf of all, saying: Lord, have mercy. Give us cause for rejoicing until we rejoice before you forever. Amen.

2

The Church, the World, and the Kingdom

✝ Once upon a time, when Solomon was king in Jerusalem, he had a faithful servant and advisor named Benaiah. He relied on him and recognized his wisdom. He would watch him as the man went about his duties—attentive, respectful, and yet assertive and bold. In fact, it was well known that Benaiah boasted that he was the most faithful of the king's subjects and that he could do anything the king requested. It did not take long for Benaiah to acquire enemies in the court. One day they approached the king, complaining of Benaiah's boasting. They wanted the king to set him an impossible task. King Solomon agreed, thinking to teach his advisor and friend a lesson in humility.

Benaiah was summoned and told he had six months to find a ring that the king desired. It was a ring that would make anyone who was happy, sad, and anyone who was sad, happy. With enthusiasm, Benaiah set forth. He prowled the back streets of the ghettos and the wider streets of Jerusalem; he even went out into the towns and villages to the houses of the destitute and those without hope. Everywhere he went, he looked and listened and learned much about his king's domain, especially about inequality and violence, human need and desire, evil and untold goodness, kindness and hospitality. Then his travels took him across the kingdom's borders into neighboring countries and further still into places he had only heard of. It was the same throughout the world. There was incredible goodness and also horror and inhumanity. But Benaiah's time was running out, and though he had asked everywhere, no one had heard of the ring that Solomon requested.

Finally he returned to Jerusalem, to the area where he had grown to manhood. He only had a handful of days left, and he was preparing himself to come before the king without the ring, humbled, knowing that his position in the kingdom and the court would never be the same. He regretted this deeply, for there was much that Solomon needed to know from his travels and he feared that his failure would cast doubt in Solomon's mind about the veracity of his insights, let alone his suggestions for remedying some of the kingdom's ills and injustices. He was musing on these thoughts as he turned into the street of the merchants and was stopped by an old grandfather and his wife, sellers of antiques. Recognizing him from childhood, they invited him in for coffee, and they questioned him about the king and the court and why he was wandering through the streets of his childhood. He told them of his dilemma, and the old man and woman smiled knowingly at one another. Wait here, he was told, we can help you.

He was only too glad to trust them, and they disappeared into a back room. He heard them rummaging about and soon they appeared with an old ring. The man handed it to Benaiah and told him to look at the inscription that he had just carved into the inside of the ring: *This too shall pass.*

Benaiah smiled. He had his treasure and Solomon would have his ring. The old couple accepted only his thanks and the promise of return visits, and Benaiah returned at last to the court of Solomon.

The court and king waited for his presentation, his enemies and detractors as well as his friends and allies. The ring was handed over to Solomon, whose face visibly changed when he read the inscription. Truly those who saw the ring would become sad if they were happy, and happy if they were sad. *This too shall pass.*

This is the old wisdom, an ancient reminder of the passage of time, of mortality, of limits and vulnerability and the inevitability of change and transformation. It is said that from that day forth Solomon wore this simple ring instead of his royal signet ring, so that he too would live daily by its wisdom. And he listened and heeded Benaiah's counsel about the state of his kingdom.

It seems that every sage has sought to live in such a way that the world becomes truer and more human because of his or her presence within it. Yet the world has proved a stumbling block and a distraction for men and women as well. In our recent history as Catholics we have undergone a sea change of drastic importance in our view of the world.

The *Pastoral Constitution on the Church in the Modern World* begins with these words on the relationship of the church to the world:

> The joys and the hopes, the griefs and the anxieties of the men of this age, especially those who are poor or in any way afflicted, these too are the joys and hopes, the griefs and anxieties of the followers of Christ. Indeed, nothing genuinely human fails to raise an echo in their hearts. For theirs is a community composed of men. United in Christ, they are led by the Holy Spirit in their journey to the kingdom of their Father and they have welcomed the news of salvation which is meant for every man. That is why this community realizes that it is truly and intimately linked with mankind and its history (no. 1).

> The Council brings to mankind light kindled from the gospel, and puts at its disposal those saving resources which the Church herself, under the guidance of the Holy Spirit, receives from her Founder. For the human person deserves to be preserved; human society deserves to be renewed. Hence the pivotal point of our total presentation will be man himself, whole and entire, body and soul, heart and conscience, mind and will.
>
> Therefore, this sacred Synod proclaims the highest destiny of man and champions the godlike seed which has been sown in him. It offers to mankind the honest assistance of the Church in fostering that brotherhood of all men which corresponds to this destiny of theirs. Inspired by no earthly ambition, the Church seeks but a solitary goal: to carry forward the work of Christ Himself under the lead of the befriending Spirit. And Christ entered this world to give witness to the truth, to rescue and not to sit in judgment, to serve and not to be served (no. 3).[1]

With this document the church begins a new age, an age that welcomes the world, accepts the world as its domain, and even admits the need to learn from the world as well as to teach and to serve the world. Now what is human belongs as much to the desire of the church as it does to the world. It is an acknowledgment that the voice of God speaks in the signs of the times as well as in the voice of the church tradition. Now the church takes up sincerely its duty of "scrutinizing the signs of the times and of interpreting them in the light of the gospel" (no. 4).

In paragraph 92 of the *Pastoral Constitution on the Church in the Modern World* various groups of people that the church can most assuredly cooperate with are listed: a) the dialogue within the church, recognizing "lawful diversity"; b) dialogue with "those brothers and communities not yet living with us in full communion" (ecumenism); c) with "all who acknowledge God"; d) with those "who cultivate beautiful qualities of the human spirit, but do not yet acknowledge the Source of these qualities." The Vatican Council ended the reign of triumphalism that had characterized so much of church/state history. And the church goes still farther in its own confession.

> [The Church] is very well aware that among her members, both clerical and lay, some have been unfaithful to the Spirit of God during the course of many centuries. In the present age, too, it does not escape the Church how great a distance lies between the message she offers and the human failings of those to whom the gospel is entrusted (no. 43).

Part of the *problem* with the world, it seems, is Christians and their lack of faithfulness to the gospel ethic of Jesus the Lord. Indeed, the church itself has been lacking in witnessing to and living out the demands of Jesus as light to the world in its own communities.

In tandem with this confession the church initiates a reign of service to the human community and presents basic principles in regard to the dignity of the human person, the necessity of human freedom, and the foundation that justice and the development of the human person and the advance of society depend upon each other (no. 25). The document underscores the belief that persons should be understood in social terms, in terms of relationships in society and community, as people of God. The interdependence of societies and communities is stressed and corporate human action on behalf of justice is accepted. Christian ethical responsibility is not just an individual responsibility but the domain of church and community.

The portions of the document that deal with economics and inequality, war and peace, culture and education, politics and church have served as the basis for many encyclicals and pastoral letters in both the universal church and local, national churches. Statements of John Paul II in his travels around the world often echo principles that first appeared in this document:

The Church . . . invites Christians to commit themselves to constructing a more just, humane and habitable world which does not close itself in, but rather, opens itself to God. . . . Making this world more just means, among other things, to make the effort, to strive to have a world in which no more children lack sufficient nutrition, education, instruction; . . . and that the economic and political never prevail over the human.[2]

A decade after Vatican II the churches were still confessing their failure to be church, as this statement from the Commission on World Mission and Evangelism Assembly in Bangkok in January 1973 reveals. "We have been deeply conscious of our failures in obedience to our Lord and our blindness to the ways he sets before us. We are moved by a profound feeling of penitence which both pains us and frees us for Christ's renewal."

The internal struggle of the church in the best sense of the word continues, a struggle to be forgiven for past failures and to be freed for renewal in the world in the future. It is expressed by bishops, priests, theologians, and lay ministers. The church itself is experiencing a time of self-criticism, self-evaluation, and self-affirmation as it struggles with being more true to the gospel in the midst of the world.

One of the greatest resources and newly rediscovered sources of renewal is the mission churches of the Third World. In *Christianity Rediscovered* Vincent Donovan describes in utter simplicity and stark possibility the power of these churches:

If the missionary truly presents God and Jesus Christ, his work is certainly finished. The rest is up to the people hearing the message. They can either reject the message entirely, or they can accept it. If they accept it, what they must do is outlined in general in the scripture, but that outline should not be considered part of the good news. I think it is rather the response to the good news. It is the church.

While the general outline of the church is certainly present in scripture, the specific details of the church, the response to the good news, will just as certainly have to be as free and diverse as all the separate cultures of the human race.

What does scripture say people must do if they accept as true God's revelation to man? First, they must believe in all that God has done, and in Christ. Then they must be sorry that they have thrown this goodness back in God's face in ingratitude; they must be sorry for the part they have played in destroying the world and their fellowmen. They must believe the unexpected good news that though they have taken part in this destruction, there is no reason to despair, there is no reason for anyone, or any people, to remain a failure forever. Because of Jesus Christ, all this can be undone, can be forgiven, and they can begin again anew. They must signify this belief and sorrow of theirs outwardly through a sign that all can see, that is, they must be baptized. They must not keep all this to themselves. They must go forth in the Spirit and witness to this good news and to Jesus, letting others see the meaning of it all, by their words and by their lives, until the time that Jesus comes again. And this is the final obligation: they must believe that Jesus will come again in consummation, and they must work in expectation of that parousia.

And that is it. That is the church. . . .

Repent, believe, be baptized, witness to Christ in the Spirit until he comes again. This is the response to the Christian message. That is the church.

Such a description of the church is both rich and deep, and yet free and open. It by no means leads us to come automatically to the form of the Western, Roman church we know, nor to the parish church we live and work in.[3]

The reality of pluralism in the church and the riches of the mission churches are becoming a wellspring for the church's understanding and development of its role in the world's future, especially among the poor and oppressed in Africa, Latin America, and Asia, where the majority of Christians dwell (even though only one-tenth of one percent of Asians are Christians).

The more the church becomes itself, the more it becomes a sacrament, a symbol that attracts and welcomes others, and the more influence and effect it will have on the world's events and histories. Only when the love of its own members for humankind becomes concretely and historically visible here and now, and is no longer confined to those immediately apparent or acceptable, will the reality of the good news be experienced in the world. Since Vatican II the church is learning to be a more concentrated, pluralistic, yet unified sacrament of the risen Lord, intent on bringing the dynamism of the gospel to bear on the lives of all peoples politically, economically, educationally, socially, and religiously.

The church is learning from the signs of the times, from the experience of the masses of people in the world, that God speaks there as clearly as in church structure, teaching, and belief.

C. S. Song, an Asian theologian, writes about learning from human beings, especially the poor:

There is such a thing as a theology with a mouth—not so much in the sense of a theology that speaks profound things as in the sense of a theology that eats the food set before it. Theology . . . cannot be choosy about what it eats. Wherever it goes, it must be able to digest the food provided by the given locality. A theology that feeds on soft bread alone is too delicate to survive the rough and tumble of Asia. Rice is definitely the staple food for theology in Asia. If theology in Asia avoids rice, it will become fragile and sick. When a church in Asia cannot celebrate the eucharist except with bread, it cannot grow into a robust church. If we continue to *break bread* instead of *sharing rice* at our theological table, our theology will be out of context and will not do justice to revelation.

"Rice is heaven," says Kim Chi Ha, a Roman Catholic poet in South Korea who suffered much for his human rights struggle. We can also turn it around and say: heaven is rice. How true this is for the starving masses in Asia! Jesus said to his disciples, "Where two or three have met together in my name, I am there among them" (Matt. 18:20). Perhaps he could also have said, "Where two or three have met together *for rice* in my name, I am there among them." Meeting with Christ is a sacramental experience. Gathering together with him is a eucharistic act. But where do we have a sacramental encounter with Jesus? Where can we be a participant in this eucharistic act with Christ? In church when the communion is celebrated? Maybe. But a most vivid sacramental experience takes place when two or three hungry persons huddle together to devour a bowl of rice. They gain a new lease on life. They can get up and walk again. Tomorrow is not just a dark emptiness, and hope is not just a luxury of the rich and the powerful. This is the real meaning of the eucharist—the eucharist where rice is heaven and heaven is rice. A theology without a mouth is far removed from such sacramental experience and eucharistic participation. A theology without rice can serve neither God nor human beings in Asia.[4]

In addition, the church is beginning dialogues with other world religions, recognizing the voice and presence of God in them as well. Two short but very vibrant selections reveal the riches most Christians have not yet tapped in their own personal spiritualities and that the church at large is still unaware of for the most part.

Have any of us heard and meditated upon these words, for example, from the "Surangama Sutra" from the Buddhist scriptures?

> May I be a balm to the sick, their healer and servitor,
>   until sickness come never again;
> May I quench with rains of food and drink the
>   anguish of hunger and thirst;
> May I be in the famine of the ages' end their drink
>   and meat;
> May I become an unfailing store for the poor, and
>   serve them with manifold things for their need.
> My own being and my pleasures, all my righteous-
>   ness in the past, present and future I surrender
>   indifferently, that all creatures may win to their
>   end.[5]

These words of heartfelt love and compassion for all the world rival the Christian story of the Good Samaritan and the words of compassion revealed in the scriptures when Jesus is "moved to pity at the sight of the lame and the sick." From the Buddhists who recite them from memory and seek to be true to them in practice we can find connection and shared vision for the future of our world.

The second selection is a short poem, "Open Secret," from the Sufi poet Rumi, who lived in the thirteenth century in Balkh, in what is now Afghanistan.

> The sufi opens his hands to the universe
> and gives away each instant, free
> Unlike someone who begs on the street for money to
>   survive,
> a dervish begs to give you his life.[6]

A Sufi parable can lead to the kingdom of heaven in four lines and remind Christians that the Spirit is to be found anywhere in the world, anywhere humans let God in and seek to uncover that presence and live truthfully.

In a religious tradition that is much closer to home, the Jewish testament, the church is learning from contemporary prophets and storytellers like Elie Wiesel, who describes himself as a witness and writes so that the world will not forget the fate of the Jewish people during the Second World War. His books ask questions, hard questions about contemporary Christian society and culture. In an interview on a Canadian television program called "Man Alive," Wiesel was asked: "Why didn't more Christians come to the aid of the Jews?"

"I have no answer," he replied. "No real answer. I don't understand what happened to them during the war. I guess God kept silent. It's easy for me to become an accuser of Christianity. It's almost too easy. And Christians themselves, those who are honest and sincere, understand that the crisis taking place now within Christianity is very profound because, it's a terrible thing to say, but Christianity failed. Christianity knew its bankruptcy at Auschwitz. You see, Auschwitz did not take place in a vacuum. It took place within a given setting, a social, philosophical and geographical setting. A setting of 2,000 years of Christianity. . . . Certainly Judaism didn't. We came out of it dead, but alive. We lost millions, but Judaism came out of it unharmed, untarnished. It withstood Auschwitz. Christianity did not."

The interview continues:

"I try to make them [both Catholics and Protestants] more Christian simply by being more Jewish. I tell them my tales and I listen to theirs. Both must have a deep concern for humanity as the basis, otherwise it is useless."[7]

Here we find clearly stated that members of other religious faiths expect and hope that we will become more of what we claim to be, truly Christians. Wiesel and others, like German theologian Dorothee Soelle, prick our consciences and demand that we deal with the ethical issues of the Holocaust and the Christian churches, even fifty years after the fact.

In the years since there have been other holocausts around the world, involving Christians and others. We have still to learn to heed the questions and to respond with swift, nonviolent, and hopeful actions and relationships.

The church also is looking elsewhere in the world for knowledge and understanding in dealing with and interpreting the ways of the kingdom of God in history. It is dialoguing with sociologists, economists, political scientists, governments, and political parties, as well as looking to science and technology to inform its pastoral applications of the gospel in contemporary life. A list of those consulted during the drafting of the bishops' pastoral letters on peace and economics is indicative of the church's trust and growth in working with the academic and scientific communities.

Artists, writers, and dramatists all contribute to the church's growing sensitivity to the world and shared community. As Willa Cather, an American author, wrote long before Vatican II:

> There are only two or three human stories and these go on repeating themselves as fiercely as if they'd never happened before. . . . An author must live, live deeply and richly and generously, live not only his own life, but all lives. He must have experiences that cannot be got out of a classical dictionary or even in polite society. He must come to know the world a good deal as God knows it, in all the pitiable depravity of its evil, in all the measureless sublimity of its good.

Writer Ignazio Silone connects literature with politics, specifically the reality of the church's dealing with communism and socialism. Silone's belief in human solidarity is reflected in his views on relations between the West and the Soviet Union, written in 1981:

> In the "difficult dialogue" with the Communist world . . . we should not consider "the other" as a remote symbol or potential instrument, but rather as "a neighbor" with whom a mutual and sympathetic relationship (in spite of all difficulties) can be established. . . . The face of Russia is no longer that of Medusa; it is a human face.[8]

Novelists such as Silone seek to deal with the realities of political and religious or liturgical life and boldly proclaim the ethical demands of belief in Jesus, in Christianity. In *The Story of a Humble Christian* Silone writes:

Try to understand me, I beg you. Even if, in a moment of weakness, I agreed to impart the blessing you ask of me, it would then
be physically impossible for me to impart it. Why? My son, it
shouldn't be difficult for you to image that. The sign of Christian
benediction is the Sign of the Cross. You know, don't you, what
the Cross is? And the words of the blessing are: in the name of the
Father, of the Son, and of the Holy Spirit. If I understand you cor-
rectly, you suggest that I give this blessing to soldiers about to go
off to war, while I am thinking of something else. Did you mean to
joke? It would be a horrible sacrilege. With the Sign of the Cross
and the names of the Trinity, you can bless bread, soup, water,
wine, and if you like, even the tools of labor, the plough, the
peasant's hoe, the carpenter's plane, and so on; but not weapons. If
you absolutely need some propitiatory rite, find someone who will
perform it in the name of Satan. It was he who invented weapons.

The pope and bishops in the last thirty years have begun to repeat
ideas such as these in their exhortations, speeches, pastoral letters, and
denunciations against war, generally and in specific instances.

The Church, however, which has no weapons at her disposal apart
from those of the Spirit, of the word and of love . . . does not cease
. . . to beg everybody in the name of God and in the name of man:
Do not kill! Do not prepare destruction and extermination for men![9]

An entire movement within the church called *liberation theologies* is
much the product of national churches dialoguing with socialism, Marx-
ism, communism, and interpreting economics and politics from a scrip-
tural perspective and seeking common ground.

Statements like this one from Dom Helder Camara could hardly have
been acknowledged or understood prior to the Vatican Council's documents on justice and the world:

Of course I'm a socialist. I don't see any solution in capitalism.
But neither do I see it in the socialist examples that are offered
today, because they're based on dictatorships. Mine is a socialism
that respects the human person and goes back to the Gospels. My
socialism is justice.

Because of the church's dialogue with the poor, the oppressed, and
those struggling for justice in many countries, the reality of the harsh-

ness and indignity of much of humanity's experience is now the subject of theology. Leonardo Boff, perhaps known best as a systematic theologian of liberation, describes this development in theology since Vatican II.

> To create a theology of liberation based on the practice of liberation, it is necessary to participate as an active member in a particular movement, a base community, a center for the defense of human rights or a trade union. This immersion in the world of the poor and oppressed gives theological discourse a passionate edge, and occasional mordancy, a holy wrath—and a sense of the practical. There is an objective concern for efficacy, because in the last analysis what counts is not theological reflection but the concrete liberation of the poor. It is this liberation-in-act rather than liberation-in-thought that anticipates the Kingdom and is pleasing to God. Oppression is not so much to be thought about; it is to be overcome.[10]

The last thirty years of church/state relations, the rise of Solidarity in Poland, a Polish pontiff, the Latin American churches' responses to Vatican II, the enormous growth in the African churches, and the coming of age of mission churches like those of Asia and India all attest to the altered and dramatically changed styles and attitudes of the church in the world.

The *Pastoral Constitution on the Church in the Modern World* has also been criticized by theologians and lay ministers because its tone, in opposition to past triumphalism, seems too all-accepting of the world. On occasion it sounds almost uncritical of the world's ways. For instance, "The church knows that her message is in harmony with the most secret desires of the human heart" (no. 21). The document minimizes the degree to which the gospel can be a scandal and a stumbling block by which men and women can be offended as well as uplifted. The church, in attempting to make common cause with others, sometimes blurred the uniqueness of the Christian message and the reality that the kingdom of God does not make its appearance easily recognizable in any nation, state, government, or people.[11] Since the mid-1960s the church has grown more sure of itself, of its need to critique society, and its obligation to stand firm in the face of the world's weaknesses, sin, and strengths.

Thomas Merton speaks to this issue:

In "turning to the world" the contemporary Church is first of all admitting that the world can once again become an object of choice. Not only can it be chosen, but in fact it must be chosen. How? If I had no choice about the age in which I was to live, I nevertheless have a choice about the attitude I take and about the way and the extent of my participation in its living ongoing events. To choose the world is not then merely a pious admission that the world is acceptable because it comes from the hand of God. It is first of all an acceptance of a task and a vocation in the world, in history and in time. In my time, which is the present. To choose the world is to choose to do the work I am capable of doing, in collaboration with my brother, to make the world better, more free, more just, more livable, more human.

But, he cautions:

To choose the world . . . is to choose the anguish of being hampered and frustrated in a situation fraught with frightful difficulties. We can affirm the world and its values all we like, but the complexity of events responds too often with a cold negation of our hopes.[12]

Merton is far from being cynical. He is a realist, acquainted with the world as well as with his monastery. Almost three decades have passed since the death of Merton, and the legacy he speaks about as our heritage from the world has continued to grow in both possibility and horror.
Contemporary theologian Matthew Lamb has outlined some of the realities of the last nine decades that have drastically shifted our understanding of anguish and the world:

Increasingly, the anguish in the world has shifted from the weary shoulders of mother nature to the proud shoulders of a male-dominated history so aptly symbolized by Atlas. Anguish has taken an anthropocentric (indeed, androcentric) turn to the subject. The countless wars and the nuclear arms race are only more evident symptoms of this turn. Never before in human history have so many humans slaughtered their fellow human beings on such a massive scale. The Lisbon earthquake pales in comparison with Hiroshima and Nagasaki. Famines and plagues can hardly measure up to the demonic intensity of the holocaust. The terrors of nature have tended to take a back seat to the horrors of history. This shift from a primacy of nature to a primacy of history as the locus of human suffering has led to a recovery of a "deprivatized" notion of human perversity.[13]

This book was written in the early 1980s, before the wars in Iran, Iraq, the national massacres in Africa and Bosnia, and the continuing killings in El Salvador, Guatemala, and scores of other places around the world.

Lamb lists other cancerous growths in our society: the phenomenal number of first-world scientists (some estimate almost three-quarters or four-fifths) involved in war-related research; the disastrous effects of world trade patterns, multinational corporations, and agribusiness; land distribution and private ownership of property; displacement of capital in third-world countries; and industrial and military expansion on the base of poverty, disease, and hunger in third-world countries. The litany of "isms" seems endless: imperialism, communism, colonialism, racism, sexism, capitalism, militarism, totalitarianism, sacralism, atheistic secularism, consumerism, multinationalism, fascism, anti-Semitism, Nazism, technocratic elitism, authoritarianism, individualism and so on. This is the reality of our world as we enter the twenty-first century. Our prejudices and violence seek out the unborn, the unwanted, the outcast, the handicapped, the alien, the poor—all those bound by categories we use to describe and constrict human beings.

These realities call theologians and Christians to acknowledge the widespread suffering of so many victims of world policy, to denounce these realities as sin, social sin, and to announce a new day, a day of justice for all in the advancing kingdom of God. For we, as Christians, profess publicly in our words, our rituals, and our ethics that Jesus is Lord, the Lord who "who humbled himself unto death, even death on a cross" (Phil 2:8). In Jesus, God lined up with the victims of suffering, evil, and injustice for all times. Theology is being reminded of such "subversive memories," a term coined by Johannes Metz to speak about both liturgy and the reality of death and resurrection. By 1971 the Synod of Bishops' document *Justice in the World* issued a stirring call for the church's active social involvement. It clearly explicated the church's growing understanding of its relationship to the world and its prophetic role in the midst of such realities and sin. "Our times demand profound changes in the very structures of society, structures which often constitute in themselves an embodiment of the sin of injustice" (no. 2).[14]

Peter Henriot describes this social sin:

A social structure which oppresses human dignity and stifles freedom; a social situation which promotes and facilitates individual
acts of selfishness and a social structure or situation which is unjust also become sinful when one is aware of the injustice but refuses to exert efforts to change it—this is the social sin of complic-
ity.[15]

How does a politically responsible Christian, genuinely worried about
such evil in our world, live with this reality. We find our answers in the
words of a sermon by Gregory the Great: "The place of battle is the heart
of the one who hears the word of God. It is called a place of battle because where the word is received makes war on well-worn ways of life."

Apathetic resignation, heroic recriminations, and guilt only trivialize
the sufferings of so many or merely heap paralyzing guilt on those who
exclude themselves from such realities. Our religion demands that we
refuse to be victims, that we bring into being a transformed vision of
reality—the kingdom of peace and justice that Jesus proclaimed.

Matthew Lamb gives us a description of discipleship that calls us to
respond as Christians to this world:

The discipleship is a life lived in a dying identification with the
victims. Prophecy is constituted by an agapic life or praxis whereby
the cries of victims are articulated into a voice protesting the vic-
timization of humans by other humans. . . . Prophetic theologies
are the narratives of the heart open to the cries of the victims, political theologies are the efforts of the mind seeking to understand
the reasons of such a heart.[16]

Lamb speaks of action on behalf of justice that is conversion, a
metanoia, that literally changes our minds and hearts and reveals to us
God's identification with the victims. Identification with the victims of
the world begins to heal the irrationalities of the biases that harden hearts
and darken human reason. These expressions are seen in prophetic story,
preaching, liturgy and sacraments, the arts, and in solidarity among
peoples that transform the human psyche and the human reality. Society,
the world, is transformed by people who believe, who celebrate the presence of God, and who transform the world using symbols, gestures, and
the old stories of belief and religion. The starting point is always in com-

munity, learning commitment in action, ethical behavior, and shared conversion, that is, celebrated in liturgy and sacraments. It is the ecclesial task of the church to act justly, love tenderly, and walk humbly with God in the world.

Another contemporary Christian, Southern writer Flannery O'Connor, reminds us of the connection between church and world and how we are to live in both:

> I think that the Church is the only thing that is going to make the terrible world we are coming to endurable; the only thing that makes the Church endurable is that it is somehow the Body of Christ and that on this we are fed. It seems to be a fact that you have to suffer as much from the Church as for it but if you believe in the divinity of Christ, you have to cherish the world at the same time that you struggle to endure.

We live with one foot in the world and one in the church. The difference lies, perhaps, in which foot takes the weight, which foot we pivot on as we move. O'Connor didn't write theology per se; she wrote stories about the world, the flesh, the devil, God, and of course, human beings in relation to all of them. She penned the following in a letter to a friend, explaining why she wrote the way she did.

> I don't think you should write something as long as a novel around anything that is not of the gravest concern to you and everybody else and for me this is always the conflict between an attraction for the Holy and the disbelief in it that we breathe in with the air of the times. It's hard to believe always but more so in the world we live in now. There are some of us who have to pay for our faith every step of the way and who have to work out dramatically what it would be like without it.

Where do we stand as Christians in the world? Enid Dinnis, in a novel written at the beginning of the twentieth century, writes: "For it is only by standing at the foot of the cross that one can view the world from God's point of view. We get his outlook if we go up close enough and stand quite still."[17] Our lives, both as individual believers and as a Christian community must be integrated, connected internally as well as to the world outside us.

In March 1934 Gandhi spoke to some of his contemporaries who wondered about mixing politics (the world) and religion:

> I could not live for a single second without religion. Many of my political friends despair of me because they say that even my politics are derived from religion. And they are right. My politics and all other activities of a person of religion must be derived from their religion, because religion means being bound to God, that is to say, God rules your every breath.

The church lives in the world. What happens in the world is as much our responsibility as what happens in the church. We still have to incorporate into our daily life, our belief systems, our celebrations, and our process of making ethical decisions the reality that we are connected to the world and its evils. We need to heed Abraham Joshua Heschel's statement: "Some of us are guilty—but all of us are responsible." We are the church. We are the world.

In the very first lines of John's gospel the earth and principally Christians are reminded that "he was already in the world and through him the world was made, the very world that did not know him. He came to his own, yet his own people did not receive him; but all who have received him he empowers to become children of God for they believe in his Name" (Jn 1:10-12). We are his own. We believe that he has empowered us to become the children of God. He comes to us yet we do not accept him fully, we do not know him for who he is. The first task for the church in the world is to be church, to be his own, who know him, accept him, and reveal him to the nations.

Stanley Hauerwas says that the church is a social ethic. He explains his position and its uniqueness thus:

> I am in fact challenging the very idea that Christian social ethics is primarily an attempt to make the world more peaceable or just. Put starkly, the first social ethical task of the church is to be church—the servant community. Such a claim may well sound self-serving until we remember that what makes church the church is its faithful manifestation of the peaceable kingdom in the world. As such the church does not have a social ethic; the church is a social ethic.

The church is where the stories of Israel and Jesus are told, enacted, and heard, and it is our conviction that as a Christian people there is literally nothing more important we can do. But the telling of that story requires that we be a particular kind of people if we and the world are to hear the story truthfully. That means that the Church must never cease from being a community of peace and truth in a world of mendacity and fear. The church does not let the world set its agenda about what constitutes a "social ethic," but a church of peace and justice must set its own agenda. It does this first by having the patience amid the injustice and violence of this world to care for the widow, the poor and the orphan. Such care, from the world's perspective, may seem to contribute little to the cause of justice, yet it is our conviction that unless we take the time for such care neither we nor the world can know what justice looks like.

By being that kind of community we see that the church helps the world understand what it means to be the world. For the world has no way of knowing it is world without the church pointing to the reality of God's kingdom. How could the world ever recognize the arbitrariness of the divisions between people if it did not have a contrasting model in the unity of the church? Only against the universality of the church can the world have the means to recognize the irrationality of the divisions resulting in violence, and war, as one arbitrary unity of people seek to protect themselves against the knowledge of their arbitrariness.[18]

Later in the same chapter he reminds us of differences:

It is particularly important to remember that the world consists of those, including ourselves, who have chosen not to make the story of God their story. The world in us refuses to affirm that this is God's world and that, as loving Lord, God's care for creation is greater than our illusion of control. The world is those aspects of our individual and social lives where we live untruthfully by continuing to rely on violence to bring order.[19]

We can be friends, fellow-travelers, enemies, or, as often in the past, ignorant of one another, fearful and distrustful. The church, the presence of the risen Lord in the world, celebrates and enacts and lives again the stories of Israel and Jesus and our stories in that history. It is a preaching church, a teaching church, and a prophetic church. Jesus' last command to his disciples before leaving the world was this: "I have been given all authority in heaven and on earth. Therefore, go and make disciples from all nations. Baptize them in the Name of the Father and of the Son and of the Holy Spirit, and teach them to fulfill all I have commanded you. I am with you always until the end of this world" (Mt 28:18b-20).

The world, according to the last command of Jesus, is to be our place of work, the place we preach, teach, and celebrate the sacraments. As Enda McDonagh has pointed out, prayer is the way we let God loose in the world. Prayer is a dangerous activity, and the liturgy and sacraments are our most powerful and fervent prayers. They are common enough activities, but dangerous nonetheless. The mystical traditions remind us in soaring and dramatic language that God's presence is wild and mysterious.

Perhaps even Jesus was reluctant to leave this world. On the grounds of a retreat center in Colorado there is a statue of Jesus ascending into heaven, but it is a remarkably different statue. He is stretched, almost like a rubber band. One arm is being dragged up to heaven by some terrible power, the other reaches just as passionately to earth, clinging to the ground. The world held Jesus, left its mark on him. It can do no less to his followers, who are cautioned that they must be like their master and teacher. Baptism is where this stretching between earth and heaven begins. There is an intimate connection between our religious rites and sacraments and our holiness as people of God in the world. Vincent Donovan tells about the Masai people, who have made the connection between their own cultural symbols and the challenge inherent in celebrating eucharist. He writes that one of the most powerful gestures in Masai culture is to offer another a tuft, a handful of grass, as a sign of peace, friendship, and trust. It is like our saying welcome, like white flags in wartime. It is a solemn pledge that there will be no violence, no hatred, no anger shown—or kept in one's heart. It is not just a sign of peace; it is peace. At the beginning of Mass all the Masai gather and begin to pray for the sick, the old and infirm, and other needs within the community; they dance and sing together. Donovan writes that he never knew if the eucharist would emerge from all of this ritual. The leaders of the village were the ones to decide, yes or no.

> If there had been selfishness and forgetfulness and hatefulness and lack of forgiveness in the work that had been done, in the life that had been led here, let them not make a sacrilege out of it by calling it the Body of Christ. And the leaders did decide occasionally, that, despite the prayers and reading and discussions, if the grass had

stopped, if someone, or some group, in the village had refused to accept the grass as the sign of the peace of Christ, there would be no eucharist at this time.[20]

The Masai witness in their lives that baptism, reconciliation, and eucharist are not isolated acts of ritual, devoid of meaning and connection to their lives as Christians. They are called by baptism to be holy people and to celebrate that holiness and unity in the breaking of bread and sharing of wine. If they are not working at being holy, they have no right, no power, to celebrate the sacrament. It does not exist in reality. It would only be an empty useless gesture. The eucharist is possible because they are becoming what they are to be, a people capable of sharing handfuls of grass and forgiveness in a world that would have us believe that no one is trustworthy and that human relations are determined by power, control, manipulation, or violence. The sacrament celebrates a living, breathing, and sometimes strained reality.

Surprisingly enough, it is the Christian community celebrating liturgy and the sacraments that is the bridge between the church and the world. It is the believers, the church, the people of God who are the link. There is a tightrope strung between the church and the world, and Christians live on it; in fact, they *are* the rope, the tie that binds the two together. A good image is found in the musical "Fiddler on the Roof." That's what we are: fiddlers picking out a tune, dancing precariously on a roof, attempting not to fall off and to make a good tune for others to hear. The roof is the church, we are the fiddlers by baptism, the tune is liturgy, sacraments, and prayer. We are called to improvise, adapt in order to get others' attention. Our balance is important, but the tune is important too. Where's the world? It's the house. The quality of the music? Some of us are good, very good; others are not so good. Some of us only know one tune. Some of us forget the music is not just for us, that it needs an audience to appreciate it fully. Some would say if there is no community, there is no liturgy, no sacraments. We need to ask ourselves— not just as individuals, but as Christian communities and as church— what tune have we been playing for the world? Is it music or is it a cacophony? How good are we at dancing? Are we a scandal to the world? Are we, worse, a scandal to the heart of our God?

In the next chapter we will begin with the first prayer of the church, the first tune, the first story of Christians who have experienced God in Jesus and have promised to follow him in the church under the watchful eyes of a world that still waits for the coming of the kingdom of peace and justice. We will look at the sacrament of initiation—baptism, eucharist, and confirmation, the rites of making adult Christians.

But first a story on why we would live with one foot in the church and one in the world.

✠ Once upon a time there was a man, rich and powerful, who owned much land in India. One of his favorite ways to spend an evening was to walk across his fields and acres surveying his property. Another of his pastimes was hunting wild game, and he dug huge pits in order to trap tigers, rhinos, and elephants. One night while he was out walking, he was not paying attention and fell into one of the holes. In the beginning he did not panic; soon someone would miss him and come looking for him. Later that night he began to wonder and look over his life—would anyone bother to come?

Night passed. Next day he yelled, hoping someone would hear. He was hungry, thirsty, cold, and a bit afraid. He thought of his wives, children, business associates, friends—and how he treated them. Would they bother to look for him? How long before someone would come? The second night passed slowly. He grew terrified. He tried in desperation to dig his way out. He became exhausted and had fits of desperation, screaming, despair. The second day passed interminably. He was painfully in need of water. He began to worry about an animal falling into the hole with him. The third night he cried, wept for his life, and gave up trying to get out. He no longer called out for help. By the fourth night he had given up hope. He was weak, broken, dying. He could no longer even talk, let alone cry out. Then unexpectedly a stranger passed by the hole and peered in. He could barely see the figure at the bottom of the pit, so he called out. No answer. He decided that whoever it was, was dead. And he walked on.

The stranger continued on his way, but it began to bother him. Perhaps he should go back and at least bury the man decently. Finally he turned around and went back. He made a rope and descended into the pit. He found the man barely alive, gave him water, and hauled him up to safety, to food and to life. Slowly the rich man revived. He was ecstatic about his good fortune and intent on repaying the stranger for coming back and rescuing him from the pit: "Sir, how can I ever repay you for my life? What can I give you— name it and it is yours, even if it is everything I own."

The stranger looked at him and answered: "How can you ever repay me for the gift of your life? You can't. There is no payment that is adequate. Instead, I ask only one thing of you—for the rest of your life make sure you look in all the holes, all the pits, and return the favor of your life to at least ten others who have fallen by the way. Then I am repaid."

Now the rich man walks with his eyes down, intent, looking for others to rescue as he once was rescued. The favor must be returned.

Let us pray:

Lord Jesus Christ, you truly contain within your gentleness, within your humanity, all the unyielding immensity and grandeur of the world. . . . I love you, Lord Jesus, because of the multitude who shelter within you and whom, if one clings closely to you one can hear with all the other beings murmuring, praying, weeping. . . . I love you as the source, the activating and life-giving ambience, the term and the summation, of the world, even of the natural world, and of its process of becoming. You are the center at which all things meet and which stretches out over all things so as to draw them back into itself: I love you for the extensions of your body and soul to the farthest corners of creation through grace, through life and through matter. Lord Jesus, you are as gentle as the human heart, as fiery as the forces of nature, as intimate as life itself, you in whom I can melt away and with whom I must have mastery and freedom: I love you as a world, as this world which has captivated my heart; and it is you, I now realize that my brother-men, even those who do not believe, sense and seek throughout the magic immensities of the cosmos. Lord Jesus, you are the center towards which all things are moving; if it be possible, make a place for us all in the company of those elect and holy ones whom your loving care has liberated one by one from the chaos of our present existence and who are being slowly incorporated into you in the unity of the new earth.[21]

3

Rites of Initiation

Baptism, Eucharist, and Confirmation[1]
The Choice for Life—Ever More Abundant for All

✟ Once upon a time three men who had been friends for a long time sought wisdom, power, and righteousness. They studied and prayed together, looked for teachers, traveled far, and listened as they journeyed. Always they sought the tiger, the symbol and the doorway to wisdom and truth. One day they were on a road, going their way and discussing all that they had experienced so far and how far they still had to go. Suddenly they saw a tiger. The tiger's eyes opened wide.

One of the men spoke: "Tiger, we would like to enter and learn the ways of wisdom."

The tiger looked at each in turn and said: "Just how far in would you like to go?"

The first smiled and said: "Thank you, this is close enough for me."

The second answered: "Not too far, but far enough so I can say that I've been there."

The third man said nothing, but he approached the tiger, who opened its mouth wide. The man put his head inside, and at that moment the tiger roared.

The other two men turned and ran back to town and safety. The third man was never seen again, though soon after there appeared one who was wise, truthful, compassionate, and just. Some say he looked vaguely familiar, but no one knew where he came from.

This ancient story from the Far East has much to say about the sacrament of initiation, which has three stages or experiences: baptism, confirmation, and eucharist. It is, however, one total experience or immersion into belief and mystery. When we discover or are discovered by the

Holy, how much do we want to experience, how much do we want to know, how much do we want to be transformed? Do we make the choice for life, ever more abundant life, as scripture describes it for us?

Poet e. e. cummings writes: "You and I can never be born enough. We are human beings for whom birth is a supremely welcome mystery, the mystery of growing . . . which happens only and whenever we are faithful to ourselves." For Christians, it happens only when we are faithful to Jesus in the world that waits for his wisdom and truth. It begins in baptism and is continued in confirmation and eucharist. These three moments of encounter with the risen Lord in the presence of the community of believers are where we all begin.

John the prophet and precursor of Jesus baptized and heralded the one who came after him, the "one more powerful than I; I am not fit to stoop before him and untie his sandal straps." John baptized with water, a baptism of repentance that led to the forgiveness of sins (Mk 1:5ff.). He warned: "Reform your lives! The reign of God is at hand" (Mt 3:2). The people confessed their sins and were baptized in the Jordan River. This baptism was for the sake of reformation. He demanded that the Pharisees and Sadducees give some evidence that they meant to reform. Not just words. Not just good intentions. John's baptism was meant to be a preparation for the one who was coming. He too would baptize, but he would baptize "in the Holy Spirit and fire" (Mt 3:11).

John baptized Jesus, and the gospel tellers recount that when he came forth from the waters "at once, the heavens opened and he saw the Spirit of God come down like a dove and rest upon him. At the same time a voice from heaven said, 'This is my Son, the Beloved; he is my Chosen One'" (Mt 3:16-17). Then this same Spirit drove Jesus into the desert to be tempted by Satan for forty days. The gift of the Spirit in baptism leads one to struggle in life-and-death situations. It leads us into dangerous and confrontational situations. It leads us to be tested, tried, and, we hope, like Jesus, found to be true. When the period of testing was over, Jesus was fed by the angels. In the life of Jesus the rites of baptism, the coming of the Spirit, the testing, and being fed from heaven were a process, an initiation into his mission, for after his sojourn in the desert the Spirit led him again, this time into his hometown to preach in the synagogue and to proclaim to his friends, family, and neighbors who he is and why he lives. The church celebrates this initiation of Jesus, this passage into public ministry, in the rites of baptism, confirmation, and eucharist. They are an integral experience that combines awareness, experience, and outer expression in the new convert and in the faithful.

This is initiation into the work of a lifetime. It is initiation into the body of Jesus, his community, his source of being with God the Father.

These rites of initiation form another chapter in a story that is ancient, mysterious, and compelling—the story of Israel. Israel, the people chosen to reveal God's glory to the nations, waiting in patient hope and expectation for the Messiah, the one who would show forth such mercy, justice, tenderness, and peace that all the kingdoms of the world would see in Israel the presence of God. The story begins by focusing on the Passover of the Jews, the Israelites, from bondage and slavery in Egypt, through the desert and the Reed Sea, to a land of promise and peace. It takes time, a whole generation, and is retold and reenacted every year. The Jews begin the narrative each Passover with the question, "Why is this night different from all other nights?" and the story happens again. The ritual ends with the glorious cry, "Next year in Jerusalem!"—that is, next year may the privilege of freedom belong to all the nations. Next year may the kingdom of peace and justice reign completely in the hearts and lives of all. Next year may the glory of the Lord shine forth as pure worship and acknowledgment of God's rule and power.

Jesus was a Jew. He celebrated the Passover thoroughly with his family and friends. His whole life was a journey toward his own Passover—his death to life, his struggle for justice and holiness, his "setting his face toward Jerusalem," his trust in his Father, his life with the poor and the oppressed, his prayer and acceptance of others' hatred, anger, and intent to kill him. He passed from earth to heaven. He passed from birth to death to life. He passed from vulnerability to power and love witnessed by God. Jesus is the Passover of God to humankind. When he passes through our earth, our humanness, he is strong enough to pull all of us with him into his Father's kingdom, the life of resurrection and glory.

We, Jesus' followers and friends, are the first invited to come after him, to experience this Passover in our persons and communities. The church celebrates Passover in baptism, confirmation, and eucharist, in liturgy, prayer, and worship, in lifestyle and community. Stanley Hauerwas describes church in this context:

> The church, therefore, is not some ideal of community but a particular people who, like Israel, must find the way to sustain its existence generation after generation. Indeed, there are clear "marks" through which we know that the church is church. These marks do not guarantee the existence of the church, but are the means that God has given us to help us along the way. Thus the

church is known where the sacraments are celebrated, the word is preached and upright lives are encouraged and lived. Certainly some churches emphasize one of these "marks" more than others, but that does not mean that they are deficient in some decisive manner. What is important is not that each particular body of Christians does all of these things, but that these "marks" are exhibited by Christians everywhere.

The sacraments enact the story of Jesus and, thus, form a community in his image. We could not be church without them. For the story of Jesus is not simply one that is told; it must be enacted. The sacraments are means crucial to shaping and preparing us to tell and hear that story. Thus baptism is that rite of initiation necessary for us to become part of Jesus' death and resurrection. Through baptism we do not simply learn the story, but we become part of that story. The Eucharist is the eschatological meal of God's continuing presence that makes possible a peaceable people. At that meal we become part of Christ's kingdom, as we know there that death could not contain him. His presence, his peace is a living reality in the world. As his people we become part of his sacrifice, God's sacrifice, so that the world might be saved from sin and death.

These rites, baptism and Eucharist, are not just "religious things" that Christian people do. They are the essential rituals of our politics. Through them we learn who we are. Instead of being motives or causes for effective social work on the part of Christian people, these liturgies are our effective social work. For because the church *is* rather than has a social ethic, these actions are our most important social witness. It is in baptism and Eucharist that we see most clearly the marks of God's kingdom in the world. They set our standard, as we try to bring every aspect of our lives under their sway.[2]

So we tell the story over and over again, until we *become* the story. Those who hear the story and come to believe it join us in the storytelling. Our lives proclaim and witness to the truth of the story. Without our story, our vision, we perish; we are, in Paul's words, "a laughingstock to the nations." We must become holy people, as Jesus is holy, as our heavenly Father is holy, if the story is to continue to come true in the world, if the kingdom is to come upon us. God has entrusted the continued work of incarnation and transformation and resurrection to us, his children, brothers and sisters of our risen and present Lord.

Baptism and the rites of initiation celebrate what has happened to us in the graciousness of God's attention. In chapter 10 of Paul's letter to the Roman Christians he describes the process of becoming a believer and the passing on of the story to others. The Word of God comes to us in the person of Jesus Christ, the justice of our God, and he saves us, loves us. He comes to anyone who believes in him. His word is always near us "on our lips and in our heart." We begin by confessing with our lips, with words of belief that Jesus Christ is Lord of our lives, and we begin to believe in our hearts that God has raised Jesus from the dead. We call on God, and we are saved in God's mercy and the Lord walks with us.

But God needs us to preach the good news, as Jesus did so clearly. We are called to be preachers and sent to others so they can hear and come to belief. "How beautiful are the feet of those who announce good news!" (Rom 10:15b, *NAB*). The process of moving from lip service to service of the heart—the essence of human life—is long and arduous. It takes a lifetime. Baptism, confirmation, and eucharist begin the journey. They open the door, point us in the right direction, put us on the road together with Jesus and his friends. Our faith teaches us how to be holy like Jesus, to imitate God's ways with us. Our lifestyles and ethics are taught to us in faith, liturgy, word, and community. It is a long journey into the ways of God. Paul explains what the relationship with God and each other will be like:

> How deep are the riches, the wisdom and knowledge of God! His decisions cannot be explained, nor his ways understood! Who has ever known God's thoughts? Who has ever been his adviser? Who has given him something first, so that God had to repay him? For everything comes from him, has been made by him and has to return to him. To him be the glory for ever! Amen (Rom 11:33-36).

We are called to *live* and witness our belief to the world by our ethical choices and lifestyles. We stand committed to Jesus' life of grace and observe God's call to life. Committed Christians see in the life of faith not merely an ethical stance with which to be consistent or a set of rules not to break, but a gracious privilege to share.

The sacraments of initiation invite believers into the community of those who have promised publicly to tell the story of Jesus Christ crucified and risen, those who have pledged to test out the implications of that story in their life and in the world. There is no assurance given that the working out will always be in accordance with the depth of the story of Jesus, or that the individual or the community will always be faithful disciples of the Lord, or that they will do all that is required by Jesus. But they will try, and the Spirit will lead them as they are tested by the world and Satan. The Spirit will also lead them into the world to preach and announce the good news in memory of Jesus. Some "practical" responses and solutions will be seen to be in error. As Stanley Hauerwas says:

> For example, it may well be that the development of the "just war" theory, which was certainly an imaginative attempt to maintain the gospel's commitments to forgiveness and peacemaking and yet respond to the Christian's increasing responsibility to wider society, was a mistake. Or it may be that the prohibition against remarriage after a "divorce" was more rigorous than it needed to be to maintain the Christian commitment to fidelity in marriage. Such matters often are not apparent at once, but depend on the working out of those developments within the people of God. The proof is definitely in the pudding as we must constantly be open to the possibility that the practice may come to distort the kind of people we are meant to be as the first fruits of the kingdom.
>
> The church is the pioneer in displaying the implications of God's kingdom of peace brought in Jesus Christ. She does so by a relentless questioning of every aspect of her life as we learn slowly what it means to be a people of peace in every aspect of our existence. The "prohibitions" that become part of that community's life must not become minimalistic rules. Rather they should charge the imagination of the community and individuals to chart new forms of response necessary to being a people of peace in a violent world.[3]

Thus the church we commit ourselves to is a place of peace, a peace that is unsettling, often in opposition to the wider society, but a peace that cares, that matures and demands imagination and creativity from its members. Like Jesus, we must speak the truth to one another and share that truth with the world, challenge the world to accept our truth, and be willing to care for those who suffer for the truth.

Our decision for the life of Jesus is a decision in favor of the cross as our power in life, in favor of life ever more abundant for all people, in favor of the defense of life. God has given us life in Jesus, and if we accept this life we accept the responsibility to share that life with others.

We commit ourselves to the belief that God stood behind Jesus and will stand behind us. Resurrection—life where there was only despair, mercy where there was sin, and love where there was only indifference or hate—is now our lifestyle. We stand together in defense of life; we choose life at all costs; we celebrate life in its myriad forms and possibilities. We commit ourselves to the grace and reality of doing just one thing and doing it well—being life for others. The sacraments of initiation are a joyous celebration of passage from our old life, which was no life at all, merely survival, into life everlasting that begins here and now. We commit ourselves in the sacraments of initiation to becoming life-giving and life-sustaining friends of all the peoples of the world, like Jesus. This commitment, this learning, takes time.

The Rite of Christian Initiation of Adults (RCIA)[4] is meant to be lengthy. In the early days of the church new believers were brought into the church in stages. Early Christians were first called Followers of the Way. As soon as they committed themselves publicly to this Way, they were considered members of the church. They had heard the good news, accepted it, and proclaimed it themselves. Their initiation was individual and thorough. The community consistently confronted them with words, choices, reflection, prayer, and action. Neophyte believers had to separate themselves from the past, from their former lifestyle, attitudes, values—and often from their families.

Initiation came in three successive stages: a period of separation from their previous lifestyle and group, a transitional period, and finally an intensive incorporation into the new group they had chosen and that had chosen them.[5] Their catechesis was communal, experiential, consisting of testimony, prayer, liturgy, community contexts, and doctrine. It was a privileged time for them and for the community, a time for sponsors and godparents to offer one-on-one teaching, shared belief, a time of developing friendships, intimacy, and support. It was a time to see people living out their belief, to take heart from them, to see how they dealt with failure and sin after baptism, and to grow in understanding of what it meant to believe in Jesus.

After their long apprenticeship—generally two to seven years up through the sixth or seventh century—they were initiated into the stages of purification, enlightenment, and illumination. They went into these stages knowing from experience the consequences of their choices, their need for the community, and their thirst for God's presence in the word, the eucharist, the community, and the sharing of faith. They knew they needed the Spirit, the first gift of God, in order to survive in their new life. And they knew they needed the community to uphold them, tell them the truth, and walk with them on the way they had chosen. They were going home together.

But the catechumenate was not just for the new believers; it was for the tried-and-true Christians too. It was a time of renewal, recommitment, and growth. In sharing their belief and struggle, they became more sure of themselves, grew in insight and understanding, and found the courage to turn more surely into the way of Jesus, which inevitably led to the way of the cross and death as well as resurrection. The catechumenate was a source of encouragement and a chance to touch again their "first love and devotion to the Lord" (Rv 2:4, *NAB*). It was the long, arduous process of making disciples that Jesus commanded at the end of his life with us on earth. It culminated in the Easter Vigil, in baptism, confirmation, and eucharist when the church was made whole and full of light on the morning of the resurrection.

Throughout the process the catechumens (those asked the questions) had the right to the word; sacramentals such as candles, books, and crosses; prayer; community relationships; blessings; and burial, marriage, and exorcism. In return they had the responsibilities of good works, prayer, and growth in their belief and in its expression. They had to learn how to be truthful, open, vulnerable, patient, forgiving, nurturing, and obedient. They learned together, new believers and old, more graceful in their behavior together.

Because of their desire and the supporting community, the rituals and stages of initiation prior to Lent and the Easter Vigil were experienced as intense, powerful, and transforming. It was literally happening to them— what had happened to Jesus. They were learning how to "do this in remembrance of me" in all its dangerous possibility and power. They were learning to move from stage to stage—perhaps best described in a prayer written by Nikos Kazantzakis, who probably never experienced the catechumenate but certainly experienced the demanding God of life:

There are three kinds of souls, three prayers:
1. I am a bow in your hands, Lord, draw me, lest I rot.
2. Do not overdraw me, Lord. I shall break.
3. Overdraw me, Lord, and who cares if I break![6]

Their attitudes toward life would henceforth be that of resurrection. "I said to the almond tree, 'Sister, speak to me of God.' And the almond tree blossomed."[7]

They learned what they were to do in the future, the impossible task before them, the adventure they were being invited to be a part of— something that Kazantzakis learned in Russia:

> One of Francis of Assisi's disciples found his shivering master walking naked one night in the heart of winter. "Why do you go naked in such cold, Father Francis?" he said to him in astonishment. "Because, my brother, thousands upon thousands of brothers and sisters are cold at this moment. I have no blankets to give them to make them warm, so I join them in their coldness."
>
> I recalled the Poor Man of God's words, but only now did I realize that to join others in their coldness was not enough. One had to cry out, "Forward all together, everyone who is hungry, everyone who is cold. There are scores of extra blankets. Take them and cover your nakedness!"[8]

His description sounds a lot like Isaiah's words of comfort and hope:

> All you who are thirsty, come to the water. All who have no money, come.
>
> Yes, without money and at no cost, come, buy and drink wine and milk.
>
> Why spend money on what is not food and labor for what does not satisfy? Listen to me, and you will eat well; you will enjoy the richest of fare.
>
> Incline your ear and come to me; listen, that your soul may live.
> (Is 55:1-3a)

The church was trying out the reality of Isaiah's vision with one another in community. The description of the early church in Acts was simple witness to the truth of the vision:

> They devoted themselves to the apostles' instruction and the communal life, to the breaking of bread and the prayers. A reverent fear overtook them all, for many wonders and signs were performed by the apostles. Those who believed shared all things in common; they would sell their property and goods, dividing everything on the basis of each one's need. They went to the temple area together every day, while in their homes they broke bread. With exultant and sincere hearts they took their meals in common, praising God

and winning the approval of all the people. Day by day the Lord added to their number those who were being saved (Acts 2:42-47, *NAB*).

They "were being saved." They believed, and it showed in their actions, in their sharing of their goods as well as their prayer. There was no racism, sexism, classism, agism, materialism, nationalism; no slaves, war, insecurity, violence.

This process of becoming a Christian has often been symbolized by the becoming of a butterfly:

> Never had I experienced the silkworm's mute agony and relief with such a sense of identification. When all the mulberry leaves it has eaten are finally transformed inside it and turned to silk, then the creative process begins. Swaying its head from side to side, it plucks out its entrails with a convulsive shudder, withdraws the silk, tiny thread by tiny thread, and with patience and mystic wisdom knits— white, gold, all of precious substance—its coffin.
>
> There is no sweeter agony, I believe, no more urgently imposed duty than for the entire worm to turn to silk, the entire flesh to spirit. Nor is there any undertaking more in keeping with the laws reigning in the workshop of God.[9]

This is the making of a Christian. It happens in baptism, confirmation, and eucharist, yet we never know for sure when it happens. The process is akin to that of the seamless garment of life, a phrase coined by Cardinal Joseph Bernardin. Just as the RCIA shapes a consistent ethic of life, so the Christian community shapes that consistent ethic of life for the world around it in words, witness, alternatives to society's ways, and the power of the Spirit. Bernardin was discussing the pastoral letter "The Challenge of Peace" in terms of the relationship of our Catholic moral vision and American culture, and he used the pastoral letter as a starting point for shaping a consistent ethic of life in our culture. He began by stating his belief:

> I believe the Catholic moral tradition has something valuable to say in the face of the multiple threats to the sacredness of life today, and I am convinced that the church is in a position to make a significant defense of life in a comprehensive and consistent manner.
>
> "The Challenge of Peace" provides a starting point for developing a consistent ethic of life, but it does not provide a fully ar-

ticulated framework. The central idea in the letter is the sacredness of human life and the responsibility we have, personally and socially to protect and preserve the sanctity of life.

Precisely because life is sacred, the taking of even one human life is a momentous event. Indeed, the sense that every human life has transcendent value has led a whole stream of the Christian tradition to argue that life may never be taken. That position is held by an increasing number of Catholics and is reflected in the pastoral letter, but it has not been the dominant view in Catholic teaching and it is not the principal moral position found in the pastoral letter.[10]

But that tradition was the prevailing, the only tradition of the church for more than three hundred years. There is the testimony of Origen in the third century in response to Celsus, a cultivated pagan who was concerned about the crumbling of Rome and who criticized the Christians, particularly for their refusal to fight in the army. Origen replied in *Contra Celsum*:

Christians have been taught not to defend themselves against their enemies; and because they have kept the laws which command gentleness and love to man, on this account they have received from God that which they would not have succeeded in doing if they had been given the right to make war, even if they may have been quite able to do so. . . . No longer do we take sword against other nations, nor do we learn war any more since we have become the sons of peace through Jesus, who is our author, instead of following the tradition-customs by which we were strangers to the covenant.[11]

This choice for life, abundant life, is the choice for the cross, a sign of folly yet the sign of power for Christians. One of the ancient prayers of the church during the baptismal liturgy states: "You will be victorious in your struggle against darkness and death, but on your knees and under the sign of the cross."

This prayer was preceded by the reading from Philippians on becoming like Christ who

humbled himself by being obedient to death, death on the cross.
That is why God exalted him
and gave him the Name which outshines all names,

> so that at the Name of Jesus all knees should bend
> in heaven, on earth and among the dead,
> and all tongues proclaim that Christ Jesus is the Lord.
>
> (Phil 2:8-11)

Leon Bloy says it succinctly: "You do not enter into paradise tomorrow or the day after or in ten years; you enter it today when you are poor and crucified."

This growing need to return to a consistent life ethic is reasonable and necessary. "The essential question today is this: In an age when we can do almost anything, how do we decide what we ought to do? An even more demanding question is: In a time when we can do almost anything with technology, how do we decide morally what we never should do? This is the crux of Bernardin's remarks. It is this consistent life ethic that cuts across all the ethical issues from the womb to the tomb: genetics, abortion, the death penalty, modern warfare, care for the terminally ill and handicapped, euthanasia, the welfare of the weak and those in need of vital necessities of life. The specifics are almost not at issue here but rather "the need for an attitude or atmosphere in society which is the precondition for sustaining a consistent ethic of life." Our moral and ethical respect for life and responsibility for life does not end with the moment of birth, but it truly begins there. Cardinal Bernardin goes on to be most specific:

> Those who defend the right to life of the weakest of us must be equally visible in support of the quality of life of the powerless among us: the old and the young, the hungry and the homeless, the undocumented immigrant and the unemployed worker. Such a quality of life posture translates into specific political and economic positions on tax policy, employment generation, welfare policy, nutrition and feeding programs, and health care. Consistency means we cannot have it both ways: We cannot urge a compassionate society and vigorous public policy to protect the rights of the unborn and then argue that compassion and significant public programs on behalf of the needy undermine the moral fiber of the society or are beyond the proper scope of governmental responsibility.[12]

One needs to be reminded that Bernardin spoke to American Christians, not specifically Catholics, and that Bernardin also mentioned that consensus within the church was the first place to begin. That consensus begins with conversion, with baptism, with the RCIA, a place to turn our hearts toward the gospel of Jesus, who came to us poor, unwelcomed at birth, hounded even as a child, and destroyed by the government in power. This Jesus was the friend of public sinners and healer of lepers and outcasts physically and spiritually. Initiation into the ethic of Jesus, into the life and heart and mind of Jesus, leaves no room for agreement or disagreement, only the question how far we will go in responding to the presence of God in Jesus Christ. In Matthew's gospel it is made perfectly clear that those of us who claim to be Christians will be judged not on doctrine or understanding of tradition but on what we have done with our lives in connection with the poor, the outcast, the prisoner, the one in need, the hungry, the homeless, the naked, and the sick (Mt 25:31-46).

Like the early Christians and Jews, we need to be touched by the words of the scriptures that call us to such accountability and commands. We still have much to learn.

Kazantzakis tells a story from his childhood that left a mark on him forty years later. We need to hear it and let it leave a mark on us too.

> I experienced my first massacre. The Turks. We were barricaded within our house. "If the Turks break down the door and enter, he told us, I plan to slaughter you myself, before you fall into their hands." My mother, sister and I had all agreed. Now we were waiting. I believe I would have seen my soul maturing during those hours if the invisible had become visible. I sensed that in the space of just a few hours I had begun to change abruptly from a child into a man. . . . The night went by. . . . I asked, "Did the massacre go away, Mother?" This frightened her. "Quiet, quiet, my child. Don't mention its name! It might hear you and return."
>
> I wrote the word MASSACRE just now and the hairs of my head stood on end, because when I was a child this word was not simply eight letters of the alphabet pasted one next to the other, it was a great droning, the feet kicking down doors, horrible faces with knives between their teeth, women shrieking everywhere in the vicinity, and men loading muskets as they knelt behind their doors. . . .
>
> Once there was a rabbi who always made his will and tearfully bade farewell to his wife and children before he went to the synagogue to pray, for he never knew if he would emerge from the prayer alive. As he used to say, "When I pronounce a word, for

instance LORD, this word shatters my heart. I am terror-stricken
and do not know if I shall be able to make the leap to the following
words: HAVE MERCY ON ME."[13]

Our own rituals, scriptures, and sacraments call us to this kind of intensity, this kind of honesty, this kind of life. It is Jesus himself who
says: "Unless the grain of wheat falls to earth and dies, it remains just a
grain of wheat. But if it dies, it produces much fruit" (Jn 12:24, *NAB*).
God wills that we are all saved. That is a hard saying for us to believe
and take to heart. John of the Cross wrote: "Where there is no love, put
love and you will find love." He was in jail when he wrote that, put there
by his own brothers.

A more contemporary monk, Thomas Merton, reminds us of the consequences of an ethic of love, of care for all life in the name of Jesus:

> In the whole world Christ suffers dismemberment. . . . His Mysti-
> cal Body is drawn and quartered from age to age. . . . As long as
> we are on earth the love that unites us will bring us suffering by
> our very contact with one another, because this love is the reset-
> ting of a Body of broken bones.

Charles Peguy put it succinctly: "We must be saved together. We must
come to God together. Together we must all return to our Father's house.
What would God say to us if some of us came to Him without the others?"

The work of being a believer, of being ethical, of being like Christ in
community is long and trying. As Christians, however, even more is asked
of us. We are asked to be the sons and daughters of God, to be Christ in
the world. And that is harder still, yet it is our glory.

The RCIA consists of three sacramental moments, gestures, words,
and symbols:

- baptism: immersion into water three times—the Passover and the
  giving of the light of Christ
- confirmation: the laying on of hands—the coming of the Spirit and
  the sealing with chrism
- eucharist: the feasting at the table of the Lord—the sharing in the
  presence of the risen Lord with his friends and the experience of
  becoming what we eat.

It is only after this extensive period of preparation and apprenticeship that the catechumen is accepted within the community as one committed to the gospel, reliable, beginning to mature in the practice of belief. Traditionally the new believer was taught the Our Father on Easter evening, and the long ordeal became a lifetime of shared struggle and joy within the community. All of the community continued to study together, to witness, and "to grow in wisdom, age and grace before God and the earth" (Lk 2). The formal term for the instruction and practice that continued after baptism is *mystogia.*

The gospel stories of the blind narrate the process by which the new believer learned to *see*—to believe. In the story of the blind man at Bethsaida (Mk 8:22-26) Jesus takes the man outside the village and lays hands on him. He can see, but indistinctly. A second time Jesus lays hands on him, and then the man can see clearly. Jesus warns him: "Do not even go into the village." Don't go back, don't lapse into old ways now that you see and believe in Jesus.

In the second story about a blind man (Mk 11:46-52, *NAB*), Bartimaeus is by the side of the road, already outside the village, and he cries out repeatedly for mercy until Jesus stops and tells his disciples to bring him over to him. These disciples were previously among those who were telling him to keep quiet and hustling him out of the way so that Jesus could pass. He is told that the Master is calling him, to have no fear. The man drops his cloak and, still blind, runs to Jesus. Jesus asks him the obvious question (ritually): "What do you want me to do for you?" and Bartimaeus answers: "I want to see [to believe]." Jesus tells him, "Be on your way. Your faith has healed you." Then we are told that Bartimaeus *started* to follow Jesus up the road (to Jerusalem). While still blind, he leaves behind his cloak, his old way of being in the world, his protection, and runs to meet the Lord. After his healing, his coming to belief, he starts to follow Jesus. It is appropriate that the very next story in Mark's gospel is Jesus' entry into Jerusalem. Jesus and the blind man, the new believer, have yet to face Jerusalem—the cross and death and resurrection. It is a process, a journey of faith.

It is Jesus, in a response to the apostle Thomas, who calls himself "the way, and the truth, and the life" (Jn 14:5, *NAB*). We come to the Father through Jesus, through his journey to Jerusalem, and through the cross in an often hostile world. Immediately after this conversation with Thomas, Jesus prays for his own disciples that they may receive the Spirit of Truth, the Paraclete, whom the world does not accept, just as it did not accept Jesus. But the Spirit will stay with them as the Comforter, and the Father will come to dwell with them, for the Father is one with Jesus and the Spirit and so one with us. The prayer for unity is the culmination of Jesus' last discourse. The new believer and the community of disciples celebrate unity together with the eucharist and pray that the Spirit will bless the new disciples with the gifts of the Spirit, so that they might show forth to the world the presence of God. The ritual is complete with the sharing of the eucharist, with the giving thanks, with the life of the believers in Jesus given back to the Father, as Jesus once gave his own life to God. The body of Jesus is "re-membered," put back together, made whole in the incorporation of new Christians, in the incarnation of new words of God in the world. This is the heritage and theology of the early church. Unfortunately the experience, even in the RCIA, is seldom the norm for today's adult Catholics, particularly where infant baptism is routine.

But there are alternatives that are pastorally powerful and conducive to conversion. If one did not experience the catechumenate before baptism, then the church can offer it before confirmation (not en masse); before marriage; before the blessing of lay ministers; at the celebration of anniversaries of marriage and religious commitment; at the ordination of deacons; and when adults return to the church or want to commit themselves to a public profession of belief and practice. The teaching and pastoral goals of a parish or diocese can focus on providing the experience of the RCIA for as many adults as possible over a period of months and years.

Since the 1980s there have been many programs of renewal in parishes and dioceses but what is needed is a *process* that incorporates members of the parish into an ongoing community characterized by studying the word as conversional, working for both personal and communal commitment to the corporal and spiritual works of mercy and the work of justice, and sharing faith and belief as a community. All of us have experienced the lack of community within our parishes and national church. All of us know in our own lives that perhaps this is due to the inadequacy of the response of individual members to the call of conversion—turning toward one another and away from the values and demands of a society that is highly distrustful, individualistic, and mobile.

There are three elements of any process—whether retreats, incorporation into base communities, or groups seeking to pray, work, and study together. The first is the proclamation of the gospel as the source of all spirituality, work, decision-making, and call to conversion. This is a call to the kingdom in a practical response of lifestyle and continual conversion alone and with others who hold us accountable. Faith is experienced not so much emotionally or psychologically but as a sharing of belief in Jesus Christ, the Trinity, the church, and the call to bring this message more deeply into our lives. It concentrates on "begin by denying your very self and pick up your cross and come after me" (Mk 8).

The second element entails looking at scripture in the context of prophetic and public calls to alternatives in lifestyle and ethical choices, as individuals and as members of various groups within the Christian community: moral decision-making, study of the teachings of the church, the practice of discipline and asceticism, penance, and a sense of wanting to be held accountable for wrongdoing and collusion with evil in the world. We look at the scriptures and what they have to say about economics, wealth and poverty, law, mercy, justice, nonviolence, and forgiveness, as well as the corporal and spiritual works of mercy and how to put these into practice as believers, alone and with others. We look more closely at how to renounce all we have so that we can be disciples (Lk 14:33, 12:33).

The third element looks at the necessity for Christians, individually and together, to resist evil and refuse to compromise with society's values. It deals with prayer, the psalms, the prophets, and a spirituality of peace and justice that knows and acknowledges the pastoral letters of the church and its long tradition of social teachings and offers alternatives to the world in these issues. It is pragmatic, practical, and demanding, depending on our finances, work, profession, vocation and status in the community.

This sort of response to the call to conversion, to becoming a Christian, to becoming the visible witness within a community of believers as an alternative to the world, requires a shift in today's tendency toward easy catechesis—a few short months of primarily teaching and/or liturgical preparation for these sacraments. We need to take a hard look also at other catechetical programs operating in our parishes, which often assume a level of commitment and dedication to the gospel and its ethic that just isn't there. Yet it is really the only option available to us. Only in the context of intense working on community and individual conversion and the demands of becoming Christian can infant baptism make any sense. When the baptism of children is considered in this larger context of the church and parish, then numerous difficulties begin to fade. In fact, adults desire even more to share their lives and the depth of their perception and conversion in order to initiate their children into a viable and caring community that has much to offer society. The baptism of children must always affirm that in the end they themselves will have to decide their lives; if the practice of the community or the lack of community were one day to become an obstacle to them, it is quite reasonable for them to leave us, as many of them have. With priorities like the pastoral options outlined above, though, they can always be welcomed back and reinitiated into a community that cares about the quality of their lives and the lives of all in society.

A Ritual Celebration of the RCIA

This rite takes approximately three hours to celebrate as a retreat or evening of reflection. It models what the RCIA might mean for people. It can also be used as a basis for a three- to four-year program that looks at specific issues of belief and what they mean practically and ethically for believers in community. Even ritualized within the context of an evening or a day-long retreat it is incredibly powerful.

Work through the ritual with a group of people who will be leading others through it. Do not try to lead others until you have experienced the ritual yourself.

Begin by telling the following story to the assembled group. (There is no limit on the number who can participate.)

✟   Once upon a time a young man heard a man preaching and was moved deeply. He decided immediately that he wanted to be one of this man's disciples and to change his life. He approached the teacher and asked to join his group of disciples and was accepted. The months went by and the young disciple continued to learn, to be touched again and again. He was grateful just to be near the master and counted as one of his own followers.

After almost a year the young man was visited by some of his friends from before. They talked for hours, catching up, and the disciple waxed eloquent about his experiences with the master, all that he had learned and what it was like to be in the master's company. He exhorted them to look hard at their own lives and to think about changing, to come and experience the transformation and the knowledge that was possible in this new life. He was sincere, open-hearted, and so intent that he didn't notice that the master was sitting close by, under a tree, quietly listening to everything that he told his friends. The day drew to a close, and it was time for his friends to leave. As they departed he was still exhorting them to reconsider and come back to join with him and meet his master.

That night he went walking in a grove of trees. It was a beautiful night and there was much to think about. The visit of his old friends had helped him realize that he was incredibly happy with his new life. To his surprise and delight, the master joined him in his walk. This was truly a day of blessing, to be honored so singularly with the master's presence and company! They walked in silence for a while, and then the master mentioned that he had overheard practically all of the young man's conversation with his friends earlier in the day. The disciple was embarrassed and tried to explain that he really meant all that he said and that he sincerely didn't know that the master was listening. He was immediately assured that the master was aware of that fact. They walked in silence again.

Then the disciple sought to put into words what the master meant to him, what this past year had meant to him, and how honored he was that he was in the company of the disciples. The master let him go on and on and on! The disciple found that he couldn't stop in his praise of the master and his gratitude at being chosen and allowed to be a disciple when so many others had come and applied and been turned away.

Then the silence and the night deepened again. This time it was the master who broke the silence. He stopped and turned to look at the young man, eyeing him for a long time. The disciple grew uncomfortable (was it something he had said?). Then the master spoke. "You know," he said, "I don't think you understand why I chose you as one of my disciples and allowed you entrance into my company." The disciple looked blank. "The reason why I chose you, rather than so many others," said the master, "was because you needed it more." The words were said quietly, seriously. He continued. "You see, you must remember, if you are to stay with me, that you are not my disciple because of anything you have done, or even because I see great possibilities in you, but because your need is so great and you lack so much."

With those words the master turned and left the young man to think about his relationship with the master and the other disciples, perhaps in a truer light than ever before. And, they say, it was the first time the young man seriously considered whether he *really* wanted to be a disciple of this man.

Leader: The story is a set-up for the ritual. Who are we, disciples of Jesus Christ, baptized for years, perhaps even decades? Do we realize why we are disciples, why we are chosen, why we are being slowly initiated into the company of believers? Do we remember that it is God who chooses us and seeks to transform us daily, and that, no matter what age we are or how long we have been baptized, we are still just novices, young Christians, would-be disciples of the crucified and risen One? In this rite we will reflect, listen, share our faith with others, take responsibility for our past, and rededicate ourselves to what we chose or what was chosen for us in our baptism. It will be a holy time, a time of insight, conversion, hope, tears, and great rejoicing. Let us begin.

Break into groups of no more than eight or ten people and sit in chairs drawn into circles. Have husbands and wives stay together. When the groups are ready, explain that this ritual will take them through the three years and stages of the catechumenate in about three hours' time. Then prepare them to choose a catechumen (just one person) from each group. Have them all sit quietly with their eyes closed and ask them to answer in their hearts the following questions:

1. Do you want to be the catechumen? The catechumen will be the center of faith sharing and prayer for the ritual. He or she will say very little but will be the focus of the community's belief and shared experiences.
2. Are you struggling with something difficult in your faith at this moment in your life? Do you need the support and verbal acknowledgment of belonging to a community that believes with you?
3. Are you usually in the role of the minister, the person who is at the forefront of an activity or there no matter what needs to be done? Do you need to be on the other end, the receiving end, right now?

Ask everyone to open his or her eyes and in silence to look at each person in the small group carefully. Say: "Do you want to be the cat-echumen? If not, does anyone look *like the catechumen to you?" (As odd as that sounds, people know exactly what it means.) "If you want to be the catechumen, say so." If no one volunteers, ask, with care, "Do you think that someone else is the catechumen?" (Invariably there is a catechumen within seconds.) Ask the catechumens to move into the center of their group, with the others moving in close about them, knees touching.*

Direct the catechumens to choose a sponsor (a godparent), a person who will be the "go-between" between the catechumen and the larger church community. They should choose someone they already know and trust, someone they think that they can trust quickly and easily, or some-

one they admire for his or her witness to the faith. Direct the sponsor to sit directly facing the catechumen. Now the ritual is ready to begin.

Instruct the group members to introduce themselves by name, stating how long they have been baptized, then to sit in silence praying for trust and openness to the Spirit. (Low lighting in the room and shadows will help people to share freely.)

Leader: Keep your eyes closed and think what it would be like for you to have searched all your life, as a child and as an adult, for a group of people who believe what you believe, to live out your life with them, sharing insights, creativity, prayer, work, money, and lifestyle. Now you have found them, and you are about to embark on a new stage of your life.

Play a piece of music that is about welcoming, such as Carole King's "Welcome Home," or something that invites all to come together, such as "Gather Us." The music does not have to be liturgical.

After the song, have the catechumen in each of the groups stand in the presence of his or her community (the group members stay seated).

Leader: What is your name? And what do you ask of the church of God? (RCIA, no. 75)

Ask both questions of each catechumen in turn. Give them a chance to think about the questions for a moment. They can answer any way they wish. After all have responded, reply:

Leader: You will be given all that you ask for and more, the gift of eternal life, if you believe.

Reading: Joshua 24:17-24 (the story of the people, ready to enter the promised land after their long journey and asked to choose life and obedience to the word).

Pick readers prior to the service; readers should not also be catechumens. The reader stands where he or she is and proclaims the reading.

Leader: You are your own witnesses that you have chosen to serve the Lord! This ritual is a gift, both for the catechumens that we have taken into our care and for ourselves, believers who have long ago chosen Jesus Christ as our Lord. Take heed that you live up to your calling and your choice.

Prayer: God enlightens everyone who comes into the world. Through the world he created, he makes known the unseen wonders of his love so that all may learn to give thanks to their creator.

You (who have come to us this day) have followed his light. Now the way of the gospel opens before you, inviting you to make a new beginning by acknowledging the living God who speaks his words of truth to all. You are called to walk by the light of Christ and to trust in his wisdom (alone). He asks you to submit yourself to him more and more and to believe in him with all your heart. This is the way of faith on which Christ (and this community) will lovingly guide you to eternal life. Are you ready to enter on this path today under the leadership of Christ (and with the guidance of this community?) (no. 76).[14]

Catechumens: I am.

Leader: My brothers and sisters gathered here and you who present them (their sponsors and godparents) are you ready to help them come to know and follow Christ? (no. 77).

All: We are.

Leader: Breathe your Spirit, Lord, and drive out the spirits of evil: command them to depart, for your kingdom is drawing near (no. 79). Go now, and take your catechumen into your homes and your hearts and teach them what they need to know in order to become true believers.

And so the first year for the catechumen would begin with the small believing community sharing with its catechumens how hard it is to change, to turn from their old ways of life, to move from their pasts, and to turn into the way of discipleship. The community members shared their own life experiences, what they had learned of change, how to cope with it, alone and in their families and work and community. Your sharing should be practical and down to earth. Realistically share with your catechumen what you are attempting to do—turn your own lives around daily. Direct all your advice and faith-sharing to the catechumen. Put yourselves in the position of the catechumens and share what you think they will need in their lives and decisions. Be simple and to the point. Let the sponsor begin.

Make sure that each member of the community is given a chance to share his or her faith and knowledge. Read the sounds of the groups. This sharing takes about twenty to thirty minutes, sometimes less. Wait for all to finish, then draw them back with these words:

Leader: And so the first year would come to a close, and the catechumens would be brought back to the larger church community to declare publicly their intention to continue the process of initiation. Catechumens, please stand in the midst of your community and face the west.

Explain that in the world of the Jews and the Greeks, the east portrayed light and freedom and the west signified evil and slavery. So the catechumens are asked to face the west and to listen to what their old way of life was like.

Reading: Galatians 21 (what proceeds from the flesh).

Leader: You have heard what your old way of life was and, with the help of God and in response to God's call, you have indicated your intention to worship and serve God alone. Now is the appointed time to renounce in public every power apart from God and every form of worship that does not offer God true honor. Do you reject every power that sets itself up in opposition to God and his Christ? If so, answer "I do" and turn to the east, the light that draws near to you.

Listen now to what your new way of life in Christ is like.

Reading: Galatians 5:22-26 (what proceeds from the Spirit).

Leader: My brothers and sisters gathered here, and you who present these candidates, you have heard them declare their resolve. Do you testify that they have chosen Christ as Lord and that they wish to serve him alone?

All: We do.

Leader: Are you ready to help them come to know and follow Christ (by following in your example and footsteps in the days to come)?

All: We are.

Leader: Father of love and mercy, we thank you in the name of our brothers and sisters who have experienced your guiding presence in their lives. Today in the presence of your community they are answering your call to faith. We praise you and bless you, Lord! (no. 82).

Ask all of the communities to rise and stand around their catechumen, laying their hands on the catechumen's shoulders. Direct them to pray for themselves that they do not hinder the growth of their catechumen by anything in their own lives and words and that their catechumen will be strengthened to follow more closely in the way of a believer. Ask them to listen to the words of the song and to pray in silence.

Song: "Turn to Me" (St. Louis Jesuits, "Earthen Vessels") or a song of repentance.

While they are praying, turn out most of the lights in the room and light candles for each of the catechumens, giving them to the sponsors while the music plays and the communities are praying. When the song is finished, direct the sponsors to give the catechumens the candles with the words: "Receive the light of Christ. Walk now in his light alone." Leave the lights out from now until the baptismal service itself. Say:

Leader: Now take your catechumens home for the second year and share with them who Jesus is for you. From your own experience and prayer and pain, share your understanding of Jesus with the catechumens, remembering that this is what they need to know to walk in the light of Christ. Share together, beginning with the sponsor.

Again, listen to the group. It will take at least a half hour for all to speak. The sound of the groups will become hushed, quiet, reverential. When it is time, tell them to take a few moments to wrap up their sharing and then to sit in silence and pray for one another.

Leader: Close your eyes now and imagine yourself in the presence of Jesus. It was at this point in the process that the community began to realize what a gift the catechumens were to the church. In sharing their belief in who Jesus was and is to them, they realized that they had forgotten much, had personalized him, and needed once again to probe the depth and richness of the reality of Jesus in their midst. No matter what they said about Jesus, there was always more to say of him. In silence, in your heart, pray to the Lord of life and tell him in your own words what he means to you and how you love him.

Give them a few moments of quiet. Then follow with these words:

Leader: There is always more to say of Jesus, and our tradition is rich with understandings that we often forget. We will listen first to a portion of scripture that proclaims a word about our belief in Jesus as Lord.

Reading: Gabriel's announcement to Mary (Luke 1:26-38); Jesus' proclamation of being the Son of Man (Luke 9:22-27); or John 1 on Jesus as the Word.

After a moment of silence, ask them to listen and to sing along with a song about Jesus.

Song: "Lord of the Dance" (Mary O'Hara, "In Concert") or another song about Jesus.

After the song, have the sponsors give a bible to the catechumens, with the words: "Receive the gospel, the good news of Jesus Christ, the Son of God (no. 93); feed now on the Word of the Lord." Then, while the sponsor holds the candle (which the catechumen has been holding all this time) direct the catechumen to read the following section from the scriptures, as if reading it for the first time, and to share this good news with their community.

Reading: Matthew 5:43-48 ("Be perfect as my heavenly Father is perfect").

Let the silence continue while all ponder what these words mean to them.

Leader: This is the third year, the hardest one, when the community members share with the catechumen their hardest moral decisions, their attempts at living the gospel, and their failures and sins. They relate why they have chosen what they did, and if they failed, how they deal with their failure to live up to their promises of faithfulness to the way of Christ. The sponsor will begin with the following exhortation to the group:

Sponsors (very quietly): Trust each other in your sharings, presenting your struggles so that the catechumen can learn what it means to follow Jesus on the way of the cross. This is not public confession of specifics or details, but confession of the fact of failure and sin.

This usually lasts a bit longer, about thirty to forty minutes. Again, listen to the sound from the groups. You'll know when to stop and bring them back together again, letting those who finish first sit in silence and pray for one another. It helps to have some Kleenex available at this point.

Leader: And so the last year would come to an end with all the community members aware that they needed forgiveness and reconciliation and the season of Lent to lead them once again into the "intensity of their first loves and commitments" (Rv 2:4).

Ask all the catechumens to stand in the presence of their communities.

Leader: These catechumens, our brothers and sisters, have already traveled a long road. Let us thank God for his loving care which has brought them to this day and ask that they may continue to hasten toward complete fellowship in our Christian way of life (no. 94).

Response: Lord, hear our prayer.

Leader: Lord, for our catechumens, that they may always remember this day when they were chosen and be thankful for the blessing they have received from heaven, let us pray to the Lord.

R: Lord, hear our prayer.

Leader: For their teachers, that they may always offer the sweetness of God's word to those who are searching for it, let us pray to the Lord.

R: Lord, hear our prayer.

Leader: For their godparents, that they may give these catechumens a good example by their consistent living of the gospel, both in their personal actions and in their duties to the community, let us pray to the Lord.

R: Lord, hear our prayer.

Leader: For their families, that, far from placing any obstacles in the way of these catechumens, they may assist them to follow the urging of the Holy Spirit, let us pray to the Lord.

R: Lord, hear our prayer.

Leader: For our community, that we may excel in fidelity to prayer and in charity, let us pray to the Lord.

R: Lord, hear our prayer.

Leader: For all who have not yet overcome their hesitation, that they may trust in Christ and one day join our community, as brothers and sisters, let us pray to the Lord (no. 148).

R: Lord, hear our prayer.

Leader: That throughout the whole world the sick may be restored to health, the broken may be made whole again, the lost found, and the found saved, let us pray to the Lord.

R: Lord, hear our prayer.

Leader: All-powerful Father, God of love, you wish to make all things new in Christ and to draw all men and women to you. Guide and govern these, your chosen ones through the ministry of your church. Keep them faithful to their calling, help them to be built into the kingdom of your Son, and prepare them to be sealed with the promised gift of the Holy Spirit. We ask this through Christ our Lord (no. 149).

R: Amen.

The Period of Lent

Leader: And so the final period of preparation would begin for the catechumens, the season of Lent, an intense time of prayer, fasting, and almsgiving. All would be exhorted to listen to the call to conversion that challenged them in the season of Lent.

The lighted candles are held in each group. Ask the catechumens to kneel in the midst of their communities.

Reading: Philippians 2:5-11 (Your attitude must be that of Christ, who humbled himself, even unto death, death on a cross).

Leader (speaking to the catechumens): You will be victorious in your struggle against darkness and death, but on your knees and under the sign of the cross.

Invite each member of the community to mark the forehead of the catechumen with the sign of the cross. The last person should help the catechumen to his or her feet. Then ask the community members to blow out their candles and put them aside and stand back to back with their catechumen wedged tightly in the middle, facing outward with their eyes closed. Explain that they are going to be taken through a prayer-experience of Lent in their minds and hearts. In the background play an instrumental piece that does not interfere with your words or their thoughts. The room should be dark.

While the music plays, speak in a very gentle, almost monotone voice, leading them within. Go slowly, distinctly, and leave them time to reflect, react, and respond in their heart.

Leader: We each stand alone, walking our way of the cross during the season of Lent, and each of us knows what we need to be reconciled for and with whom. In your heart, look back over the last few months and get in touch with those from whom you need to ask forgiveness. (*Pause.*)

Who has hurt you, whom do you need to forgive? (*Pause.*) In your heart, ask forgiveness for all that stands between you and your neighbors and loved ones and your God. (*Pause.*)

Now it is Good Friday, and the church gathers to celebrate the death of Jesus and his unfailing trust in the Father. Put yourself in the position of Christ on the cross and gather in your heart all the things of the earth that you love: places you have been, sunrises and sunsets, the change of seasons, mountains, deserts, rain, the ocean. As you gather them together in gratitude, let them go, one by one.

Now think of all the material possessions that have made your life rich: books, music, a home, photography, a car, musical instruments, good food, art, small gifts, and one by one let them all go.

In your mind's eye look at the faces of the people you love and who have loved you—children, parents, trusted and dear friends, husbands, wives, lovers. One by one give them back to God until you are alone in the presence of God.

Breathe deeply and touch the heart of your life. Breathe the spirit in and out. Know how much your life means to you and, when you are ready, use the words of Jesus and say in your heart: "Father, into your hands I give my spirit." Then let go of your life and fall into the arms of God.

> *The music should last about another four to six minutes, depending on how slowly you speak when you direct them in the meditation. Leave them in silence after the music ends for a moment or two. Then put on another song to lead into something of resurrection and Easter life, not fast, but a song that builds, like Rory Cooney's "Do Not Fear to Hope." When the song is over, ask them to renew their baptismal promises together.*

Leader: Do you promise to live in the freedom of the children of God?
R: We do.
Leader: Do you promise to reject sin and to resist evil?
R: We do.
Leader: Do you promise to take up your cross daily and follow in the footsteps of Jesus your Lord? (no. 217, adapted).
R: We do.
Leader: Do you believe in God the Father, maker of heaven and earth?
R: We do.
Leader: Do you believe in Jesus Christ, his only Son, our Lord who was born of the Virgin Mary, was crucified, died and was buried, rose from the dead, and now is seated at the right hand of the Father?
R: We do.

Leader: Do you believe in the Holy Spirit, the holy Catholic church, the communion of saints, the forgiveness of sins, the resurrection of the body and life everlasting?

R. We do (no. 219).

The Rite of Baptism

Ask the community members to turn and face their catechumen. Turn up the lights. Explain that the rite of baptism was done by immersion, three times, pushing the catechumen down into the waters. Ask them to put their hands on the catechumens' shoulders and push them down at the name of the Father, Son, and Spirit.

Leader: I baptize you in the name of the Father (*"immerse" them for the first time*). I baptize you in the name of the Son (*immerse them for the second time*). I baptize you in the name of the Holy Spirit (*immerse them the third time*) (no. 220).

Leader: God, the father of our Lord Jesus Christ, has freed you from all sin, given you a new birth by water and the Holy Spirit, and welcomed you into his holy people. He now anoints you with the chrism of salvation. As Christ was anointed priest, prophet, and king, so may you live always as a member of his body, sharing everlasting life.

R: Amen

Have small bowls of oil and cotton available and ask the sponsors to anoint the newly baptized persons with the sign of the cross with oil. Be generous. Also have a bowl of water and a branch or sprig of green ready and bless the water of baptism and sprinkle the whole group after the baptismal promises. Use blessing no. 215 from the RCIA over the water.

Leader: Godparents, please come forward and give your newly baptized Christian the kiss of peace. Let us all welcome our new brothers and sisters into our community.

As they finish up the welcoming and the kiss of peace, reform the small communities with the newly baptized as a part of the group. Explain that after the sacraments of initiation and the celebration of the eucharist, the new Christians returned on Easter Sunday night to pray and to learn together the prayer of believers, the Our Father.

Leaders: Teach your new Christians the Our Father now, realizing that this is the first time they have heard the prayer of a beloved child of God. Go line by line and let them repeat after you.

Ask all the groups to come together and sing the Our Father.

Leader: My brothers and sisters, sing glory to the Lord of the universe. Your garments have the brightness of the sun and your faces shine like those of the angels. Gladness, today is pressed upon your lips. . . . You have received the grace of God; watch, lest the evil one take it from you. God is your father, your friend and love. Go in peace, children, and adore the cross, which will watch over you forever. In the name of the Father and the Son and the Holy Spirit.

R: Amen.

Song: End with something that will pull the group together, one that all know by heart.

Follow-up

Gather the small groups and ask them to talk about what happened to them, what touched them. After they have had a chance to talk and share emotions (about five to ten minutes), have the larger group answer these questions:

1. What is it like to be a catechumen?
2. Did you get what you asked from the church of Christ—or more?
3. What is it like to be a sponsor or godparent? What was hard about it?
4. What was it like to be a member of the Christian community?
5. What did you experience during the ritual?
6. What part of the ritual touched you most? Why?
7. What is the church?
8. How did you feel about the people in your group before? Now?
9. How do you feel about not having been the catechumen?

Close with the reminder that this is a small segment of the ritual. Ask what it would be like to experience this over a two- to three-year period with the same people studying the scriptures weekly and sharing the faith.

Closing Prayer (from an ancient liturgy):

Lord Jesus, you have joined me to yourself through the waters of baptism. Make me a true sheep of your flock, a worthy hymn of your church, a consecrated vessel, a child of light, an inheritor of your kingdom. May I ever acknowledge you as Son of the Living God, with the Holy Spirit, living forever in the Father. Amen.

4

Confirmation

The Choice of the Cross and Truth-Telling

✝ Once upon a time there was a man called Matajura, who wanted to be a great swordsman. But his father and brothers told him he wasn't quick enough or agile enough and would never learn. So Matajura went to the most famous swordsman in all of Japan, a man by the name of Banzo, and asked to become his pupil. "How long will it take me to become a master?" he queried. "Suppose I became your servant, in order to be with you every minute?"

"Ten years," said Banzo.

"Ten years," Matajura gasped. "My father is getting old. Before ten years have passed I will have to return home and take care of him, since I am the youngest and that is my duty. Suppose I work twice as hard, practice, and do more than is required of me. How long will it then take me?"

"Thirty years," said Banzo.

"Thirty years," Matajura gasped again. "How is that? First you say ten years. Then when I offer to work twice as hard you say it will take three times as long. Let me make myself clear: I will work unceasingly. No hardship will ever be too much. How long will it take me then?"

"Seventy years," said Banzo. "A pupil in such a hurry learns very slowly."

Matajura began to understand. Without asking for any promises in terms of time, he became Banzo's servant. And Banzo ordered him to do three things. First, he was not to pick up a sword. Second, he was not to watch the others practicing. Last, he was not to speak of fencing or study books in the library or look at pictures of swords. This caused him a great deal of pain, and, though he did not understand, he obeyed. He was a servant. He cooked, washed, cleaned, swept, worked in the garden, did the laundry.

Matajura kept his word. A year passed and he learned much of discipline, honesty, integrity, obedience, and respect. He found he had no desire to read about swords and battles. Another year passed, and he learned more discipline of body and mind. He grew strong and agile, fast and graceful, and sure of himself; he no longer desired to watch the other students as they fenced and practiced. A third year passed, and he learned the seasons of the year, rituals, prayers, asceticism, silence, almost to disappear as a servant. He realized then that he had no desire to even pick up a sword. What had happened to him, to his dream?

Then one day while he was in the garden, digging up carrots for lunch, Banzo came up stealthily behind him and without warning gave him a terrible whack with a wooden sword. Matajura turned, surprised, stung to find Banzo with a broad grin on his face. Banzo left him in the garden, wondering. The next day it came while he was washing dishes—a terrible blow to the back of his legs. He turned to find Banzo doubled over with laughter. And the master left him again. That night as he lay fitfully asleep, Banzo came again and the blow fell across Matajura's shins. Matajura saw Banzo smiling softly.

The blows kept coming, raining down on him, night and day. There was no place, no time, where he was safe. The attacks were relentless, daunting, and he was sore from the crown of his head to the soles of his feet. He was constantly on guard, watching, waiting. He learned to live on the balls of his feet, to move at a moment's notice, to spin, dance, jump, slip away, dodge any blow. He became like the wind, like air, like silence. Not a word was spoken. He lived for the encounter with no desires, no thoughts, only quickness, readiness, attentiveness, awareness. Nothing else. Soon the blows missed him once in a while, then almost all the time. And with that, Banzo seemed to smile more and more deeply.

Then they started the formal lessons. It was quick. Soon Matajura was the greatest swordsman in all Japan. Even Banzo loved to fight with him. No one ever landed a blow. No one was ever there. Both smiled a lot and very deeply (from the *Annals of Zen*).

Welcome to the school of the Spirit, the sacrament of confirmation, the choice of the cross, of obedience even unto death. It is a school for adepts, for servants, and for those who want to be holy, to be saints, to be warriors of God, men and women of wisdom and Spirit.

Jesus is baptized by John in the River Jordan. The gift of the Spirit is given to him, the fullness of that gift, and he is acknowledged by the Father to be own beloved child, the chosen one of God. He is described by Isaiah as making justice shine on every race, never faltering, never breaking down, planting justice on the earth (Is 42:3-4). Then the Spirit leads him into the desert for forty days to be tested, and proven true, he is led by the Spirit back into his own home synagogue to take hold of the scroll of the Book of the Prophet Isaiah and announce who he is in truth and in spirit. He is given the words, insight, and strength to become who he is by the gift of God.

Jesus speaks only once about his baptism: "I have come to bring fire upon the earth and how I wish it were already kindled; but I have a baptism to undergo and what anguish I feel until it is over!" (Lk 12:49-50). Suffering, as we were told earlier in Luke's gospel, is the destiny of the Son of Man: "The Son of Man must suffer many things. He will be rejected by the elders and chief priests and teachers of the Law, and put to death. Then after three days he will be raised to life" (Lk 9:22). His legacy is to be the suffering servant, the one who will put things right in our world. He will be compassionate, just yet merciful, full of gentle, nonviolent power and love for the truth. Through him, all the nations will know that God is among the people, especially the poor, the outcast, and the oppressed of the earth. As Paul reminds us, there is no partiality in God's great love and invitation; God cares deeply for those that we do not attend.

Jesus' baptism is immersion in death, anointing for power, and resurrection to a new life of reconciliation, peace, and justice. By his death, Jesus gives forth his Spirit to the world and we are baptized with water and the Spirit. This is our faith, and it "has meaning because it is linked essentially with the fate of Jesus Christ, whose violently aborted life and broken body reveal to us a completely different God and a completely different life."[1] He came to his own and to the world and the world refused him, refused his good news, refused his God as Father, refused to hope, love, and obey. This "world" is in each of us, "this bastion of resistance to God lies deep in the marrow of the Church itself and deep in the heart of every Christian."[2] The kingdom of Jesus is here, but it has not finished coming yet. Gabriel Marcel puts it starkly: "We live in a world where betrayal is possible at every moment and in every form." Christians should feel the incongruence between the earthly and heavenly kingdoms in themselves, in the church, and in the world.

The Christian lifestyle involves an indication of the still impending reality of the kingdom of God. We who choose the kingdom often contradict the lifestyles and ideals of the world. We are caught between yesterday and tomorrow, and we freely choose to live there, hung between reality and graced possibility. We do not lead "normal" lives, but we choose out of love for Christ a kind of life into which many are thrust involuntarily. We live as models, as a holy people, so that others can share the meaning of our lives and take heart from us. As we are warned often in the scriptures: the disciple will not be better off than the Master (Mt 10:24). "No slave is greater than his master. They will harry you as they harried me. They will respect your words as much as they respected mine. All this they will do to you because of my name" (Jn 15:20-21, *NAB*).

In order to live in the world but not of it, Jesus prays that his Father give his friends a gift, the Paraclete, the comforter to be with us always (Jn 14:16). That gift of the Spirit, who is the Spirit of Truth, will continue to instruct the disciples in everything and remind them of all that Jesus did and told them (Jn 14:26). The Spirit will guide them to all truth and announce to them the things to come and will give glory to God (Jn 16:13). The Spirit will be an abiding presence of comfort, strength, insight, and hope to the disciples.

As for the world, the Spirit will be an abrasive one, "He will prove the world wrong about sin, about justice and about judgment—he will condemn the powers of this world and in the face of persecution he will not leave the disciples orphans" (Jn 16:8ff., *NAB*). In Luke's gospel the power of the Spirit is clearly and precisely spelled out: "When they bring you before synagogues, rulers and authorities, do not worry about how you are to defend yourselves or what to say. The Holy Spirit will teach you at that moment all that should be said" (Lk 12:11-12, *NAB*). Jesus does his best to warn his friends, to make them realistic about their future. Life with God in public will not be without its dangers, struggles, doubts, and insecurities. It is a life still to be fulfilled, a life of yearning and desiring, of dreaming and hoping, of commitment to God's reign. It is a life of consciously endured unfulfillment freely chosen and shared with others who wait, especially with those who have most need of the kingdom's comforting presence: the poor, the lame, the prisoner, the blind, the broken-hearted (Lk 4). The world will hinder the kingdom's coming and hinder our lives, dangle in front of us anything that might stave off the "hunger and thirst for justice, righteousness, and singleheartedness." Baptism and our faith demand a great deal of us. They invite us to live like Jesus, to "wish to totally and consciously live the reality of human existence, of humanness as a pilgrimage toward God; of humanness as an existence of seeking, a questioning, wrestling; of humanness as a life of suspension, of waiting for the coming of God."[3]

In *Nomad of the Spirit: Reflections of a Young Monastic* Bernardin Schellenberger points out that he is not writing about monks but about Christians in the world. He describes the life of a Christian in drastically insecure and demanding terms.

> The element that has always kept Christianity alive is the tension between the "already here" and "the not yet here" of the kingdom of God. There is a meaning, a necessity, a sublime grandeur in living the "already here." Yet today, without giving up this aspect or being permitted to resolve the tension we should be admitting the aspect of the "not yet here" more powerfully and making it the formative principle of our lives. Quite simply, we are pushed into this by the situation of the world, of the Church, and of our own monastic communities.
>
> What does it mean in practical terms? First of all, we should accept the experience of living with crises and problems positively, as an essential component of our calling. We should not regard it as an interference factor, repressing it and lamenting it as something that should not be and allowing it to paralyze us. Instead, we should, paradoxically, view it as the source of our strength and inspiration. That which chafes us keeps us awake.[4]

Or, as Thomas Merton once said to a questioner in response to the rather blunt query of who he was: "If you want to know who I am, then ask me, 'What are you living for, very concretely, here and today, in your everyday life? What do you think keeps you from living fully for what you would like to live for?'" There is an ancient, mystical, even romantic image for this very tenuous and realistic way of life: the cross. Jesus was the first who "offered his sacrifice with tears and cries" (Heb 5:7) and "who was the first to hang between heaven and earth . . . as a sign of our true situation."[5] We must learn to live with what happened to Jesus, in life and in death.

Dostoyevsky in his "Grand Inquisitor" interprets the devil's three proposals (Mt 4:1-11) as the temptations to miracles, mystery, and power. They also can be seen as temptations to take care of immediate needs, using the powers of the world to make the kingdom come or relying on our privileged relationship with God to save us from suffering (Lk 4:1-13). We are told, rather ominously, that the tempter left Jesus only to await another opportunity. In his life and in his death Jesus must deal with obstacles to the kingdom, to his mission. Jesus is a sign of peace and contradiction. We are called to both signs as well. We are to continue the approach of the kingdom, the work of mercy and justice in the world. He relies on us. He gives us the Spirit to sustain us. In the open prayer of the rite of confirmation we are reminded of why we are to receive the power of the Holy Spirit.

> The gift of the Holy Spirit which you are to receive will be a spiritual sign and seal to make you more like Christ and more perfect members of his Church. At his baptism by John, Christ Himself was anointed by the Spirit and sent out on his public ministry to set the world on fire.
>
> You have already been baptized into Christ and now you will receive the power of his Spirit and the sign of the cross on your forehead. You must be witnesses before all the world to his suffering, death and resurrection; your way of life should at all times reflect the goodness of Christ. Christ gives varied gifts to his Church, and the Spirit distributes them among the members of Christ's body to build up the holy people of God in unity and love.
>
> Be active members of the Church, alive in Jesus Christ. Under the guidance of the Spirit give your lives completely in the service of all, as did Christ, who came not to be served but to serve.
>
> So now, before you receive this Spirit, I ask you to renew the profession of faith you made in baptism (no. 22).[6]

It is in the Acts of the Apostles, often called the gospel of the Holy Spirit, that we see the workings of the Spirit in the apostles and disciples and the effect it has on the world: some hear and come to belief, others are enraged. Peter, who is first seen in the Acts huddled in a back room, is filled with the Holy Spirit and begins to preach. Suddenly he is self-assured and dynamic (Acts 4:8). Stephen witnesses to Jesus and preaches that God has always witnessed the sufferings of the people and come to their aid (Acts 7:34). As Stephen gives up his own spirit to God in death by stoning he sees the glory of God revealed (Acts 7:59). He dies because he has provoked others to anger in accusing them of opposing the Spirit of God in the prophets and again in the person of Jesus Christ. He calls them stiff-necked people who have the law but do not obey it (Acts 7:51).

Paul too knows the touch of the Spirit. He is described as "growing steadily more powerful and could reduce the Jewish community of Damascus to silence with his proofs that this Jesus that they had crucified was the Messiah" (Acts 9:22, *NAB*). But the Spirit gets one in trouble too. Peter and John are preaching soon after the feast of Pentecost and the elders in the Sanhedrin make it clear to them that they are to stop speaking in the name of Jesus or teaching about him. And Peter replies: "Judge for yourselves whether it is right in God's sight for us to obey you rather than God. Surely we cannot help speaking of what we have heard and seen" (Acts 4:19-20, *NAB*). The act of witnessing makes them public nuisances. But they are obeying the command that Jesus gave them: "The Spirit bears witness on my behalf; you must bear witness as well" (Jn 15:26, *NAB*). It is the Spirit who gives words, courage, and endurance to the followers of Jesus and makes them bold.

But the Spirit is not given only to individual believers; it is given also to the church, for the church. We are church by the power of the Spirit. Acts gives a description of the work of the Spirit in the church: "Meanwhile throughout all of Judea, Galilee and Samaria the church was at peace. It was being built up and was making steady progress in the fear of the Lord; at the same time it enjoyed the increased consolation of the Holy Spirit" (Acts 9:31, *NAB*). The Spirit speaks to the community and says: "Set apart Barnabas and Saul for me to do the work for which I have called them" (Acts 13:2-3, *NAB*). So they set apart Saul and Barnabas, lay hands on them, and sent them off on the first missionary journey. Finally, it is the Spirit who both pushes Paul to go to Jerusalem and at the same time warns him that chains and hardship await him there (Acts 20:23).

The Spirit is given in confirmation to individual believers to sustain them in faith, to build up the church, and to witness to the world the death and resurrection of Jesus. The closing prayer of the sacramental celebration says it simply.

> God our Father,
> complete the work you have begun
> and keep the gifts of your Holy Spirit
> active in the hearts of your people.
> Make them ready to live this gospel
> and eager to do his will.
> May they never be ashamed
> to proclaim to all the world Christ crucified
> living and reigning for ever and ever. Amen (no. 33).

The sacrament of confirmation is a sacrament for in-between times— in between the future fullness of the kingdom and now, ordinary time.

There is a story by Madeleine L'Engle that reminds us why we need the Spirit.

> There's a story of a small village . . . where there lived an old clockmaker and repairer. When anything was wrong with any of the clocks or watches in the village, he was able to fix them, to get them working properly again. When he died, leaving no children and no apprentices, there was no one left in the village who could fix clocks. Soon various watches began to break down. Those whose continued to run often lost or gained time, so they were of little use. A clock might strike midnight or three in the afternoon. So many of the villagers abandoned their timepieces.
>
> One day a renowned clockmaker and repairer came through that village and the people crowded around him and begged him to fix their broken clocks and watches. He spent many hours looking at all the faulty time pieces and at last announced that he could repair only those whose owners had kept them wound, because they were the only ones which would be able to remember how to keep time.
>
> So we must keep things wound: that is, we must pray when prayer seems dry as dust; we must write when we are physically tired, when our hearts are heavy, when our bodies are in pain. We may not always be able to make our clock run correctly, but at least we can keep it wound, so that it will not forget.[7]

The Spirit in the sacrament of confirmation is given to us so that we will remember who we are, learn to endure, and steadfastly grow, as Jesus did, "in wisdom, age and grace before the world" (Lk 2).

The Spirit is first of all a teacher. What do we learn from the Spirit? The Spirit teaches that the most important thing is the struggle to be holy. Dorothy Day wrote: "We live in a time of gigantic evil. It is hopeless to think of combating it by any other means than that of sanctity. To think of overcoming such evil by material means, by alleviations, by changes in the social order only—all this is utterly hopeless." And what does that holiness consist in? "Common sense in religion is rare, and we are too often trying to be heroic instead of just ordinarily good and kind. . . . On the one hand, we have to change the social order in order that men might lead decent Christian lives, and on the other hand, we must remake ourselves."[8]

What is sanctity? Thomas Merton quotes Georges Bernanos:

The saints are not resigned, at least in the sense that the world thinks. If they suffer in silence those injustices which upset the mediocre, it is in order better to turn against injustice, against its face of brass, all the strength of their great souls. Angers, daughters of despair, creep and twist like worms. Prayer is, all things considered, the only form of revolt that stays standing up.

Merton comments on these words.

There may be a touch of stoicism in Bernanos' wording here, but that does not matter. A little more stoic strength would not hurt us, and would not necessarily get in the way of grace![9]

Merton prays in his journal, struggling with his place and times:

Father, I beg you to keep me in this silence so that I may learn from it the word of your peace and the word of your mercy and the word of your gentleness to the world; and that through me perhaps your word of peace may make itself heard where it has not been possible for anyone to hear it for a long time.
    To study truth here and learn here to suffer for truth.

Life is, or should be, nothing but a struggle to seek truth: yet what we seek is really the truth that we already possess. Truth is mine in the reality of life as it is given to me to live; yet to take life thoughtlessly, passively as it comes, is to renounce the struggle and purification which are necessary.

I think I will have to become a Christian.[10]

The Spirit gives us the courage to become Christians. We must keep at it, endure. We must pray like the Yokut Indians in their death-song: "All my life I have been seeking, seeking, seeking." And we must learn to take the struggle lightly, and laugh at ourselves. I recall an anecdote from a short book on parables written by Bishop Anthony Bloom. The martyr Hermas is being cheered up by his guardian angel, who tells him: "Be of good cheer, Hermas. God will not abandon you before he breaks either your heart or your bones." The other translation for the word *martyr* is "witness," and the Spirit helps us to be witnesses. A card from Vatican II carried this quotation by Cardinal Suenens: "To be a witness does not consist in engaging in propaganda, not even in stirring people up, but in being a living mystery. It means to live in such a way that one's life would not make sense if God did not exist."

What are we to witness to? First—to courage and hope. The word *hope* in Hebrew means to "twist, to twine around," like strands to braid a rope. We need to tie each other together, to haul each other up out of danger, to throw each other lifelines, to give support and courage to those who need it. We need to witness to justice, encourage others to work for justice, and help victims of injustice survive with gracefulness and some joy instead of despair. Why? Because by raising Jesus from the dead, God not only brought about an invincible hope in the ultimate victory of the divine kingdom but also identified with this poor man from Nazareth, who died in godforsakenness as a condemned blasphemer and thorn in the side of the government and the religious institution. To live resisting injustice and identifying with the poor and the powerless is to shout hope and resurrection; it is to continue the mission of Jesus. The Spirit proceeds from the cross and resurrection, and the Spirit sides with the destitute, the forgotten, the lost, the spurned and alienated, those persecuted for justice's sake, the downtrodden, and those broken in spirit. It is the Spirit who continues to move in protest against injustice, sin, and the world's ways of power and contempt. This Spirit is dangerous. This Spirit is prophetic.

Abraham Heschel describes the character of the prophet:

> To us a single act of injustice—cheating in business, exploitation of the poor—is slight; to the prophets a disaster. To us injustice is injurious to the welfare of the people; to the prophets it's a death-blow to existence: to us, an episode, to them, a catastrophe, a threat to the world. Their breathless impatience with injustice may strike us as hysteria. . . . to the prophets even a minor injustice assumes cosmic proportions.[11]

Elie Wiesel makes the link among prophets, martyrs, and witnesses in our society. "A witness is a link. A link between the event and the other person who has not participated in it. A witness is a link between past and present, between man and God, between man and Man."[12] The Spirit witnesses to Jesus. We also are told to witness to his death and resurrection. We witness for the world's sake. This witness is desperately needed. Dom Helder Camara, a former archbishop of Recife, Brazil, prays:

Come Lord. Do not smile and say you are already with us. Millions do not know you, and to us who do, What is the difference? What is the point of your presence if our lives do not alter? Change our lives, shatter our complacency. Make your word flesh of our flesh, blood of our blood and our life's purpose. Take away the quietness of a clear conscience. Press us uncomfortably. For only thus that other peace is made—your peace.

We need to care for our neighbor as Jesus did. Amnesty International is based on just one command: to visit the imprisoned. It obeys by giving strength, encouragement, and care to prisoners of conscience and by hounding governments and individuals to stop inhumane treatment of prisoners, restore rights to political prisoners, and abolish the death penalty. A story is told of what that kind of relentless, everyday witness can mean to someone.

During the final days of World War II, a captured resistance member sat alone in a black prison cell, tired, hungry, tortured, and convinced of approaching death. After weeks of torture, and torment, the prisoner was sure that there was no hope, that no one knew or cared.

But in the middle of the night the door of the cell opened, and the jailer, shouting abuse into the darkness, threw a loaf of bread onto the dirt floor. The prisoner, by this time ravenous, tore open the loaf. Inside was a matchbox, and inside the matchbox were matches and a scrap of paper.

The prisoner lit a match. On the paper there was a single word: *Coraggio!*

Coraggio. Take courage. Don't give up, don't give in. We are trying to help you. *Coraggio!*

The name of Amnesty International's newsletter, *The Matchbox*, is based on this story.

The Spirit teaches us to tell the truth. The place where everything is laid bare, exposed, and the truth that rules all other truths is told is in the cross. It is here that Christians learn that, as Emily Dickinson wrote, "power is only pain, disciplined." What is the meaning of the cross? It certainly isn't a glorification of suffering or even a way to tread on the edges of God's mysterious presence and ways among us. It is to remind us to uncrucify the earth in living persons—to take them all down from their crosses and set them free. We are to acknowledge their human dignity, care for them, embrace them, be compassionate with them. The meaning of the cross is to undo injustice, hatred, poverty, and war.

The cross is a word of judgment against our priorities, projects, and lifestyles. It is a word of hope and mercy for the poor, the powerless, and the unimportant. It sets us at odds, draws the sword of distinction more surely than any other interpretation of scripture, tradition, and spirituality. Jesus died on a garbage heap, reminiscent of Job on his dunghill. Why? There is no simple answer. What is important is that this subversive memory of Jesus is kept alive in words and in deeds. Dan Berrigan reminds those who speak out on justice and peace issues: "If you're going to get involved with justice, you'd better look good on wood!"

The Spirit urges us to speak out courageously for others, in compassion. This speaking on behalf of the truth is never easy. But Roger Schutz, the prior of Taizé, tells us what happens when people do speak.

> During the darkest periods of history, quite often a small number of men and women, scattered through the world, have been able to reverse the course of historical evolutions. This was only possible because they hoped beyond all hope. What had been bound for disintegration then entered into the current of a new dynamism.

Not to speak is a sin, a crime against humanity, against the Spirit of God. Pastor Martin Niemoller of Germany reminds us of our excuses and their consequences in the world:

> In Germany they first came for the Communists and I didn't speak up because I wasn't a Communist. Then they came for the Jews, and I didn't speak up because I wasn't a Jew. Then they came for the trade unionists, and I didn't speak up because I wasn't a trade unionist. Then they came for the Catholics, and I didn't speak up because I was a Protestant. Then they came for me—and by that time no one was left to speak up.

Those who are confronted or caught in the web of injustice often have to ask themselves difficult questions and decide how to live or die. Nadezhda Mandelstam in her book *Hope against Hope: A Memoir* recalls her terror when her husband was jailed and sent into exile. She was not to learn what happened to him for over thirty years.

Later I often wondered whether it is right to scream when you are being beaten and trampled underfoot. Isn't it better to face one's tormentors in a stance of satanic pride, answering them with contemptuous silence? I decided that it is better to scream. This pitiful sound, which sometimes, goodness knows how, reaches into the remotest prison cell, is a concentrated expression of the last vestiges of human dignity. It is a human's way of leaving a trace, of telling people how you lived and died. By one's screams, one asserts his right to live, sends a message to the outside world demanding help and calling for resistance. Silence is the real crime against humanity.[13]

As Christians we need to learn to speak and break our silence long before it reaches such a level of anguish if we are to tell the truth, obey the commands of Jesus and witness to the power of the cross and resurrection in the world. We need to speak out and remind the world of the presence of the gospel of Jesus long before it reaches the brink of persecution and martyrdom.

The role of the Spirit today is protest, resistance that is nonviolent and imaginative, and the making of peace and unity among peoples. It is in the arena of racial differences, the political process, and getting people to face their national and religious separations and forge harmony out of them. It is in places like the Middle East, Ireland, South America, the ghettos of the first-world countries, and Africa. The Spirit calls us from Native American reservations, the castes of India, and the classes of people in every country. The real prophets of the Spirit, ones who tell us the truth, sometimes forcefully, are the real heroines and heroes of holiness. We are church; we must learn to *conspire* together, to breathe together, to share life together. In the words of Nikos Kazantzakis:

And I strive to discover how to signal my companions . . . to say in time a simple word, a password, like conspirators, let us unite, let us hold each other tightly, let us merge our hearts, let us create for earth a brain and heart, let us give a human meaning to the superhuman struggle.

It is this struggle in the world that saves us and brings to fruition our baptism. Merton prays: "The world without storms and our lives without agony would give us nothing to grow on. Make us glad for stormy weather."

At the very beginning of the Second Vatican Council John XXIII received the diplomats in the Sistine Chapel, pointed up to Michelangelo's scene of the Last Judgment on the ceiling, and said, "Well, gentlemen and ladies, what will it be?" The choice still lies before us.

The sacrament of confirmation is for discipline, for speaking, for facing the realities of life in our times in the world as believing, practicing Christians. The Dalai Lama says that it is religion, freely accepted and lived, that gives us strength and endurance.

> The practical test comes when occasions of sorrow or suffering arise. The person whose mind is conditioned by the study and practice of religion faces these circumstances with patience and forbearance. The person who does not follow the path of religion may break under the impact of what he regards as calamities, and may end in either self-frustration, or else in pursuits which inflict unhappiness on others. Humanitarianism and true love for all beings can only stem from an awareness of the content of religion. In whatever name religion may be known, its understanding and practice are the essence of a peaceful mind and therefore of a peaceful world. If there is no peace in one's mind, there can be no peace in one's approach to others, and thus no peaceful relations between individuals and between nations.[14]

The Spirit and the practice of our commitment to Christianity change our attitude toward life. We come to realize that it does not really matter what we expect from life—it is what life expects from us, what the Spirit expects from us. Life means taking responsibility with others for the care of the world. The deeper we go into life, the more we are a disciple of Jesus.

Near the end of World War II Etty Hillesum wrote in her diary: "Here I always come back to what one should strive after with all one's might: one must marry one's feelings to one's beliefs and ideas. That is probably the only way to achieve a measure of harmony in one's life."[15] She was twenty-seven, a linguist, a writer, a translator. She was Jewish, though she did not consider herself practicing, just a member of her people. She was caught in Amsterdam in 1943, when the Nazis invaded. Her diaries were written during the occupation and deportation. The Holocaust enters her journals obliquely, slowly, as it came into the core of her life. She struggled to keep her hope and humanity alive, and, as she describes it, learned to pray:

I draw prayer around me like a dark protective wall, withdraw inside it as one might into a convent cell and then step outside again, calmer and stronger and more collected again. I can imagine times to come when I will stay on my knees for days on end waiting until the protective walls are strong enough to prevent me going to pieces altogether, my being lost and utterly devastated. . . . [Surrender] does not mean giving up the ghost, fading away with grief, but offering what little assistance I can wherever it has pleased God to place me.

As conditions worsen she writes in her journal to God:

But one thing is becoming increasingly clear to me: that You cannot help us, that we must help You to help ourselves. And that is all we can manage these days and also all that really matters: that we safeguard that little piece of You, God, in ourselves. And perhaps, in others as well. Alas, there doesn't seem to be much You Yourself can do about our circumstances, about our lives. Neither do I hold You responsible. You cannot help us but we must help You and defend Your dwelling place inside us to the last.

She rescues a few branches of jasmine from a tree drenched by rain the night before and continues:

I have strength enough, God, for suffering on a grand scale, but there are more than a thousand everyday cares that leap up on me without warning like so many fleas. So I scratch away desperately and tell myself, "This day has been taken care of now. . . . You can see, I look after You, I bring you not only my tears and my forebodings on this stormy, grey Sunday morning, I even bring you scented jasmine."

She has never been confirmed, but she learned from the Spirit.

I shall become the chronicler of our adventures. I shall forge them into a new language and store them inside me should I have no chance to write things down. I shall grow dull and come to life again, fall down and rise up again and one day I may perhaps discover a peaceful space around me which is mine alone and then I shall sit there for as long as it takes, even if it should be a year, until life begins to bubble up in me again and I find the words that bear witness where witness needs to be borne.

Two months before she disappeared into a concentration camp she wrote:

> Ultimately, we have just one moral duty: to reclaim large areas of peace in ourselves, more and more peace and to reflect it towards others. And the more peace there is in us, the more peace there will also be in our troubled world. . . . I shall try to be a prayer. . . . There is no poet in me, just a little piece of God that might grow into poetry.
>
> A soul is forged out of fire and rock crystal. Something rigorous, hard in an Old Testament sense, but also as gentle as the gesture with which his tender fingertips sometimes stroked my eyelashes.[16]

Her last words, written on a postcard, were: "We should be willing to act as a balm for all wounds." Etty Hillesum died in Auschwitz on November 30, 1943. By the time she had finished her brief pilgrimage, as revealed in her diaries, she had undergone a radical conversion that enabled her to face the Nazis, her future, and her peoples' future with compassion for others and forgiveness for her enemies. She had learned in her flesh many of the fruits of the Spirit.

At confirmation we are given seven gifts: wisdom, understanding, counsel or right judgment, courage, knowledge, reverence, and fear of the Lord or awe. Confirmation triggers the process of endurance and faithfulness, as we become what we profess and believe. The fruits of devotion to that task are recognizable to all. They are the fruits of obedience to the Spirit: charity, joy, peace, patience, kindness, goodness, longsuffering, gentleness, faith, truthfulness, self-control, and chastity. These form the essence of holiness, righteousness, and justice. Perhaps the most obvious of the effects of the Spirit's growth in us is joy. The quality of joy comes hard to us. Bernardin Schellenberger taps some of its illusiveness.

> Who can say how much hidden suffering and how much quietly borne loneliness and wretchedness this outwardly cheerful person has endured or must secretly endure over and over again? And who can say that an outwardly careworn person who looks tense

and unredeemed does not know joy? His joy may be very deeply hidden. Perhaps it is only a pebble under a mountain of suffering and skepticism—a final certainty, in the midst of darkness, that his condition must be *thus* and not otherwise, and that it *thus* has its meaning, albeit ungraspable and ineffable. His certainty can be a realization that is bare and naked and does not reach feeling and emotion: the joy of the fish at being caught in God's net, and yet a writhing and struggling with all the fibers of its being against the death that must be died.

The Christian can have a calling to participate very intensely in the passion of his Master. His disciple is even all the more one with Him the deeper he plunges. This kind of "joy," which can be shrouded in great sorrow, is not something that such a person will wish to exchange for any other joy. And it will be perceptible to anyone around him who has a feel for it. For one really needs a special feel. It can't be found for sale to everyone in the market-place.[17]

Baptism and confirmation must be seen in the framework of the whole history of Christ. In these sacraments (and with eucharist) we are stamped with the cross, the sign of the gospel of the Lord. We are reborn.

This concept of rebirth is to be understood eschatologically. Matthew (19:28) means by it the renewal and rebirth of the world in the future of the Son of Man and his glory. Titus 3:5 talks about regeneration of believers in the Holy Spirit according to the mercy of God through Jesus Christ, which makes them already heirs of eternal life "in hope." When the Johannine writings talk about new birth "from God" and "from the Spirit" they are talking about the new source of new life. Born again of the Spirit, believers acquire a share in the kingdom of God. The first epistle of Peter talks about being born again "to a living hope" (1:3) by the mercy of God through the resurrection of Jesus Christ from the dead. Jürgen Moltmann describes this concept:

> In the rebirth of life the new creation of the world into the kingdom of God in an individual life is already experienced and anticipated *here*. This has its foundation in the prevenient mercy of God, it is manifest in the resurrection of Christ from the dead; and it is efficacious in the Spirit, which moulds life in faith to the living hope. . . . "The one who is born again is, as it were, ahead of himself; he lives from the thing that is coming to him, not from what is

already in him." The one who is born again cannot, therefore, be scrupulously and anxiously preoccupied with himself, although he lives in this experience. His life has become new because, being orientated towards the new creation, he lives in the presence of the Spirit and under his influence, the "earnest of glory." At the same time the eschatological orientation of the individual's rebirth opens him for the community and for the world. The experience is his own—irreplaceably so; but it sets him in the movement of hope and in the fellowship of the messianic community. Rebirth does not isolate a person, even though it affects the individual in his unrepeatable character. On the contrary, it links his life with the future, giving that life, limited as it is, a meaning that transcends it.[18]

This is, in essence, the crux of the theological reality of the sacrament of confirmation. It forms individuals within the church to be disciples of the Messiah, to pick up their cross and come after Jesus. But what does this discipleship mean for individuals today? In a collection of sermons entitled *The Christian Disciple*, John F. Skinner writes:

What are some of the possible lures for the actualization of discipleship? What are some of the possibilities which may arise from the acceptance of one's personal, finite reality derived from the practice of self-denial [the cross]?

1. It may be some special burden of the care of others, or of the service to humankind which can be declined [to take up your cross on behalf of others].
2. It may be some lot in life you cannot escape [a situation most would find intolerable].
3. It may be some limitation or poverty which you can leave behind by accepting some lower ideal of life [accepting one or more of the temptations to power, authority, acceptance, greed, etc.].
4. It may be some share in the life of others which keeps you back from a career or the development of your own powers [a limit in the direction and options for personal growth].
5. It may be some mode of life, humbling and difficult, which you might avoid [in job possibilities, location, pay, etc.].
6. It may be some refusal of place, or power, or ease, or home, or love which in conscience you are compelled to make [to refuse such control and social status].

7. It may be some sacrifice of a high aim, an alluring ambition, a heart-satisfying purpose and a meek acceptance of obscurity and toil [to refuse the production-consumption model of life, to align oneself with "minority groups," service jobs, an option for "downward mobility"].
8. It may mean the silent acceptance of some wrong, or the stepping down from a place you could have occupied [to be sensitive, understanding and loving, to know when to make an issue of an event and when not to].
9. It may be the passing into some mean estate which one word could prevent [to stand against injustice by standing with those oppressed and victimized].

The preceding nine instances are only a small selection from the possibilities that have occurred and can occur as lures for a Christian future. Whatever shape such a lure or cross may take, one thing is certain. The disciple must freely accept it as a lure for his life. It cannot be thrust upon the disciple as an inevitability of existence. W. M. Clow observes: "Your cross is something you can take or you can refuse."[19]

Later Skinner extends this lure, this acceptance of the cross, to the church as a corporate entity, as an ecclesiastical reality:

Is the Church willing to embrace these lures, actualize these possibilities, take up these crosses, or will the Church lapse back into the protection of the many fantasies, pretensions, and illusions which often accompany the claims it makes about itself? Does the pattern of Jesus' life and death inform the life of the Church or not? Out of the vast number of crosses available to the Church corporate today, three will be cited: They are: 1. the urban poor, 2. women and 3. gay people. . . .

These are explosive issues for the church and society. No easy solutions will come to these difficult and compelling human dilemmas. Much study, prayer and fasting is needed in approaching these sensitive questions. But two observations should be made. The leaders of the Church corporate should consider the implication of an [existing] position . . . that is unacceptable to a portion of the Church. . . . Secondly, the Church corporate in most cases acts decisively through individuals, and smaller groups with it. The leaders of the Church corporate should at least permit and support individuals, groups and schools who are working on the cutting edge of this issue who are launching out into the deep, who are taking up this lure or cross on behalf of the entire Church. When an individual, group, or school is willing to risk itself in this way, the leaders of the Church corporate should not become adversaries to those who are taking this needed risk. Instead they should permit and support it.[20]

Skinner, a United Methodist, deals with issues that his church has neglected to confront or has partially considered. Some of the crosses that need to be shouldered within the Roman Catholic Church, along with those of the poor, women, and gay people, are the crosses of the divorced, widowed, remarried, single persons, the handicapped, and those who struggle for peace and justice education in a society that does not look kindly on mixing church/state issues, especially those issues that have a bearing on American policies: the death penalty, the penal system, interracial and intercultural education and rights, foreign policy, apartheid at home and abroad, nuclear arms proliferation, war-related research, escalation of new defense systems, and a climate of national defense that cripples human services within our own country. Skinner concludes, "The pattern of Jesus' life and death should become dynamically a part of the life of a Church which denies itself, of a Church which takes up the Cross, and of a Church which follows in the way of its Lord."[21]

We begin with ourselves. As Audre Lorde, a black essayist and poet, said in a talk entitled "The Transformation of Silence into Language and Action":

I have come to believe over and over again that what is most important to me must be spoken, made verbal and shared, even at the risk of being bruised or misunderstood. . . .

In becoming forcibly and essentially aware of my mortality, and of what I wished and wanted for my life, however short it might be, priorities and omissions became strongly etched in a merciless light and what I most regretted were my silences. Of what had I ever been afraid? To question or to speak as I believed could have meant pain, or death. But we all hurt in so many different ways, all the time, and pain will either change or end. Death, on the other hand, is the final silence. And that might be coming quickly, now, without regard for whether I had ever spoken what needed to be said, or had only betrayed myself into small silences, while I planned someday to speak, or waited for someone else's words. . . . I am the face of one of your fears.[22]

When she spoke these words she was struggling with cancer, and so the sense of her silences was acute. Her confrontation with her own death makes her courageous in facing the many deaths of humanity and specifically in American society. She continues,

I'm doing my work—come to ask you, are you doing yours? . . . And of course I am afraid because the transformation of silence into language and action is an act of self-revelation, and that always seems fraught with danger. . . . In the cause of silence, each of us draws the face of her own fear—fear of contempt, of censure, or some judgment, or recognition, of challenge, of annihilation. But, most of all, I think, we fear the visibility without which we cannot truly live. . . . For to survive in the mouth of this dragon we call america, we have had to learn this first and most vital lesson—that we were never meant to survive. Not as human beings. And neither were most of you here today. Black or not. And that visibility which makes us most vulnerable is that which also is the source of our greatest strength. Because the machine will try to grind you into dust anyway, whether or not we speak. We can sit in our corners mute forever while our sisters and our selves are wasted, while our children are distorted and destroyed, while our earth is poisoned; we can sit in our safe corners mute as bottles, and we will still be no less afraid.

For all of us, it is necessary to teach by living and speaking those truths which we believe and know beyond understanding. Because in this way alone we can survive, by taking part in a process of life that is creative and continuing, that is growth.

. And it is never without fear—of visibility, of the harsh light of scrutiny and perhaps of judgment, of pain, of death. But we have lived through all of those already, in silence, except death. . . . I am attempting to break that silence. And there are so many silences to be broken.[23]

Audre Lorde lived almost another decade after these words. There have been many who have spoken—in words, action, affiliations. "A cup of coffee never tastes so good as when coming out of an ice cold room into a warm kitchen," said Dorothy Day, the founder of the Catholic Worker, who up until the very end of her life protested and resisted injustice, war, violence, poverty, homelessness, and despair. Over and over again she reminded her workers of the lines from Dostoyevsky that "love in practice is a harsh and dreadful thing compared to love in dreams, but if we see only Jesus in all who come to us . . . then it is easier." She was a journalist, a Catholic who believed in simple human kindness and charity; her life showed a standard of values that offended the world in which she lived and oftentimes even embarrassed her church.

Another woman, Hannah Senesh, Israel's national heroine, is remembered as a poet and martyr in the struggle against Nazi Germany. She was safe in Palestine during World War II, yet she volunteered for a mission to help rescue Jews in her native Hungary. She was captured by the Gestapo, stood up to imprisonment and torture, and was executed at the age of twenty-two.

A third woman, Sophie Scholl, her brother Hans, and their friend Christoph Probst were executed in Munich, Germany, for high treason against Hitler. They were the leaders of the White Rose, an underground student organization dedicated to awakening fellow Germans to the immorality of the Hitler regime. In a state that no longer tolerated free expression or dissent they repeatedly accumulated the paper, stencils, and stamps for their angry leaflets of protest and traveled separately throughout Germany to distribute them. They knew the danger they were in and acted anyway. At twenty-one Sophie wrote: "With all those people dying for the regime, it is high time that someone died against it." She often wanted to escape Germany. "Oh how I wish that just for a little while I could live on an island where I could do and say whatever I wanted to." She had once belonged to the Hitler Youth, as had all the others in her age group, but slowly eased her way out. She read Augustine, early Christian writers and testimonies, and learned from another of the group, Werner, about the great religions of the world; she became intensely preoccupied with Christianity. She became convinced that Germany had to lose the war and even wrote that to her boyfriend, an officer in the army, Fritz Hartnagel, who is today a judge in Stuttgart. She began by refusing to donate clothing, money, or food. She served her alternative service in a camp and began consciously to "make decisions against herself." She told a friend, "You must have a hard spirit and a soft heart." She was beheaded after a public trial on February 22, 1943, with her brother and a friend. The White Rose was crushed. Eventually some fifty people were arrested, eight killed. But resistance within

Germany was spurred and began in earnest. The last words between her and her mother are simple and telling: "Oh, Mother, those few short years! We took all the responsibility, for everything. That will fan the flames." Her mother spoke: "Remember, Sophie, Jesus." And she replied: "Yes—but you must remember too." And then she left to face her execution.[24]

There are others, many others. Sheila Cassidy abandoned the rat-race for success in surgery and volunteered to do clinic work in poor sections of Chile. She returned to the practice of her faith after years away, because of her contact with missionaries who worked with her. In November 1975 she was arrested by the DINA, Chile's secret police, for treating a wounded revolutionary. A period of interrogation and torture was followed by three weeks in solitary confinement and then five weeks in a detention camp with one hundred other political prisoners. Found guilty of a minor infringement of Chilean law at a trial after her arrest, she was held for fifty-nine days and then expelled from the country. At thirty-five she discovered the realities of politics—that giving aid to those in need can be dangerous to one's health and well-being. She returned to England and worked for a while for Amnesty International, speaking on behalf of torture victims, then as a recluse attached to a monastery, and then for more than a decade in hospices for those with incurable diseases. She writes, remembers, lives, and tells the truth.[25]

The list can become a litany of resistance and nonviolence and truthtelling: Jim and Shelley Douglass at Ground Zero, then in Birmingham, Alabama, and in Bosnia and the Palestinian West Bank; Jim Wallis and the Sojourners community; Daniel, Philip, and Elizabeth Berrigan and Jonah House; the many Ploughshares communities; John Dear; the L'Arche communities, and Catholic Worker Houses; Sister Helen Prejean and those active against the death penalty and prison reform; AIDS hospices and those who work for rights and dignity for all regardless of sexual orientation; houses of hospitality in communities in El Salvador, Guatemala, and other countries. There are countless nameless voices who continue to obey the promptings of the Spirit and obey what they know to be the truth in regards to issues of peace, mercy, justice, and human rights. They seek to live lives of charity, kindness, and community within the church. This maturing of Christian faith is often in response to the Spirit given in baptism and confirmation and accepted as strength and courage in life. They have taken the Spirit seriously, and so others must take them seriously.

The sacrament of confirmation is meant primarily to be an intimate part of the sacrament of baptism and to be celebrated before full participation in the eucharist. In reality, confirmation exists as a separate sacrament, and this baffles theologians, liturgists, and religious educators. It is almost impossible to explain confirmation apart from the other sacraments of initiation and community. Now that the RCIA is once again stressing for believers the interconnectedness of the initiation rites, we need to look at pastoral options for celebrating this sacrament effectively.

There is no reason confirmation can't be celebrated apart from baptism. But it is not a rite of adolescence or transition, as often taught. Its character is adult, demanding, and singular, not meant to be done collectively in an age group. The church needs to confront honestly the fact that most if not all high school students and young adults are not ready to embrace the demands of Christian life in our culture. The church itself is partially to blame for that fact because of its stress on education and information rather than conversion and ethical conduct and its own debilitating lack of real adult community. But it is a place to begin—by demanding that those to be confirmed enroll in a rigorous and time-consuming apprenticeship and discipleship of initiation and preparation for commitment to the cross and resurrection of Jesus in their lives. No young adult *deserves* confirmation, and no program of six months to a year with a weekend retreat is adequate preparation for it, especially in light of the lack of development of the faith in the past years.

Another alternative, in conjunction with the bishops' recommendations, is to put off the reception of the sacrament until individuals are ready to enroll themselves in the adult catechumenate and receive the sacrament of confirmation with others who are initiated into the full communion of the church at the Easter Vigil liturgy of a parish. Or the diocese can begin a confirmation catechumenate for adult believers who wish to recommit themselves to their baptismal promises and life in the community after a rededication and apprenticeship within the larger church. This is the idea behind religious communities' novitiates and pre-formation programs. The church can institute such a catechumenate for those who wish to be confirmed. But to introduce confirmation prior to eucharist and reconciliation in the lower primary grades is to water down any ethical understanding of the sacrament and to perpetuate the disintegration of the sacramental structure focused primarily on children who are not in a position to know or understand what they are being initiated into or what they are committing themselves to. The coming of the Spirit is for adults; it shows the dangerous, adventurous side of God's working in us.

Nikos Kazantzakis writes of his conversation with an artist, who says:

> They paint the Holy Spirit descending upon the Apostles' heads in the form of a dove. For shame! Haven't they ever felt the Holy Spirit burning them? Where did they find that innocent edible bird? How can they present that to us as spirit? No, the Holy Spirit is not a dove, it is fire, a man-eating fire which clamps its talons into the very crown of saints, martyrs, and great strugglers, reducing them to ashes. Abject souls are the ones who take the Holy Spirit for a dove which they imagine they can kill and eat. Some day, God willing, I shall paint the Holy Spirit above the Apostles' heads, and then you'll see. . . . That flame is what I want to paint. I don't want to paint the ashes. I am an artist, not a theologian. The moment I want to paint is the moment when God's creatures are burning, just before they turn to ashes.

That was his final dream, and the book and his life end with one more wondering:

> The battle is drawing to a close. Did I win or lose? The only thing I know is this: I am full of wounds and still standing on my feet. . . . Grandfather, hello![26]

The pupil should be glad to become like his teacher, the slave like his master (Mt 10:25). Jesus has called us his friends. The whole world and life are our text. Those who have gone before us in faith are our comrades, and the Spirit of God befriends us on our journey.

But now another story. I am grateful to my friend Tony Cowan for telling me this one.

✠ Once upon a time there was a master violin maker. His instruments were exquisite, and the sound that could be drawn forth from them was beyond description. He only accepted a small number of apprentices, and he took them through the long and arduous process of making a violin from the choice of the tree to how to string the piece at the very end, after the varnish. There was one apprentice, an especially adept one, who had trouble with only one aspect of the process: the choice of wood. He had mastered all the other levels but would balk at the choice of which tree to mark and cut to form the base of the violin. Finally the master took him out to the forest again.

It was the dead of winter, a frightfully cold and windy day, with snow swirling and ice thickly hung in all the trees. They walked north and the master starting marking out the trees.

"Why?" the apprentice queried. "Why these?"

The master answered, "They face due north and they take the brunt of the wind, the chill, and the ice. They make the best violins."

They returned. The storm grew stronger, and the student asked his teacher, "Master, doesn't it bother you to think about the trees that you marked standing alone in the wind, standing against all this ice and fury? Have you no pity for them?"

The Master eyed him and smiled, "No, not at all. You see, they are being tuned!"

Confirmation sets us up for the Spirit to start tuning us. What music are we making?

5

The Eucharist

The Choice for Shared Bread and Solidarity

There is a delightful and thought-provoking children's story I heard decades ago from a Maryknoll missioner home from Japan. It is called "The Chopsticks Story."

✟ Once upon a time a man died. He hadn't been all that bad, but he hadn't been all that good, either. He arrived at the pearly gates and asked Peter: "Where am I going?"

Peter threw up his hands and said: "Will you people never learn? I don't decide, you do. Where do you want to go?"

"Uh, can I see my choices first?" the man asked.

"Sure," Peter answered. "Which one do you want to see first?"

"Uh, hell."

So off they went, down alleyways and stairways, winding around in the depths of the clouds. Finally they came to two huge brass doors. They were intricately carved with panels from scriptures, from the past, present, and future. "This is it," Peter exclaimed. "Ready?" He opened the doors. The man couldn't believe his eyes. The place was marvelous: huge banquet tables laden down with food and drink; flowers, piped-in music; chandeliers—anything a person could want.

"This is hell?" the man gulped.

"Yes," Peter replied. "Want to stay?"

"Uh, let me look around a bit, OK?"

"Sure," said Peter, "I'll be back in about fifteen minutes." And the man was left alone in hell.

As he looked more closely, it wasn't as beautiful as it had appeared at first glance. All the people were skinny, nasty, and very upset. The banquet tables were twelve feet off the ground, but the people were only two feet high. Each had a set of ten-foot-long chopsticks to get the food from the tables to his or her mouth. They kept dropping the food or other people stole it off the chopsticks before they could get to it. Still other people were hitting each other over the head with the chopsticks and poking each other with them, screaming and yelling. They were bruised and starving, dying to eat. The man gulped and said to himself: "This really is hell, I have to get out of here."

Just then Peter returned and asked him: "Have you seen enough? Want to check out heaven now?"

"Sure," the man answered gratefully, and the doors of hell swung closed behind him. Up and up they climbed, retracing their steps, and finally they reached another set of carved bronze doors, again carved with scenes from scriptures of past, present, and future.

"This is heaven," Peter said. The doors opened. Again the man could not believe his eyes. The place looked just like hell! Huge tables laden down with food and drink; piped-in music; chandeliers. The tables were twelve feet off the ground, the people were two feet tall, and everybody had ten-foot-long chopsticks. Flabbergasted, the man turned to Peter and gasped: "Are you sure this is heaven?"

"Sure," said Peter. "Look a little more closely because it's getting time for you to make your decision on where you're going to stay."

And the man did look a bit closer. Everyone was fat, rosy-cheeked, healthy, happy, and at peace. Why, he wondered to himself. Same set-up. And then it hit him. These people had realized that with ten-foot-long chopsticks there was no way to get the food to their own mouths. So they fed each other. The only difference between heaven and hell is whom you feed. And so it is to this day!

Mahatma Gandhi has clearly stated the condition of God's revelation: "To the poor man God dare not appear except in the form of bread and the promise of work. Grinding pauperism cannot lead to anything else than moral degradation. Every human being has a right to live and therefore to find the wherewithal to feed himself."

In reality, one day we will all be poor. For in the kingdom of God there are no possessions. The encyclical *On the Development of Peoples* describes the condition of the world simply: "The world is like an uneven load. On one side, many people and little food. On the other side, lots of food and few people. An uneven load is dangerous. It is apt to tip over at any moment" (Brazilian translation).

Jesus was vitally concerned with the poor, with the question of bread for the hungry. As he went about his ministry he often met great numbers of hungry people. And he fed them, four or five thousand at a time, not even counting the women and the children. But his disciples failed to see any deeper meaning in these events. For them, the bread was bread, fish was fish, something for an empty stomach that would get empty again. Nothing more. When Jesus warns the disciples to be on their guard against the leaven of the Pharisees and the yeast of Herod, all they can think of is their own scarcity of bread—one loaf. In Jesus' reply to them he sounds irritated.

> Aware of this, Jesus asked them, "Why are you talking about the loaves you are short of? Do you not see or understand? Are your minds closed? Have you eyes that don't see and ears that don't hear? And do you not remember when I broke the five loaves among five thousand? How many baskets full of leftovers did you collect?" They answered: "Twelve." "And having seven loaves for the four thousand, how many wicker baskets of leftovers did you collect?" They answered: "Seven." Then Jesus said to them: "Do you still not understand?" (Mk 8:17-21).

And of course, they don't. They must have looked at each other, embarrassed. They remembered every detail of the events but did not grasp their meaning.

Memory of the past does not necessarily help us to understand the meaning of the present; sometimes it actually gets in the way of understanding or believing. Yahweh had fed the people in Moses' time—"It is the bread that Yahweh has given you to eat" (Ex 16:15)—and the chosen people had not understood.

C. S. Song comments on the disciples' misunderstanding of Jesus' actions.

> Imprisonment in the memory of the past causes a chain reaction. It leads to this: "blindness" is "deafness" is "hardness of heart" is "misunderstanding." The disciples were blind and deaf to the deeper meaning of Jesus' feeding five thousand and four thousand persons: namely, that God loves and cares about these hungry crowds. In the disciples' minds, daily bread and God's salvation could not become connected. They saw the bread distributed to the hungry, but did not see God's promise to feed the hungry realized by their ministration.

They heard the excitement of the hungry gathering around the food, but they did not hear Jesus' good news for them. To see God's promise fulfilled in others, to hear Jesus' good news for them, the disciples needed "the seeing-hearing-understanding heart." But they were not to have this kind of heart until the dark night of the cross was over and the bright morning of the resurrection had dawned.[1]

It is often poets and singers who make the connections between symbol and theology, between food and God, as reflected in these lines:

> As you cannot go to heaven alone,
> Food is to be shared.
> As all share the sight of the heavenly stars,
> So food is something that must be shared. . . .
> Ah! food is something that must be shared.[2]

Those who struggle to worship in spirit and in truth while living lives of hope and meaning often see the connections among worship, food, and God's concern for those who hunger, whether for bread or justice. Rabindranath Tagore writes:

The Hidden God

Leave this chanting and singing and telling of beads.
Whom do you worship in this lonely dark corner of the
    temple with all the doors shut?
Open your eyes and see that God is not in front of you.
He is there where the farmer is tilling the hard ground
    and where the laborer is breaking stones.
He is with them in the sun and the rain and his garment
    is covered with dust.
Put off your holy cloak and like him come down on to
    the dusty soil.
Deliverance?
Where will you find deliverance?
Our master himself has joyfully taken on the bonds of
    creation; he is bound with us forever.
Come out of your meditations and leave aside the
    flowers and the incense;
What harm is there if your clothes become tattered
    and stained?

Meet him and stand by him in toil and in the sweat
of your brow.[3]

Mary, the mother of Jesus, heralds the wonders of what her child will
do for the earth in echoes of Hannah's (mother of Samuel) song: "He has
acted with power and done wonders, and scattered the proud with their
plans. He has put down the mighty from their thrones and lifted up those
who are downtrodden. He has filled the hungry with good things but has
sent the rich away empty" (Lk 1:51-53).

Jesus in Mark's gospel seems to echo her feelings: "Beware the leaven
of the Pharisees and the yeast of Herod," he says, referring to the arro-
gant elite and the monarch of his day. God, not those in positions of
power, is the one concerned about the poor, the hungry, the masses of
people in the world.

We are human. We are always hungry. Food occupies a great deal of
our thoughts and reveals much about our priorities. "Things are getting
worse, please send chocolate," says a contemporary greeting card. Food
and families are intimately tied together. TV commercials promote fast
food restaurants, make suggestions on what to serve at a party, and tell
us where to get the best deals on food. Yet it is only in a few countries
that people enjoy the luxury of a wide choice of food, the reality of a
supermarket. The experience of bringing foreign visitors into a first-
world grocery store and watching them weep uncontrollably at the dis-
play of fresh fruit and vegetables is a sobering experience. So is the
experience of bargaining for food each day in a country where prices
fluctuate drastically, or standing in line for rationed staples and bread.

Food has played a huge role in the tradition of spirituality, prayer, and
worship. A few quotations from various times remind us of its centrality.

I've suddenly discovered that the exploitation of men by men and
undernourishment relegate luxuries like metaphysical ills to the
background. Hunger is a real evil. I've been getting through a long
apprenticeship to reality. I've seen children die of hunger. What
does literature mean in a hungry world? Literature like morality
needs to be universal. A writer has to take sides with the majority,
with the hungry—otherwise he is just serving a privileged class
(Jean-Paul Sartre, 1905-1980).

We may be misled in many ways by worldly peace. For instance—
some people have all they require for their needs, besides a large

sum of money shut up in their safe as well, but as they avoid mortal sin, they think they have done their duty. They enjoy their riches and give an occasional alms, never consider that their property is not their own, but that God has entrusted it to them as His stewards for the good of the poor, and that they will have to render a strict account of the time they kept it shut up in their money chests, if the poor have suffered from want on account of their hoards and delay (St. Teresa of Avila).

You will find out that charity is a heavy burden to carry, heavier than the bowl of soup and the full basket. But you will keep your gentleness and your smile. It is not enough to give soup and bread. This the rich can do. You are the servant of the poor, always smiling and always good humored. They are your masters, terrible, sensitive and exacting masters, as you will soon see. The uglier and dirtier they will be, the more unjust and insulting, the more love you must give them. It is only for your love alone, that the poor will forgive you the bread you give them (St. Vincent de Paul).

Bread is given to us not that we eat it alone but that others who are indigent might be participants. When we eat bread acquired unjustly, we eat not only our own bread but another's—for nothing that we have unjustly is ours (Meister Eckhart).

You are not making a gift of your possessions to the poor person. You are handing over to him what is his. For what has been given in common for the use of all, you have arrogated to yourself. The world is given to all, and not only to the rich (St. Ambrose).

Those who make private property of the gifts of God pretend in vain to be innocent, for in thus retaining the subsistence of the poor, they are the murderers of those who die every day for want of it (St. Gregory the Great).

What is a man if he is not a thief who openly charges as much as he can for the goods he sells? (Gandhi).

Share everything with your brother and sister. Do not say, "It is private property." If you share what is everlasting, you should be that much more willing to share things which do not last (*Didache*).

The obvious contradiction between the waste involved in the over-production of military devices and the extent of unsatisfied vital needs is in itself an act of aggression which amounts to a crime, for even when they are not used, by their costs alone, armaments kill the poor by causing them to starve (Pope Paul VI, speech at the United Nations).

All these connections come from the stories of Jesus and the consequences of meaning that are the basis for our liturgical celebrations. In John's gospel a simple story is told. It will be repeated many times throughout the gospel and in history:

> Then lifting up his eyes, Jesus saw the crowds that were coming to him and said to Philip: "Where shall we buy bread so that these people may eat?" He said this to test Philip, for he himself knew what he was going to do. Philip answered him, "Two hundred silver coins would not buy enough bread for each of them to have a piece."
>
> Then one of the disciples spoke to Jesus. Andrew, Simon Peter's brother, said: "There is a boy here who has five barley loaves and two fish; but what good are these for so many?"
>
> Jesus said, "Make the people sit down." There was plenty of grass there so the people, about five thousand men, sat down to rest. Jesus then took the loaves, gave thanks and distributed them to those who were seated. He did the same with the fish and gave them as much as they wanted. And when they had eaten enough, he told his disciples, "Gather up the pieces left over, that nothing may be lost."
>
> So they gathered them up and filled twelve baskets with bread, that is with the pieces of the five barley loaves left by those who had eaten (Jn 6:5-13).

It is here in John's gospel that we are told something very specific: there were five *barley* loaves and some fish. In Israel, barley is the bread of the poor; it symbolizes obduracy. The dough is heavy and requires a strong yeast before it will rise properly. There are three stories of barley in the Hebrew scriptures, all intertwining elements of stubbornness, hunger, and generosity. The first is found in Judges 7:13-14, where Gideon is threshing his grain in hiding. God is patient with stubborn, slow, and unbelieving Gideon, who after three signs of God's presence and power is told to go and overhear a dream. The dream is about a barley cake that flattens the camp of his enemies.

The second is the story of Ruth, who comes to Bethlehem ("House of Bread") at the beginning of the barley harvest and goes gleaning in the barley fields, where grain is left for the poor. There she meets her future husband, Boaz, and he gives her six measures of barley in gratitude for finding a wife in the fields of the poor.

The last story, found in Ezekiel 4:13-17, is harsh. Ezekiel prepares a special barley cake dough at the request of Yahweh, bakes it on human dung, and eats it, an exact measure each day, as the foretelling of the punishment and hunger of Jerusalem, terrible words of deprivation but a deserved punishment for their insensitivity to the poor and their unfaithfulness to God.

And Jesus, in John's gospel, feeds the people barley loaves that belong to the hungry, the poor, his own people. He himself will become finest wheat ground for Israel's eating, his peoples' Bread of Life. Jesus' life will be forfeit in society because he aligns himself with the poor and seeks to respond to their hunger with the good news of God's presence with them in his own person, in his life and death.

We are given a memorial of Jesus' life, passion, death, and resurrection in the eucharist. At the Last Supper Jesus gives a sign, a symbol, a way of being present to us through our own identification with the poor and the suffering in solidarity with him. He shares his liberation and new life with his followers and tells them to share it with others. He shares his last meal with his friends, giving himself to them before he suffers and dies. He tells them: "I shall not eat it again until it is fulfilled in the kingdom of God" (Lk 22:16). It is fulfilled in the cross and resurrection and in the lives and belief of his friends, the church, which celebrates his life and truth until the end of time. Each Christian's first communion is meant to be celebrated along with baptism, the promise to "put on Christ." Communion, thanksgiving, sharing life, food, and hope are the gifts given to those who follow Jesus' way of having pity and compassion on the crowds of poor and needy people. The simple, central action of eucharist is the sharing of food—not only eating but sharing. Our capacity for hunger is parallel to our capacity to know compassion and to hunger and thirst for justice. Sharing reminds us and lets us experience the need of always being hungry and never satisfied. Hunger brings into focus our human dependency on other human beings. We do not live by bread alone, but we must begin with bread. The very gesture of sharing bread does more than alleviate starvation; it gives company, dialogue, companionship, solidarity, and hope. It gives communion.

The ritual of eucharist, of thanksgiving for what God has done for us in the person of Jesus, is not just repeating his words and gestures; it is living his life and sharing his compassion and worshiping his God as he did, in service and humble obedience. Economy and eucharist are linked and bound together in the believing community. It has been so in history and tradition in Israel and the early Christian communities. Listen to the prophet in the Book of Sirach 34:18-22:

> An offering to God from stolen goods is a stained offering; such sacrifices do not please God.
>
> The Most High takes no pleasure in the offering of the godless. It is not the number of victims that obtains pardon for sin.
>
> Offering to God from what belongs to the poor is like slaughtering a son in the presence of his father.
>
> Bread is life to the poor; he who takes it from them is a murderer. He who deprives others of a livelihood kills them, and whoever withdraws the salary of a worker is guilty of blood.

Other prophets' words of warning from Yahweh are even more precise on the kind of sacrifice that God wants from us:

> "Your endless sacrifices—
> What do I care about them?"
> says the Lord.
> "I have had more than enough
> of whole-burnt offerings
> of rams and the fat of fatlings;
> the blood of bulls and lambs and he-goats
> does not delight me anymore. . . .
> When you stretch out your hands
> I will close my eyes;
> the more you pray,
> the more I refuse to listen.
> Your hands are bloody;
> wash and make yourselves clean.
> Remove from my sight
> the evil of your deeds.
> Put an end to your wickedness and learn to do good.

Seek justice,
give hope to the oppressed;
give the fatherless their rights
and defend the widow" (Is 1:11, 15-17).

Is that the kind of fast that pleases me,
just a day for a man to humble himself?
Is fasting merely bowing down one's head,
and making use of sackcloth and ashes?
Would you call that fasting,
a day acceptable to Yahweh?

See the fast that pleases me:
breaking the fetters of injustice
and unfastening the thongs of the yoke,
setting the oppressed free
and breaking every yoke.
Fast by sharing your food with the hungry,
bring to your house the homeless,
clothe the man you see naked
and do not turn from your own kin.

Then will your light break forth as the morning
and your healing will come speedily.
Your righteousness will be your vanguard,
the Glory of Yahweh will be your rearguard.
Then you will call and Yahweh will answer,
you will cry and he will say, I am here (Is 58:5-9).

I hate, I reject your feasts, I take no pleasure when you assemble to offer me your burnt offerings. Your cereal offerings, I will not accept! Your peace offerings and your fatted beasts, I will not look upon!

Away with the noise of your chanting, away with your strumming on harps. But let justice run its course like water, and righteousness be like an ever-flowing river (Am 5:21-24).

Israel, like the church today, had developed economically and forgotten the plight of the poor. The people had become barbaric in their relationships with each other. Perhaps that word *barbaric* seems too harsh, but the reality of the United States church today is that it is the richest of the religious groups. One-third of the world dominates and keeps in destitution the other two-thirds of the world. Our affluence is paid for with an enormous price: the life and death of other people. We must examine our consciences on whether our worship is empty and shallow (though often correct and creative) or whether it celebrates the truth: that the "hungry are given food, the thirsty are given drink, those away from home are given welcome, those in prison are visited and freed, those who are naked are clothed and those who are in need are given compassion" (Mt 25:31-46). We have to keep asking ourselves as individuals and as communities if our worship and our lives are in tandem; if "we do what is good and what the Lord requires of us, that we do justice, love kindness and walk humbly with our God?" (Mic 6:8, *NAB*). The eucharist "re-members" the presence of Jesus in our world and invites us to respond to his sacrifice and commit ourselves to the society of our time. We must reenact not only the liturgy of his life and death but live it ourselves by the power of his grace and the Spirit, given to us in our baptisms. Our commitment to living with the community does the work of Jesus now. It is a fundamental imperative, in imitation of Jesus, to die rather than compromise his values and belief in his Father's kingdom and its reality in his life. Just as Jesus is our sustenance, we are sustenance for each other and for the world. We are to become the bread that we share together.

Monika Hellwig makes the connection among food, death, and service even clearer. In John's gospel Jesus is called the Lamb of God, an allusion to the lamb sacrificed in worship at the Temple during the feast of Passover. Jesus will purify his Father's house (of buying and selling and cheating the poor) prior to his own bitter death. Hellwig writes:

> A lamb only becomes food because it is killed. Its "vocation" is to exist for the life of others; in a sense its fulfillment is to be slaughtered and eaten. The lamb for Passover was to be very carefully chosen, certified free of blemish, because its eating was an act dedicating the people to God. There is a certain ruthlessness in it. The focus of the message is that it is in his death that Jesus becomes the bread of life for others, and that it is in total engagement with his death that others are to find the ultimate satisfaction of their hunger, so that they will not hunger or thirst again.[4]

A second powerful meaning of eucharist is service, giving one's life totally to others. Surprisingly enough, it is John's gospel that makes this most clear. John's account of Jesus' life is filled with discourses and sermons on the eucharist, the bread of life and love. At the very beginning of the Last Discourse John has Jesus washing the feet of his disciples, an action that distressed Peter terribly. He did eucharist, served them as a slave would, washing their feet, not an empty gesture in the Jewish world but the work of slaves. Jesus is blunt in his explanation:

"Do you understand what I have done to you? You call me Master and *Lord*, and you are right, for so I am. If I, then, your *Lord* and Master, have washed your feet, you also must wash one another's feet. I have just given you an example that as I have done, you also may do.

Truly, I say to you, the servant is not greater than his master, nor is the messenger greater than he who sent him. Understand this, and blessed are you if you put it into practice" (Jn 13:12b-17).

Immediately after this Jesus reminds them that one of them will betray him, even though he dips a piece of bread in the dish with him. Even today the Bedouins of the East have an understanding of breaking bread with one another that we have lost long ago. When visitors come to their tent and share a meal with them, they dip a piece of bread in wine or oil and share it. If after eating and an evening of sleep the host should rise and find that his guests have robbed him, he cannot go after them. Because they have eaten together, they have shared the same life and are bound closer than blood. Only after three days, when all the food has passed through the guests' stomachs, can the host go after them.

Judas, who had shared many meals with Jesus, would betray him. Eating and drinking with Jesus does not automatically make one a Christian or a good follower. Jesus' words are simple: "Why do you call me 'Lord, Lord' and not put into practice what I teach you?" (Lk 6:46, *NAB*).

Often in our history and tradition the reception of eucharist was a very private matter between the believer and God. Receiving communion meant withdrawal from the community's awareness, even to the point where we often hid our faces from each other. This ritual reception of eucharist often mirrored the reality within the community rather than what the eucharist was truly meant to be. But the Second Vatican Council reminded us of the ethical demands of the eucharist upon every believer and upon the Christian community. It seems we need to be reminded often. Like the community at Corinth, we tend to separate according to social class in order to celebrate our sharing of the life of Christ in bread and wine (1 Cor 11:17-34). We also separate our religion from our economics, politics, and care for one another. Yet more than anything else, the eucharist symbolizes our human solidarity, one with another—with *any* other. We have a corporate responsibility for the acts of justice and mercy. To reach out and take eucharist is to adopt a lifestyle that involves an aggressive search for justice for the unloved and unneeded ones of the earth. Whom we eat with becomes a judgment on our faithfulness and love for one another in a world that watches to see with whom we choose to stand as followers of Jesus, the bread of life.

We stand before a minister of the eucharist. A piece of bread is held before our eyes, and we hear the words "Body of Christ" proclaimed to us. And we answer, often without thinking, "Amen." But what is the Body of Christ? It is the church, the people of God—*all* the people of God, especially the poor, the outcast, the hungry, and those who struggle for freedom and human dignity. Do we accept the responsibility for each other, for all the body of Christ, when we "eat this bread and drink this cup"? Gustavo Gutiérrez writes:

> Without a real commitment against exploitation and alienation and for a society of solidarity and justice, the Eucharistic celebration is an empty action, lacking any genuine endorsement by those who participate in it. This is something that many Latin American Christians are feeling more and more deeply, and they are thus more demanding both of themselves and of the whole Church.[5]

Our resistance to the world's culture of materialism and consumerism—as evidenced in alternative ways of living and eating—will effectively change the quality of our eucharistic celebrations. Sacraments celebrate what has already happened in reality: there must be a reality to our sharing the bread of life before we come to the table and break bread with one another. Our individual and communal lifestyles must show that the poor are cared for and the feet of all who need it are washed. A lifestyle of care and feeding, nurturing and being compassionate must be present if we are to celebrate with clean hearts and pure minds and spirits, ready to "love one another as I have loved you" (Jn 15:12). This is the tradition of the early church, which has faded over the years as the church has become strong, rich, and powerful, a force to be reckoned with on a state and national level. St. Augustine reminds us: "Find out how much God has given you, and from it take what you need; the remainder which you do not require is needed by others. The superfluities of the rich are the necessities of the poor. Those who retain what is superfluous possess the goods of others."[6]

We need to begin simply—with ourselves, our families, and our small circles of connections. Dorothy Day describes why she lived the way she did: "I wanted life and I wanted the abundant life. I wanted it for others too." After long years with the poor and the hungry she wrote:

> The mystery of the poor is this: That they are Jesus, and what you do for them you do for him. It is the only way we have of knowing and believing in our love. The mystery of poverty is that by sharing in it, by making ourselves poor in giving to others, we increase our knowledge of and belief in love.[7]

What Day refers to as "poverty" is simplicity freely chosen and surplus shared in thanksgiving. This means learning a personal generosity, both on an individual level and as a community with priorities professed on a public basis. We need to learn, even vicariously, the song of the Kiowa: "Because I am poor, I pray for every creature." And we learn by giving, practically, consistently, ever more. Day writes:

> The act and spirit of giving are the best counter to the evil forces in the world today, and giving liberates the individual not only spiritually but materially. For in a world of enslavement through installment buying and mortgages, the only way to live in any true security is to live so close to the bottom that when you fall you do not have far to drop, you do not have much to lose.

We have much to learn from other traditions, like those the Jewish sages and the Quakers practice. The following selections are both thought-provoking and practical:

> Rabbi Shmelke of Nicholsburg said: "When a poor man asks you for aid, do not use his faults as an excuse for not helping him. For then God will look for your offenses, and He is sure to find many of them. Keep in mind that the poor man's transgressions have been atoned for by his poverty while yours still remain with you."[8]

> Rabbi Chayim of Sanz had this to say about fraudulent charity collectors: "The merit of charity is so great that I am happy to give to one hundred beggars even if only one might actually be needy.

Some people, however, act as if they are exempt from giving charity to one hundred beggars in the event that one might be a fraud."[9]

Though you may have given already, give yet again, even a hundred times, for it says, "Give, yea, give thou shalt" (Dt 15:10-11).

In the Jewish community there is a common fund called *Tz'dakah*,
"alms for unity." The directions for giving (as enumerated by Mai-
monides) are shown in stages. The order is enlightening.
- giving grudgingly;
- giving less than you should, but cheerfully;
- giving after you are asked;
- giving directly before you are asked;
- giving so that the recipient knows who you are;
- giving so that you know who the recipient is;
- giving anonymously;
- helping another become self-sufficient by giving the person a loan,
  a gift, or setting him or her up in business.

The Shakers founded their communities on the four principles of a
classless society:

1. total equality of the sexes;
2. some form of practical sharing of goods;
3. total pacifism;
4. celibacy (no exclusive relationships).

Their practice is conveyed in a line from an 1840 Shaker hymn: "Break
off, shake off, take off, every bond and fetter."
The Society of Friends (the Quakers) describes simplicity thus: "True
simplicity consists not in the use of particular forms but in foregoing
over-indulgence, in maintaining humility of spirit, and in keeping the
material surroundings of our lives directly serviceable to necessary ends
even though these surroundings may properly be characterized by grace,
symmetry, and beauty."[10]
But simplicity also means realigning our church and our national priorities toward care and compassion rather than defense and insecurity.
Statistics need to reflect reality: "The money required to provide adequate food, water, housing, health and education for every person in the
world has been estimated at $17 billion a year. It is a huge sum of money

. . . about as much as the military spends on arms worldwide every two weeks."[11]

We need to start making *bread connections*, working with all our hearts and souls for daily bread for all, especially the poor. "Breaking the bread" is a call to action. People like Sheila Cassidy, Mairhead Corrigan and Betty Williams, Kim Chi Ha, Molly Rush, Daniel Berrigan, Jean Vanier, Dom Helder Camara, the four women of El Salvador, Rutilio Grande, Oscar Romero, the Jesuit martyrs and their housekeeper and her daughter, and so many others are the present-day communion of saints in solidarity, the body of Christ, bread for the poor. Action with and for those who suffer is the concrete expression of the compassionate life and the final criterion of being a Christian. In a Lenten homily John Paul II commented on the life and death of Oscar Romero, martyred bishop of El Salvador:

> A year has passed since the tragic death of Archbishop Romero, that zealous pastor who was murdered on 24 March 1980, while he was celebrating holy Mass. He crowned his ministry, devoted particularly to the poorest and most marginalized, with his blood. It was a supreme witness, which has become the symbol of the tribulations of a whole people; but also a motive of hope for a better future.

These are some of the more obvious symbols of eucharist today, but many people reveal in their ordinary relationships and charity and work for justice what eucharist means for the world. It is witnessed most clearly in community. The church at the time of Tertullian (second century) was something to take heart from and look to for hope. John Chrysostom described this church centuries later:

> In the churches at that time there developed a marvelous practice when all the faithful met together, after hearing the Divine Word, after the prayers and the communion of the mysteries, after the liturgical meeting; they didn't return immediately to their homes, but the rich, who had prepared the food and drink, invited the poor and set a common table, a common feast, a common invitation in the church itself, so that the community of the table, and the piety of the place and a thousand and one other circumstances joined to make charity very close; their pleasure was great and so was their gain. This practice was the source of countless benefits—the main

one being friendship—becoming daily more warm after each liturgical meeting since benefactors and beneficiaries felt united by such great love.

Today this description seems strange to much of our celebration of the eucharist, but there are instances of this love and care and sharing. In a talk given in Latin America Pope John Paul II spoke of charity within the base Christian communities of the world:

> Charity as lived by a base Christian community can take many different forms. In the first place it can help all to increase their faith and then, after that, it can be realized in act for the human promotion of oppressed persons or groups, for the integration of those on the fringes of society, for the defence of human rights when these are being violated, for justice in situations of inequality, for the overcoming of inhuman conditions, for the creation of greater solidarity within a given society, and so on. All this of course, must be taken as a sign of true charity, as described by St. Paul: patient, kind, forgetful of self, caring only for others, incapable of rejoicing in wrongdoing; or by St. John: a man can have no greater love than to lay down his life for his friends.

Father José Alamiro Andrade Silva, who works in Brazil with base Christian communities, describes the "four breads of community":

> In the base community we say that we must share four kinds of bread. First the bread of friendship. We must have a deep friendship among us. Second, we share the bread of God's word. For this two books are important—first, the Bible and second the book of life. Not only personal life, but the life of the people. This meaning of community is very important. Third is the bread of the eucharist—fourth the bread of freedom, the bread of liberty—liberty to have a house, to have work, to have free unions, free political parties, free media. We work with these four breads.
> A base community is a very small group. For example in the favela there are seven hundred families. Maybe the base community has twenty people. These twenty people are known by everyone, and when an important moment comes, the others support them. The community is a small group and they do what they can to know the social structure, the economic structure, the political.

They begin trying, themselves and with other people, to confront this structure of power with love.[12]

This is a good model for any parish in the United States. The issues would perhaps be different, but perhaps not. Hunger exists in every city and rural area in the United States. In 1984 Mark Fitzgerald wrote:

> The commission found that hunger is growing in the U.S. and that it is no longer restricted to the once typical poor or to disadvantaged ethnic groups. Now hunger afflicts Americans who a few years ago were in comfortable circumstances. Far from being confined to Appalachia or the South or to Indian tribes, hunger is found today in the industrial areas of the Northeast, the Middle West and even in middle-class suburbs. Without discrimination, hunger draws within its net the elderly on fixed incomes, teenagers and infants, unemployed parents as well as those who work at wages inadequate to support their families to the end of the month. The street people in our large cities, men, women and youngsters, know hunger daily.[13]

That was over a decade ago, and statistics indicate that each year the situation grows more critical. Our experience of eucharist and our experience of community begins with conversion in our attitudes, beliefs about people, and behavior. A friend of mine, Jeannette Easley, once a lay missioner in Ecuador, wrote of an experience she had in a restaurant.

> Recently, after having dinner at an outdoor chicken restaurant in Guayaquil, we had one piece of chicken left with everyone too full to eat it. I immediately thought I would like to take it with us and give it to a beggar in the street. (This was a new thought for me; previously I would have left it.) As we were walking down the street, I saw a woman huddled in a doorway with all her worldly possessions and her five children (two months to six years old). I thought "I can't give this chicken to her. There is only one piece, and there are six of them.
>
> The words of Jesus flashed in my mind and I went over to the family, knelt down, introduced myself, offered what I had and was welcomed by warmness and cheer. We talked a few minutes and then prayed together. The woman ended up giving me her blessing and the kids thanked me and kissed me. I don't know what hap-

pened after I left, who ate the chicken but I know beyond a doubt that God's grace was enough.

As Christians we must reflect Christ. United as the Body of Christ, in community support, we can start transforming our world where we live, with the little we have, in the love, grace, and power of the Spirit. In many ways I have been ignoring the reality of grace and making excuses why I don't do anything, saying "what little I give won't change their situation." What I have realized lately, is that I was reacting at a very human level and making human comparisons instead of faith.[14]

Eucharist is the celebration of our commitment to Jesus through baptism. Eucharist, the breaking and sharing of the word, bread, and wine in community is our life, our example to the world. Our worship of God, our way of giving thanks "through Jesus, with Jesus, in Jesus" is for the world's salvation. The ethical demands of eucharist mirror the demands of Christian life, of Jesus' values and work in the world. They include:

- Search aggressively for justice;
- Admit that we are not yet free and united, that we are working for the kingdom that is "not yet";
- Receive the eucharist in community; not privatizing the sacrament;
- Share the kingdom—the kiss of peace, small bits of bread, our excess—with anyone, especially those we don't meet in church;
- Stand personally in human solidarity with those who are oppressed, minorities, third-world peoples, the hungry, and so on;
- Realize we have a corporate responsibility as church to stand in solidarity and share our resources; this conversion is radical and takes a great deal of time, effort, and struggle.
- Work for unity among the churches;
- Do something about church land, bank accounts, resources, and educational and hospital facilities on a universal scale for the poor; we as a church must put our influence, reputations, and persons into the struggle for justice and human rights;
- Work for peace and against war and arms proliferation; our beliefs in national security and in personal individuality and selfishness are alien to Christian belief in the God who protects us; we can never kill.

In the words of Gustavo Gutiérrez,

Our conversion process is affected by the socio-economic, political, cultural and human environment in which it occurs. Without a change in these structures there is no authentic conversion. We have to break with our mental categories, with the way we relate to others, with our way of identifying with the Lord, with our cultural milieu, with our social class, in other words, with all that can stand in the way of a real, profound solidarity with those who suffer. . . . Only thus, and not through purely interior and spiritual attitudes, will the "new person" arise from the ashes of the "old."[15]

It is only our quality of resistance, conversion, and unity with others that will change the quality of our eucharist, our liturgical celebrations. We must commit ourselves in small groups to sharing prayer, bread, housing, education, medical expenses, and other living expenses in dedication to the coming of the kingdom. Individuals and groups can make a difference, within both church structures and political structures. Charity and justice must be practiced together in word and deed as thanksgiving, as worship, as community if the presence of the risen Lord is to be a reality in the church. We must become bread for life, for others. We—the Christian community—are the promise of God to the world. Jesus radically transformed the possibilities of the world and real human life, and the Spirit that bonds us together in true community is our gift. With the Spirit we continue to grow and permeate the world with the presence of Jesus, with his compassion and love.

Lastly, the eucharist is blessing, thanksgiving, extravagance, and worship. The ritual takes and blesses God, then breaks and shares. The blessing cannot be forgotten. It is our form of worship in the world. God has blessed us in Jesus. We are blessed so that we might become a blessing for others. Monika Hellwig touches upon the understanding of Jewish blessings:

The effect of such a blessing (*berakot*) is not to make the bread holy but to hallow those around the table who share and eat the bread, making their act of eating a moment of communion with God in heightened awareness and receptivity of his blessing which must not come to rest in those who are here at table but must overflow in them to become a blessing for others.[16]

Later she touches on Jesus' unique blessing on his friends:

In that last supper he is blessing them not only with what he is and with what he has done; he is blessing them with the death that he is yet to die. It is in that death that he becomes the ultimate blessing for others.[17]

Nicolai Berdyaev has said: "Bread for others is always a spiritual question." It is always a question of love. Most of us are sure we love. In James's letter to his community he warns that there is no meaning in love for the hungry person which leaves that person hungry, love for one who is cold and without shelter that does not supply the necessary clothing, fuel, and housing. Jesus' message is good news, hope for the poor that their suffering is to be alleviated. It is to be alleviated in the kingdom, by those who follow his ways and share. As the feeding stories attest, there is always more than enough to go around when we share and when we remember to gather up what is left over so that it does not go to waste. Ministry begins with these leftovers. The community is gathered in the act of sharing.

The early Christians saw this as a reality in history and took it upon themselves to ease the hardships of the poor and excluded. This led to large-scale social change that has historically worked toward eliminating certain forms of suffering—slavery; abandonment of lepers, the sick poor, and orphans; education for women; and more. Community was expressed in concern for the poor of other churches, the concern that none should go hungry while any had wealth to share, even in collections sent from one local church to another to relieve need. The Acts of the Apostles reveals that no one should be in need and that Christian society should be structured so that the needs of all are amply taken care of without embarrassment or the need to beg. This behavior toward others is the act of doing "this in memory of me," as Jesus commanded. It often means standing in opposition to the values of the world and can put oneself and one's family at risk, even within the larger church. Our message and good news as Christians is communicated in how we relate to others, by who we are, by our lifestyle, concerns, priorities, affiliations, and by the real difference we attempt to make in any situation. In the world of despair we have bread, abundant life, and the love of our God to share.

Jesus is sometimes sung about as the "Lord of the Dance," dancing forever in the presence of God, leading us in the dance of resurrection that cannot be stopped or turned aside from its ecstasy. Eucharist teaches us to dance in trying situations, in the face of a world that has forgotten Jesus' dance of glory, and with others who have never learned to dance. The meaning of the dance, the meaning of the eucharist, is the doing of it. First, we invite others to share it with us, and only then are we able to speak about it, to theologize. The more we seek to be eucharist, as Jesus is, the more we will understand our calling as Christians. There is an ancient prayer of the church that is apropos here. It was sung and danced during the resurrection cycle of liturgies.

> Grace makes the dance
> I will make the music
> and we shall all dance in a ring. Alleluia.

> Glory to thee, Father
> Glory to thee, Word
> Glory to thee, Grace
> Glory to thee, Spirit
> Glory to thee, Holy One
> Glory to thy Glory.
> We praise thee, Father
> We praise thee, O Light
> We praise thee, in whom there is no darkness.

> A lamp I am to thee, beholding me
> A mirror am I to thee, perceiving me
> A door I am to thee, knocking
> A way I am to thee, a traveler.

> Join now in my dancing
> Alleluia Alleluia.

Eucharist is described by a story that was told in many immigrant communities of Irish, people who left their homeland in droves hoping for a better life, and knowing that most likely they would never return to those they left behind. Always such leaving was a desperate measure, an act of risk, a chance at freedom and dignity.

✠ Once upon a time there was a man who agonized about taking his family to the new world. He scrimped, saved, sold, and borrowed money until he had the price of the tickets. They would have only the clothes on their backs and a few coins; nothing else was left. They would start from scratch after the long sea journey.

The night before they left, their neighbors, relations, and friends came to sing and weep and send them off. It was a party to remember during the long days and nights on board ship. As they set off the next morning, tight-lipped, faces betraying their fear and loss, they were met along the road by their neighbors again, this time with bags of bread and bits of cheese and potatoes. They were reminded that the trip was long and arduous, and this was the best gift they could give them: food. It truly was their best gift, for they would go hungry in the days to come. The family was filled with gratitude and tears. They set off with the love of their community.

Once on board ship they found themselves on the lowest deck: the grandmother, mother and six children, father, and three cousins. The father was frantic, gathering them about him and exhorting them to be careful, stay close, and not to get lost. He especially eyed one of his younger children, a boy of about six, who was forever going off to discover things. The trip dragged on, day after day. They soon ate much of the bread and cheese and even the now-moldy potatoes. The food was being doled out by the grandmother, a piece or two here, more for the younger ones. They were always hungry, dreaming and talking endlessly of what they would eat when they got to America. The last few days of the trip were the hardest. After months at sea they were tired, afraid, near starving.

Then one morning, as he did every morning, the youngest boy pleaded with his mother for something fresh and good to eat. This time, however, he kept at it, whining, pleading, begging until the mother was near her wits' end. They had those few pennies, coins saved in case of emergency when they arrived. She looked at her husband, pleading with her eyes, and finally spoke softly: "We can buy one or two oranges to share among us. Let him go and get them, and we can celebrate that we only have a few more days until we land."

The father took a few of the precious coins out of his bag. He handed them to the young boy, who by now knew every corner of the great ship, and told him to go and get two oranges up on one of the higher decks. It should only take fifteen minutes or so if he didn't tarry. So off the boy ran, bursting with expectation and thrilled with being given permission to go to the upper decks.

He was gone longer than fifteen minutes. The mother and grandmother began to worry. What could have happened to him? The father calmed them. It was a long way up the decks and perhaps he had trouble finding the fruit vendor. Half an hour went by, and both parents were frantic with worry. It was such a huge ship, and there were so many things that could happen to a youngster. After another ten minutes the father climbed to the upper decks himself, looking for his lost son. Deck after deck he searched for him, more fearful and praying more to the Virgin for his safety.

Finally, painstakingly going from room to room, he reached the top deck, which was crowded with people. At last he found his son sitting at a table in a huge sprawling dining room, eating everything in sight! He grabbed him by the collar and hauled him out of the chair, sputtering in anger. "How could you worry your mother and grandmother, frighten them so? And how can you do this, eat so much? You will destroy us. We have no money to pay for all this food." The boy sputtered, trying to talk with his mouth full. "Papa! Papa! You don't understand. The food is free. The food is ours. It came with the price of the ticket!"

Stunned, the father turned, and the steward nodded affirmatively. The young boy was sent below to bring his grandmother, mother, cousins, and brothers and sisters up to eat. They ate in silence, thankful, thinking of the past weeks of being hungry, below decks, fearful of speaking to anyone, doling out their neighbors' bread and parting gifts. The words kept thundering, pounding in their heads: *The food is free. The food is free. It came with the price of the ticket!* If only they had spoken to someone, shared their food, reached out to others. That night, below deck again, full for the first time in weeks, they promised that in their new life they would share, they would trust, they would reach out to others, they would speak to all around them and not live in fear and scarcity.

The food is free. It comes with the price of the ticket. Baptism draws us into the body of Christ where the food is free, the hope is lavish, the possibilities of sharing limitless, and there are always leftovers, more than enough to go around. The price was paid ages ago in the life, love, death, and resurrection of Jesus, shared with us all now in eucharist and in our commitment to feed the world on the bread of justice, the bread of hope, the bread of life. We feast on the word, bread, and wine of the Lord so that the world can feast on our faith, hope, and love shared freely, with great gratitude. How long it takes us to learn the basics, the simple things!

6

Reconciliation

The Choice for Life with Nonviolence

There are so many stories of forgiveness. The good news itself is the proclamation of God's forgiveness, which is expressed as clearly as possible in Jesus Christ incarnated in our midst. Let us begin with some stories of forgiveness, the first step in the experience of reconciliation.

✟ Margaret Mary, a Visitation sister in France, was having visions of the Sacred Heart, but she was also being sorely beset by her own community. They were persecuting her and making life as unbearable for her as possible. She had been told by the Sacred Heart that she must do penance for the sins of the convent and that she must tell the sisters that she lived with that she was doing this in obedience to the Lord. She obeyed, and they retaliated with anger. But Jesus also told her that he would send her a friend to be her support and a help to her soul, one who would aid her in spreading the devotion to the Sacred Heart.

Soon after, Claude de la Columbière, a Jesuit, arrived at the village and was assigned as confessor to the nuns at Paray. Her friend had arrived. However, he didn't believe her. It seems that God had informed her of his friendship and support, but had not yet told him! He steadfastly refused to acknowledge her visions as authentic, though he questioned her ceaselessly on their content and what Jesus had said in relation to specific issues. Finally, he devised a way to find out if these were really visions of God. The next time Jesus appeared she was to ask him a question and relay the answer immediately to Claude de la Columbière alone. The question was one that only he and God would know the correct answer to: what were Claude de la Columbière's worst sins? Margaret Mary obeyed.

After another vision Claude was impatient to question her on Jesus' response. When he asked her if she had put the question to God, she replied that she had. "Well?" he prodded her. She looked at him strangely and responded: "The Sacred Heart said, 'Tell him I forget!'" In that instance Claude de la Columbière, now Blessed Claude, knew that she was indeed seeing and listening to Jesus. He became her ardent friend, admirer, and a constant source of hope to her as well as the first to speak of the devotion to the Sacred Heart and the love and mercy of Jesus in public.

A second story is based on an actual occurrence as well.

✟ It seems that King Philip of Aragon in Spain was going through the market district with a number of his advisors, nobles, generals, and attendant staff. The king was looking for a birthday gift for the queen, so they stopped at a number of stores to admire the goods. They had just left a jeweler's shop when the owner ran out and followed the king and his entourage down the street in obvious distress. The king halted and listened to the man's complaint: a number of gems were missing from the selection that the king and his men had been look- ing at just moments before. Obviously, someone in the group had stolen them.

The king had all of them return to the shop. He then asked the owner to find him a large bowl, big enough for a man to put his fist inside, and to fill it with salt. Puzzled, the owner obeyed. When the container of salt was prepared, the king looked at all his compan- ions and told them that each of them would put his hand in the con- tainer in turn. They obeyed. When every man had put his hand in the salt, the king commanded the owner to empty the container onto the table. Lo, there in the midst of the salt were the missing jewels! The king's mercy and imagination had allowed the thief to repent, the owner to reclaim his property, and all to be treated with dignity and respect. The thief was forgiven anonymously, without violence.

These stories reveal much about forgiveness. The sacrament of rec- onciliation allows us to learn of our continuing need for forgiveness, recommitment, and "the intensity of our first love" (Rv 2) in the practice of our baptismal promises. Because God extends forgiveness and mercy over and over again to us, we, in turn, extend it to others.

Perhaps this sacrament demands the most of Christians; it stands in opposition to the world's ethic of "looking out for Number One," of seeking revenge against our enemies and those we perceive as having wronged us. But a Christian believes that it is God who looks out best for us, if we look out for all others. The sacrament touches specific situations, relationships, and promises, as well as more demanding attitudes, ethical stances, and public witness, alone and in communion with the universal church of believers. Reconciliation is the Christian's ethical choice for nonviolent living, for a life steeped in mercy, a tender life lived with conscious regard for the other, no matter what the personal cost. It is for looking at the past and asking forgiveness and celebrating God's ever-present love, and for looking to the future to grow in the awareness and practice of being an adult child of God, a brother and sister to Jesus and others in the kingdom. It is a call to the realization that we are bound together in Jesus' life, death, and resurrection, and that our actions, weaknesses, and strengths are bound to the lives of others. Jesus came to save sinners, and first and foremost we are sinners—loved and forgiven and challenged sinners.[1]

From the early days of the church, penance, the sacrament of reconciliation, has been called "second baptism." For the first century of the church's history the sacraments of baptism and eucharist forgave sin; there was no specific sacrament of healing, forgiving, and strengthening after sin. The process of the catechumenate and the rites of initiation were so intense, demanding and powerful that there was little need of another sacrament of forgiveness that specifically dealt with sin and liberation. The good news is that we are forgiven, liberated from all sin, death, and darkness of soul. That good news was a daily reality shared in community response to the proclamation of the scriptures. It was only after the passage of years that the intensity wore off and the need for forgiveness began to assert itself individually and within the community's fabric. Aside from the celebration of eucharist, prayer, fasting, and almsgiving had been the usual ways to atone for sin and failure to live up to one's baptismal commitment.

When the sacrament of reconciliation was begun, it was celebrated for only three sins: being unfaithful in marriage; murdering another; and betraying one's community by betraying one's belief in public (apostasy). These three realities destroyed the fabric of the Christian's individual relationship with God but also tore the community's bonds and discouraged other believers so much that reconciliation was needed on a public as well as private basis. The sacrament was celebrated only once in a lifetime. It was considered a second baptism, a second conversion experience, and it demanded at least as much time and intensity and endurance as the first process.

Still, the reality of forgiveness was the constant backdrop for a believer's life and growth within the community. Jesus' message and life was a startling proclamation of forgiveness; it has tangible effects in a person who accepts such love and forgiveness and "repents."

Jesus' words at the beginning of his ministry are: "Repent and believe the good news for the kingdom of God is close at hand" (Mk 1). It is close—present in Jesus' words, touch, and in his offer of forgiveness and acceptance. His last words in Luke's gospel are "Father, forgive them, for they know not what they do" (Lk 23:34, *NAB*). Immediately afterward he assures a common thief dying next to him that he will be remembered and be the first to be with him in paradise that very day. After the resurrection Jesus' first words of greeting to his friends are those of peace: *shalom.*

Peter, soon to be leader of the believing community of Jesus, experiences Jesus' forgiveness firsthand. At the Last Supper Jesus prays for him, that his faith will not fail, but it does. After Jesus is arrested, Peter betrays Jesus, exclaiming that he does not "even know the man. And seeing Jesus leaving the high priest's house, he leaves, weeping bitterly for his words and lack of faithfulness" (Lk 22:62, *NAB*).

Peter, like the other apostles, deserted Jesus. They were not at the execution site to hear the last words of Jesus. These words would have come to them secondhand, as hearsay: "Father, forgive them, for they know not what they do" (*NAB*). Peter would have taken them to heart, like a knife cleaning out a wound, knowing that his friend and Lord forgave him as he died, forgave his cowardice and betrayal of their friendship.

In John's gospel we are given the story of Jesus' meeting with Peter and the other disciples on the beach. They have been out all night and caught nothing (a usual experience with this group of fishermen). Then, in response to the directions of the lone man walking on the beach, they catch a record number of fish. This is a pattern that they have known before in the presence of Jesus, and he feeds them breakfast on the beach. It is eucharist; they are forgiven. They are friends again.

Then Jesus takes Peter for a walk down the beach. Three times Jesus questions him: "Simon, son of John, do you love me more than these?" And three times, Simon answers. "I do, you know I do." The text tells us that the third time Simon is offended that Jesus would ask him three times (Jn 21:15-17). Has he forgotten the past few days so soon? He is hurt. How hurt would he have been if instead of being given three chances to say "I love you" to Jesus, he had been coldly reminded that three times he had betrayed his friend's trust the very night he broke bread and shared the cup of the covenant with him and the others? We notice that he is called Simon, not Peter, for he has reverted back to the identity he had before he met Jesus. He is not a disciple, not a leader in the community, but one who has betrayed the Lord and disheartened the entire community of believers. He is in sore need of reconciliation.

Reconciliation in Greek literally means "to walk together again," and Jesus takes him for such a walk. Simon Peter has the chance to start over again with the intent and proclamation: "I love you. I love you. I love you." He speaks of his love and repeats it so that he begins to believe it again. In reply he is told, "Feed my lambs, feed my sheep." He is told to share that forgiveness—that gracious and meek response to evil and betrayal—with his own community and all who might betray him in the future. As he has known the loving kindness and mercy of God, so he must return the favor and forgive, give others a chance to say, "I love you, I do love you," and to begin again to walk with the Lord and one another. The reality of forgiveness has blossomed into the reality of reconciliation.

Earlier in Luke's gospel (5:1-11) Peter experiences his sinfulness not as something he has done or failed to do, but as a state of being, a lack. He is out fishing and can catch nothing. He obeys Jesus' directions and hauls in so many fish that the boat almost sinks. He falls to his knees in front of Jesus in the rocking boat and declares: "Leave me, Lord, for I am a sinful man." He sees himself in Jesus' eyes. *Sin* means "missing the mark." It is not so much something done or undone but a sense of not measuring up, not fulfilling a promise or commitment, not living up to an ideal. Reconciliation is not so much concerned with mistakes as with the lived reality of our lives in relation to our baptismal promises.

Our promises are threefold: to live in the freedom of the children of God, committed to the life of God; to live under the power of the cross and the Father's kingdom and not bend to any other; and to shun evil. Reconciliation is concerned with life, life as a Christian called to live it, share it, put it at the service of others. It is concerned with following the will of God, not of human beings, as Peter learns in Mark's gospel when he takes Jesus aside and tries to remonstrate with him, talk him out of the cross and going to Jerusalem (Mk 8). It is then that Jesus turns on Peter and "eyeing the disciples, reprimanded Peter: 'Get out of my sight, you satan! You are not judging by God's standards but by other men and women's standards'" (Mk 8:33, *NAB*). Reconciliation is concerned with Jesus' standards of good and not with an individual's sense of duty or behavior. It is concerned with the spirit and the letter of the law. For when Jesus is approached later in Mark's gospel he is called "good" by the teacher who approaches him and Jesus responds: "Why do you call me good? No one is good but God alone" (Mk 10:18). The criterion for reconciliation is how we have followed Jesus in our baptismal promises and grown as children of light, sons and daughters of one Father.

Some of this sacrament's commandments and exhortations are found in Matthew's gospel: the merciful are blessed, they will be given mercy, shown mercy, know mercy (Mt 5:7). "If your brother has anything against you, leave your gift at the altar and go first to be reconciled and then come and offer your gift" (Mt 5:23, *NAB*).

Christians are to offer no resistance to injury. If a person strikes you on the right cheek, offer him your other; should anyone press you into service for one mile, go two miles (Mt 5:38). There is to be no retaliation in kind, no "eye for an eye." And the commands go further, often, seeming to us, beyond reason: "love your enemies, and pray for those who persecute you" (Mt 5:44). This is a *command*, not an option. Christians are reminded: "*If* you forgive the faults of others, your heavenly Father will forgive you yours. *If* you do *not* forgive others, neither will your Father forgive you" (Mt 6:14-15, *NAB*). Even when we pray we call upon God, our Father, to forgive us the wrong we have done, as we forgive those who wrong us (Mt 6:11). It gets heavier: "Your verdict on others will be the verdict passed on you. The measure with which you measure will be used to measure you" (Mt 7:1f., *NAB*). We are to beware of the planks in our own eyes while looking for the specks in someone else's. All of these exhortations could easily fall under the blessing of "the meek who will inherit the earth," those who, like Jesus, respond to evil and violence nonviolently.

Jesus tells his disciples plainly: "I have come to call sinners, not the righteous" (Mk 2:17, *NAB*). To the rich young landowner who wants to follow him more closely by becoming a disciple, Jesus says that there is one more thing he must do (Mk 10:20). Indeed, after the fulfillment of the law there is always one more thing to do and that is to follow Jesus more closely, deny ourselves, pick up our cross, and come after him to Jerusalem. When his disciples want to rain down destruction on the Samaritan towns, Jesus reprimands them (Lk 9:55), and when Peter asks him how many times he is to forgive another, he is told seventy times seven. There is no end to how many times one is to forgive, for there is no end to the times we have known forgiveness from God. God will deal with us as ruthlessly or as generously and mercifully as we have dealt with one another.

Perhaps the story that makes this most clear is that of the merciless official. In anger at the official's unjust behavior, his master exacts all from the man and Jesus' disciples are told, "My heavenly Father will treat you in exactly the same way unless each of you forgives his brother from his heart" (Mt 18: 21-35, *NAB*).

And Jesus forgives anyone, everyone. His gift is extended to all. He forgives the Samaritan woman and her entire nation, the woman caught in adultery, the man lowered through the roof by his friends. He forgives his disciples, Peter, the thief hanging beside him, his murderers, even Judas. There is no limit to the forgiveness of God. We are called by baptism to stake our very lives on that forgiveness and to extend it to others in imitation of God and in gratitude. There is hope for us all; in fact, throughout the older and new testaments it seems that God does more with sinners than with those who claim to be righteous. God works through Abraham and the slave woman Hagar and his wife, Sarah, in spite of brutality, subterfuge, and even intent to kill; Jacob with his lies and thieving deceptions; Moses, a murderer; Rahab, a prostitute; David, who murdered a man to take his wife; Matthew, a tax-collector; Peter, a coward; and Paul, a self-righteous persecutor. There is an old saying that nothing can be truly loved that does not contain some element that needs to be forgiven. We, as sinners and Christians, often need to be reminded, using words of Dietrich Bonhoeffer, that "we have the Exalted One only as crucified, the Sinless One only as the one laden with guilt, and the Risen One only as the humiliated one." Our baptism exhorts us to "put on the Lord Jesus Christ," to become like our Redeemer. Paul urges his new Christians to

> be imitators of God as his dear children. Follow the way of love, even as Christ has loved you. He gave himself for us as an offering to God, a gift of pleasing fragrance. . . .
> There was a time when you were in darkness, but now you are light in the Lord. Well, then, live as children of light. Light produces every kind of goodness and justice and truth. Be correct in your judgment of what pleases the Lord. Take no part in vain deeds done in darkness; rather, condemn them. It is shameful even to mention the things these people do in secret; but when such deeds are condemned they are seen in the light of day, and all that then appears is light. That is why we read:
> > "Awake, O sleeper,
> > > arise from the dead,
> > > and Christ will give you light."

> Keep careful watch over your conduct. Do not act like fools, but like thoughtful men and women. Make the most of the present opportunity, for these are evil days. Do not continue in ignorance, but try to discern the will of the Lord (Eph 5:1-17, *NAB*).

In baptism we sense that God has great expectations of us. His word takes root in us, and we become novices learning to live honorably in the daylight (Rom 13:13). The Spirit is given to us to form us anew in the image of God in Jesus. God consciously saves us by becoming one of us, with us, in the Incarnation. We begin to admit the truth about ourselves and the world, the unbelievable goodness that resides within us waiting to be born of love and the equally unbelievable cruelty, violence, and evil that reside within us and need to be crucified in love and redeemed.

In the Christian community the heart and history are redeemed together. Persons and powers, sinners and structures are called to repent as one. The perversity of the human heart and the malice of historical evil merge. Time and eternity interlock in our souls and bodies and politics and economics. Baptism and reconciliation and eucharist call us to a change of heart and mind, to move from apathy and ignorance to resistance and to political, economic, and social liberation. We are committed to a *metanoia*, a turning away from idolatry toward the face of Jesus as found in the faces of the earth, especially in the wretched and needy, prisoners, the sick, the lame, the blind, the sinners.

We are saved individually and together. In the stories of scripture we are caught by the violence and sinfulness of those who were closest to Jesus and the abruptness and depth of their transformation after his death and resurrection. Archbishop Oscar Romero, with Bishop Rivera y Damas, writes:

> We wish to end our reflection gazing at the splendid vision of peace that is the Transfiguration. It is noteworthy that the five who were chosen to accompany the Divine Savior in that theophany were five people violent in deed and temperament. What was said at Medellín about Christians could be said of Moses, Elijah, Peter, James and John: They are not simply pacifist, because they are capable of fighting, but they prefer peace to war. Jesus directed the aggressiveness of those rich temperaments toward the work of constructing justice and peace in the world. We ask the Divine Patron of El Salvador to transfigure in this same sense the rich potential of our people, who wish to share with Him His name.[2]

We are the people who celebrate forgiveness and greet each other before receiving eucharist with the word "peace." But daily we must learn to make what we celebrate a reality in our lives and in the world. Pope John Paul II in his 1984 World Day of Peace Message says:

> If we celebrate forgiveness can we fight one another endlessly? Can we remain enemies while we invoke the same living God? If Christ's law of love is our law, shall we remain silent and inert while the wounded world looks to us to join the front ranks of those who are building peace?

What we do individually in our lives and relationships is mirrored in the world in which we dwell. Anger, violence, and hatred in our hearts are the individual characteristics of murder in society, whether personal or collective. George MacDonald says something remarkable and jolting to Christians:

> It may be an infinitely less evil to murder a man than to refuse to forgive him. To him who obeys, and thus opens the door of his heart to receive the eternal gift, God gives the Spirit. . . . The true disciple shall thus always know what he ought to do, though not necessarily what another ought to do. A man is in bondage to whatever he cannot part with that is less than himself.

We must forgive. It is our lifeline to the community, to the Spirit of God, to Jesus and the Father's mercy. We must look kindly on the weaknesses of others as God looks on ours. There are dragons and terrors within each of us. Rainer Maria Rilke's words on dragons are well worth taking to heart:

> How should we be able to forget those ancient myths about dragons that at the last minute turn into princesses who are only waiting to see us once beautiful and brave. . . . Perhaps everything terrible is in its deepest being something helpless that wants help from us.

The Jews have a tradition about the strongest of men and women. "Who is the mighty one?" asks Abbot de Rabi Natan. "He who converts his enemy into his friend. . . . For the loving kindness of our God has overpowered us. We are to seek peace and pursue it (Psalms). It is only friendship and the meeting of the just rights of one's opponents that can do this."[3]

After baptism we are still sinners in need of redeeming grace and forgiveness. We learn best by sharing forgiveness and mercy with others and practicing nonviolent resistance to the evil within and around us. Baptism is a choice for life, the forgiving, redeeming, loving life of Jesus. Eucharist and confirmation are the extension of that choice for life with and for others. Reconciliation tells us to try again, to act again on the grace given to us in baptism. We are the ones who put the borders there, call the halt, say "no more!" In the eyes of God the borders are not there. Virgil Elizondo, when he was director of the Mexican American Cultural Center, said: "Borders are always difficult. They limit the frontiers of belonging. Traditionally, we have had military, economic, political, ethnic, religious, linguistic, racial and cultural borders. There is nothing uglier than hatred of others for the love of God, and yet many of our borders are typified by just that."[4]

We are all brothers and sisters, not enemies. In our Lord's life and death all hatred and condemnation ends. In Luke's opening ministry statement Jesus quotes the prophet Isaiah about bringing a year of favor from the Lord, but he chooses to leave out a crucial line in the original text— that of condemnation, the day of vengeance (see Lk 4 and Is 61). Jesus' demand is for life, life everlasting, life abundant, open to all. We are called first of all to love, forgiving love. This call connects political issues of war, arms buildup, capital punishment, and imprisonment with the community's capacity to love and forgive and repair. Our present society reveals our lack of life, our lack of love. Pope Paul VI, in his address to the United Nations on October 4, 1965, said:

> If you wish to be brothers, let the arms fall from your hands. You cannot love with weapons in your hands. Long before they mete out death and destruction, those terrible arms supplied by modern science foment bad feelings and cause nightmares, distrust, and dark designs. . . . But you . . . are seeking means to guarantee the stability of international relations without the need of recourse to arms. This is a goal worthy of your efforts; this is what the peoples of the world expect from you.[5]

It is a dream that is shared with many, a work that is undertaken across boundaries and borders. It is the nitty-gritty of the work of reconciliation. Vo Van Ai, a Vietnamese poet, writes:

If I could close up
all the hatreds of the world
into a single bullet
last bullet in the last gun
So that my breast could receive it
as the hand gathers the last grape
rotted on the cluster
Then the lute of a thousand voices
would sing.

The Vow[6]

Our fear, hostility, and lack of love are both individual and communal. To unlearn the lessons of war and killing and hate takes time, courage, and insight; it takes being forgiven over and over again. Our Christian-Jewish tradition appears to be conflicting and vacillating, but perhaps it is more that we have failed to live up to it. In *Beggar in Jerusalem* Elie Wiesel tells two stories, one of a Jew and the other of Jesus.

Afraid of suffering, afraid of dying?

Yes, Father, I'm afraid.

The rabbi sighed. You still have a lot to learn, my son. What you should fear is to inflict evil, to cause death. To die for God and his commandments is nothing: our ancestors, the saints and the martyrs did just that. But to kill for God, to cause blood to flow in his name, is serious and difficult. It is alien to us, it goes against our nature and tradition: that is what should frighten you.[7]

The second story is told of a man who meets Jesus, Yeshua, years after his death:

May I tell you about my meeting with Yeshua? Do you remember him? The innocent preacher who had only one word on his lips: Love. Poor Man. I saw him the day he was crucified. Not far from here. . . . He seemed serene, at peace with himself and the whole creation. I tried to make him understand that this was not the first time a Jew was dying for his faith. There were other martyrs before him. But they had gone to their death crying, screaming with pain. For them, for us, no death is worthy of being invoked or sanctified. All life is sacred, irreplaceable; it is inhuman for any person to renounce it joyfully, it is blasphemous to abandon it without remorse.

"Are you angry with me?" he asked.

"No," I answered. "Not angry. Just sad."

"Because of me?"

"Yes, because of you. You think you are suffering for my sake and for my brothers; yet we are the ones who will be made to suffer for you, because of you." Since he refused to believe this, I began to describe what actions his followers would undertake in his name to spread his word. I painted a picture of the future which made him see the innumerable victims persecuted and crushed under the sign of his law. Whereupon he burst into tears of despair: "No, no! This is not how it will be! You are wrong, you must be. This is not how I foresee the reign of my spirit! I want my heritage to be a gift of compassion and hope, not a punishment in blood!" His sobs broke my heart and I sought to comfort him. I begged him to retrace his steps, to return to his people. "Too late," he answered. "Once the stone is thrown, it can no longer be stopped. Once the spark is lit, it must burn itself out." I was overcome with pity and ended up weeping not only for us but for him as well.[8]

Wiesel's stories are tantamount to an examination of conscience for the church. History makes it clear that we have failed as Christians. But the call to repent, to live in peace, and to love all others is still a reality.

There are other stories, though, testaments to the power and validity of Christianity. Hugh of Lincoln, who lived in the late 1100s, was a Carthusian monk, a recluse for a time, then a bishop. He worked with children and lepers, and he loved the sick and the poor. He defended Jews in a time of hatred. Then in 1197 Richard III called the Third Crusade. Richard wanted his barons to subsidize this war and expected his bishops to collect the tax from the poor. Hugh of Lincoln refused. He then proceeded to rebuke the king for oppressing the people and taxing them for his war. A historian described him as the "first clear-cut case of the refusal of a money grant demanded from the crown and a most valuable precedent for future times." He then proceeded to rebuke the king for oppressing the people and taxing them for his war. Others, in our own time, in the United States, imitate his lead.

And, of course, there is the story of Thomas More, popularized in the play "A Man for All Seasons." More pays a stiff price for his beliefs. Margaret, his daughter, comes to "reason" with him:

Margaret: In any country that was half good, you would already be raised on high.

Thomas: If we lived in a country where virtue was profitable, common sense and reason would make us good. And good would make us saints.

Margaret: But in reason! Haven't you done as much as God could reasonably want?

Thomas: Well . . . finally . . . it isn't a matter of reason. Finally it is a matter of love.

Finally, for Christians, in all ethical decisions and demands, it is a matter of love and mercy.

Christians are called to practice forgiveness and mercy, both in atonement for our own lack of love and on behalf of our neighbors. We are to feed the hungry, give drink to the thirsty, clothe the naked, visit the sick, shelter the homeless, visit and set free the prisoners, bury the dead, and pray for the living and the dead. *The Catholic Worker* periodically prints the "works of war" that oppose these works of mercy: to destroy crops and land, seize food supplies, destroy homes and villages, scatter families, contaminate water, imprison dissenters, inflict wounds, and burn and kill the living. War is lack of forgiveness on a grand scale. Murder, whether committed in anger or greed or inflicted legally is an individual's and a society's way of waging war on individuals. As individuals and communities we must learn forgiveness and nonviolence. John Howard Yoder gives an example in *The Christian and Capital Punishment*:

On July 18, 1957, a young farmer was murdered in Ohio by an ex-convict. The reaction of the community, mostly Amish Mennonite, to the brutal deed of this intruder was not one of hostility but of forgiveness. Twenty-eight persons, most of them Amish, were refused for jury duty because of their conscientious unwillingness to inflict the death penalty. During the trial, numerous Amish families invited the murderer's parents into their homes. After the conviction was final, the Amish signed petitions and wrote to Governor C. William O'Neill requesting a commutation of the sentence, in such numbers as to surprise those who thought the Amish cared nothing for the outside world.

The commutation was granted by Governor O'Neill seven hours before the time scheduled for the execution. Meanwhile, a few Amish Mennonites had been attempting to draw a spiritual lesson from the event which had so deeply shaken their community. "God has been speaking to many of us Amish people through this act," some of them concluded. "We believe that God allowed this, especially to call us back to Him in the work of winning souls to His kingdom." Soon after the commutation, two ministers visited the murderer in the Ohio penitentiary, bearing a letter from which the above words were quoted. There they learned that he had become a Christian a few months earlier, and was deeply appreciative of letters he had received from the Amish people, some of them as far away as Iowa, among them, the widow of his victim.[9]

To most people this response seems heroic—or stupid. To Christians, it is to be expected. Jesus Christ was crucified, the legal form of the death penalty used by Rome. Crucifixion was also an example to the Jews and others of Roman power, cruelty, and disregard for the life of anyone who resisted authority. The state may have the right to protect itself from individuals, but to take life in order to protect life is absurdity. In reality, the death penalty is vengeance and hatred; it discriminates and is selective. It is worth nothing that the thief who died with Jesus is assured that he will be with Jesus in paradise that day, more assurance than most people ever have.

The issue of capital punishment is closely aligned with those of imprisonment, human rights, and torture. No one deserves what we dish out in our fear, ignorance, and hatred. No one ever recovers from jail—the cruelty, lack of privacy, hatred and fear, pain, and lack of decency, companionship, and self-respect—whether it is "legal" or part of a regime of destructive power. Karl Menninger says: "Jail means misery to a prisoner's body, mayhem to his personality and assassination to his humanity. There is no such thing as 'curative cruelty.'" We are lying to ourselves when we speak of rehabilitation, deterrence, and justice. The reality of the prison situation and the system of justice belies our words. The prison system reminds us that there is a streak of vengeance within all of us that is evil. We waste human beings under cover of the law. And our methods do nothing for the victims who need to be healed, given justice, reconciled to the community in the person or persons who wronged them. We seem instead to be obsessed with punishment and putting our hatred on scapegoats for certain crimes and actions. There is always another way to deal with violence, deviation, suffering. Our belief in the power of the cross attests to this. The role of the Christian in society is to offer that alternative and believe in its power on a practical level and offer the witness to others. One of the primary groups of people that Jesus is concerned with is prisoners.

The kingdom today is still about sin, wealth and poverty, power, and the kingdoms of this world warring with little people's lives at stake. The church in the kingdom is to be the ally of the poor and the prisoner, sharing power, justice, food, a second chance, housing, health, and all possibilities due to human beings. We are subversive in the sense that we want everyone to have more than an equal chance at that humanness. We are even called to be willing to give over our own so that others may have a taste and experience of it in love.

The kingdom is not of this world, but it is moving in on this world in us and in the presence of the risen Lord's Spirit with us. We speak liberation for all. We stand, like Jesus, with the defeated, the forgotten, and the unwanted, with victims and those condemned, justly and unjustly. We do not align ourselves with power, but with weakness. This is the way of God's coming.

The revolution is that *we turn around* and stand with those who are outside. If we preach the good news, we must believe it and ante up for others. We cannot be cautious and timid in forgiveness and mercy. In the kingdom peace and justice come nonviolently, in the persons who love and are willing to suffer for and with others—both victims and those who do evil. We are called to constant change and just as constant reconciliation and forgiveness for all. We are to suffer with all but choose those most in need first. If we are to be prophetic we must begin with those who have no one to care for them or love them. Always it is time to turn.

We are not alone in sharing this hope and commitment to life and mercy. The Buddhists of Vietnam in 1974 offered their belief in the Four Vows to all who would share their hope for peace: demonstration of love and reverence for life; acceptance of truth and justice; determination not to speak, not to listen to, and not to do anything which can create division, hatred and conflict; and determination to refuse taking up arms to attack our brothers.

This sense of nonviolence, of all being brothers and sisters called to live together, begins with a change in attitude and has a long apprenticeship in practice. Thich Nhat Hanh, a Buddhist monk and poet, talks about the practice of awareness, nonviolence, enemies, and friends:

> We still think that the enemy is the other, and that is why we cannot really see him. Now, everybody needs an enemy in order to survive. The Soviet Union needs an enemy, perhaps the United States. China needs an enemy. Vietnam needs an enemy. Everybody needs an enemy to the extent that without an enemy we can-

not survive. In order to rally people behind them, the governments need an enemy and are very ready to approve that. They want us to be afraid in order for us to rally behind them. And if they do not have a real enemy, they would invent one in order to mobilize us.

Non-violence has another name, awareness. We should be aware of what we are, of who we are, and of what we are doing. That is what I was taught the day I became a novice in a Buddhist monastery. They taught me to be aware of every act during the day. Since that day I have been practicing mindfulness and awareness. The purpose of Buddhist meditation and practice is to see into your own nature and to become a Buddha (a compassionate one). Buddha comes from the verb *buddh*. It means aware. . . . Are we really awake in our daily life?

We need people who are awake, serene, calm. We need such a person to inspire us with calm confidence to tell us what to do. And who is that person? The Mahayana Buddhist Sutras have the answer. All the Buddhist Sutras tell you one thing, you are that person. And only with such a person, calm, lucid, aware, solid, can our situation change and our danger be avoided. So please, good luck, be yourself, and be that person. Thank you.[10]

Perhaps the attitude set before us is most clearly outlined in the United States bishops' peace pastoral:

It is clear today, perhaps more than in previous generations, that convinced Christians are a minority in nearly every country of the world—including nominally Christian and Catholic nations. In our own country we are coming to a fuller awareness that a response to the call of Jesus is both personal and demanding. . . . To be disciples of Jesus requires that we continually go beyond where we are. To obey the call of Jesus means separating ourselves from all attachments and affiliation that could prevent us from hearing and following our authentic vocation. To set out on the road to discipleship is to dispose oneself for a share in the cross (cf. John 16:20). To be a Christian, according to the New Testament, is not simply to believe with one's mind, but also to become a doer of the word, a wayfarer with and a witness to Jesus. This means, of course, that we never expect complete success within history and that we must regard as normal even the path of persecution and the possibility of martyrdom. (no. 276)

We readily recognize that we live in a world that is becoming increasingly estranged from Christian values. In order to remain a Christian, one must take a resolute stand against many commonly accepted axioms of the world. To become true disciples, we must undergo a demanding course of induction into the adult Christian community. We must continually equip ourselves to profess the full faith of the Church in an increasingly secularized society. We must develop a sense of solidarity, cemented by relationships with mature and exemplary Christians who represent Christ and his way of life. (no. 277)

The bishops are realistic, aware of the personal and communal difficulties facing American Catholics in issues that deal with life and death. They propose practical responses to help in the changes, solidarity, and responses that are needed in the world today. They suggest the following:

1. Educational Programs and Formation of Conscience

We must keep in mind that questions of war and peace have a profoundly moral dimension which responsible Christians cannot ignore. They are questions of life and death. True, they also have a political dimension because they are embedded in public policy. But the fact that they are also political is no excuse for denying the Church's obligation to provide its members with the help they need in forming their consciences. We must learn together how to make correct and responsible moral judgments. We reject therefore, criticism of the Church's concern with these issues on the ground that it "should not become involved in politics." We are called to move from discussion to witness and action. (no. 281)

2. Reverence for Life

All of the values we are promoting in this letter rest ultimately in the disarmament of the human heart and the conversion of the human spirit to God who alone can give authentic peace. . . .

No society can live in peace with itself, or with the world, without a full awareness of the worth and dignity of every human person, and of the sacredness of all human life (James 4:1-2). When we accept violence in any form as commonplace, our sensitivities become dulled. When we accept violence, war itself can be taken for granted. Violence has many faces: oppression of the poor, deprivation of basic human rights, economic exploitation, sexual exploitation and pornography, neglect or abuse of the aged and the helpless, and innumerable other acts of inhumanity. Abortion in particular blunts a sense of the sacredness of human life. . . .

Pope Paul VI was resolutely clear: "If you wish peace, defend life." (nos. 284, 285, 289)

3. Prayer

As believers we understand peace as a gift of God. This belief prompts us to pray constantly, personally and communally. . . . We seek the wisdom, through these means and others, to begin the search for peace and the courage to sustain us as instruments of Christ's peace in the world. (no. 293)

4. Penance

Prayer by itself is incomplete without penance. Penance directs us towards our goal of putting on the attitudes of Jesus himself. Because we are all capable of violence, we are never totally conformed to Christ and are always in need of conversion. . . . We are called to turn back from this evil of total destruction and turn instead in prayer and penance toward God, toward our neighbor, and toward the building of a peaceful world. (nos. 297, 300)

In the following section, the bishops look at the reality of the challenge and our hope, and speak specifically to the Catholic community:

After the passage of nearly four decades and a concomitant growth in our understanding of the ever growing horror of nuclear war, we must shape the climate of opinion which will make it possible for our country to express profound sorrow over the atomic bombing in 1945. Without that sorrow, there is no possibility of finding a way to repudiate future use of nuclear weapons or of conventional weapons in such military actions as would not fulfill just-war criteria. (no. 302)

It is this last exhortation that calls American Catholics to specific repentance and change in working for the fullness of reconciliation that is peace, the peace of Christ. We must come to examine our consciences collectively as well as personally for our contribution to hatred, insecurity, anger, violence, and divisiveness in our world. We are reminded repeatedly in the pastoral letter that Christ is our peace and that we are called to be that peace in the world. Paul in his letter to the Ephesians says:

> At that time you were without Christ, you did not belong to the community of Israel; the covenants of God and his promises were not for you; you had no hope and were without God in this world. But now, in Christ Jesus and by his blood, you who were once far off have come near.
>
> For Christ is our peace, he who has made the two peoples one, destroying in his own flesh the wall—the hatred—which separated us. He abolished the Law with its commands and precepts. He made peace in uniting the two peoples in him, creating out of the two one New Man. He destroyed hatred and reconciled us both to God through the cross, making the two one body.
>
> He came to proclaim peace; peace to you who were far off, peace to the Jews who were near. Through him we—the two peoples—approach the Father in one Spirit (Eph 2:12-18).

The sacrament of reconciliation calls us to walk together again to look back and do penance for our past, and to recommit ourselves to living in peace, unity, and freedom.

Our liturgical year even has seasons for reconciliation: Advent and Lent. Advent is our time for turning into the future coming of the Kingdom and incarnation and repenting of our old sins and weaknesses. Lent is a time of the struggle between entrenched power and the prophetic spirit that dares to cry out. It is a time of active confrontation when Christians learn to endure and to be faithful to the call of Jesus to imitate his ways. It is a time for dwelling in an uncharted wilderness—a desert—learning to be mature, carrying the burden of the world and making up what is lacking in the sufferings of Christ. We Christians are called to accept the pain inherent in being forgiving, merciful, nonviolent, and facing evil with the strength of the Spirit, with truth and peace.

We all live daily with the serious struggle of good and evil in our hearts and relationships, even within the structures of the church and society. Some acts betray our thoughtlessness and ignorance, some betray the core of our belief, some are habits, some are signs of living in a dominant culture, and some are deliberate acts of malice and injustice. Sin is both internal and external, with a context in relation to the challenge and the call of the good news of the scriptures. We have the ability to reach for evil as well as for good. Yet the good news reminds us repeatedly that we are forgiven, saved and liberated from all that binds us, that makes us less than human, that oppresses us and others. Acceptance of that belief and reality drastically alters our life, our responsibilities, and our priorities. To accept the forgiveness and mercy of God is to accept the demand that we live justly and mercifully, forgiving as God does, with no strings attached. God relents with us, and we are to relent with others, so that they too can experience the mercy and loving kindness of God. God seeks us out in forgiveness and reconciliation and we, as baptized believers, are called to share that reconciliation.

Often it is the celebration of the eucharist that reveals to us the paucity of our love, the lack of unity and care that is the reality of the Christian community. When we break bread together and drink of the same cup we often realize that we are not what we proclaim to be. Instead we are broken, divided, violent, destructive, and unforgiving. The eucharist forgives us—the shared meal tightens the bonds between God and us and one another—but we need the healing, strengthening, and challenging of the rites of reconciliation to keep us struggling to live up to our baptismal promises: to live as the children of God, trusting in our Father, like Jesus; to live as brothers and sisters in a large family, aware of our commitments to each other; to live the way of the cross with the values and ethic of Jesus uppermost in our lives; to nonviolently resist evil; and to practice forgiveness, mercy, and justice that are undying and all-inclusive as we seek to repair the damage that we have done. There is always more to change, to grow into together. Conversion happens to us, in us, until we die. We are called to die to ourselves and put on Christ— the new person, the new creation. The rites of reconciliation allow us to do that in the context of the scriptures, prayer, and community. Reconciliation is the embrace of the church that allows us to look long and lovingly at what we promised to be and what we are not yet—and move unerringly toward that reality, individually and as community.

We have known the favor of God in Christ through his forgiveness, reconciliation, and mercy. We have cause to rejoice and give thanks and to forgive one another graciously. Reconciliation is a chance to look again at "the one more thing" we are called to in love and to turn our faces resolutely toward the cross and dying to ourselves. Reconciliation is the way of the cross, the way of truth and life, the way of Jesus. Reconciliation is a clear teaching, a prophetic challenge, good news, and a hard reality. It is a chance to practice being ministers of reconciliation—to act like God, forgive, and say to an enemy become friend: "I love you."

Our covenant with God is simple. If we are forgiven and accept the mercy of God, then we are required in justice to forgive all who walk with us. We can exclude no one from the experience of that forgiveness, seventy times seven, whether for trivial slights or monstrous injustices. We are to be peacemakers, signs of the cross to the world in need of hope and forgiveness and the love of God. We are saved and liberated; it is up to us now to minister to and liberate our world. This is the task given us by God in Jesus, with Jesus and through Jesus.

There may be people we find very difficult to forgive. On the other hand, some of us may carry around things within us that we are sure others will not forgive, because no one has ever shared our guilt, anguish, and remorse. Even our communities and nations have "Judases" that we dump things on, scapegoats that we blame so that we do not have to look at ourselves and forgive one another and live in unity. But Jesus forgave Judas. There is no one who does not deserve forgiveness, reconciliation, and mercy. No one.

There is an old Welsh legend that when Judas hanged himself no one would take his soul in, not even hell. And so Judas was condemned to wander the barren reaches of the north in ice and snow and cold and darkness for all time, living alone with what he did. The story tells that finally Judas comes upon a house alit with candles, ready for a feast. A bridegroom with a lighted taper stands at the door. He hears Judas as he prowls in the guise of a wolf outside the doors and windows, moaning and howling in anguish. Then the soul of Judas comes to the door and falls at the feet of the bridegroom. At that the bridegroom, Jesus, says that he has waited long for him before beginning the feast of the kingdom.

Perhaps this is the justice of God as well as God's mercy. The reality of the good news is that *if* we accept the forgiveness of our God then we *must* forgive others. We cannot refuse another what God has shared with us so generously and without reason. In the end it is a question of love.

There is a story told of Tomas Borge, who was active in the Nicaraguan struggle for freedom. After the revolution he went to a prison and met the man who had tortured him for five hundred hours under Somoza's regime. He extended his hand to the man, who was absolutely terrified, and said to him: "This is my revenge. I forgive you." Later, when the man who had helped rape, torture, and kill Borge's wife was on trial, he asked that the man not be judged for this particular crime. During the trial he asked that they look away from the past and look to the future—

to the wedding feast of the kingdom of peace, mercy, and justice in a society that is a reality if we make it so.

This is the sacrament of reconciliation: foregoing revenge; living with the reality of sin, evil, and violence in our lives and enduring what is done to us with compassion for others' pain; remembering our own sin and the times we have hurt others; forgetting what others have done to us and allowing them a future; and extending our hand in peace. We walk together again, doing what is necessary to balance what has been divided and destroyed.

Restitution follows upon this offer of forgiveness and the work of reconciling with one another. It allows us to face the evil done to us and the evil that we do with truthfulness and the possibility of redeeming all of us. It reminds us that we are to choose nonviolent resistance to evil, peaceful solutions to conflict, forgiveness, and freedom.

Let us pray together in the words of Daniel Berrigan:

> Christ our brother, you welcome the repentant to
>   your side.
> You sit at the table with social outcasts.
> Your healing embraces illness of body and soul; you
>   judge the secret sin, even as you forgive. Your
>   forgiveness is judgment.
> You bid us forgive our debtor before we offer gifts at
>   the altar. Forgiven by you, may we win
>   forgiveness of those we cruelly wrong.
> Bid us turn. Bid us return.
> Turn our hearts from coercive blindness, fury of
>   destruction, our mad race to oblivion.
> You know us to the quick. Your glance penetrates the
>   dark declivities of the heart, the self-blinded
>   conscience.
> You know us. Hell bent, sowing the earth with
>   dragons' teeth, hapless and misled, victimized
>   even as we multiply the victims, self deceived
>   amid our spoiled paradise.
> Bid us turn. Bid us return.
> Disarmed Christ, sole hope of the self damned, light
>   amid blindness, straight way in wilderness; bid
>   us return.[11]

Benediction

Send us forth now as you sent Mary Magdalen, to
announce the good news, the only news, the
news forever new; your resurrection.

Send us forth as you sent the twelve to confront
murderous power, to walk peaceably amid the
fires of violence.

Send us forth as you sent the first Christians, to act
as fools for your Christ's sake.

Send us forth; that reviled, we may bless; that
persecuted, we may endure; that slandered, we
may reconcile.

Send us forth, to places likely and unlikely; to the
seats of power and strife, that we may deny
their ascendancy with a fearless word; to the
dwellings of the powerless, that we may bring
hope, and win hope.

Send us to those who love, to those who fear, to
those who are indifferent. That we may sow
love where there is no love and so bring forth
love.

Send us forth, as your word goes forth, and returns
heavy with a harvest of peace.

Send us forth, bid us return. Knowing that far or
near, our names are written in your heart.
Amen.

7

Anointing and Pastoral Care of the Sick

The Choice for Life with Compassion

There is a children's story called "The Magic Pomegranate" or "The Best Gift." It is a good place to start.

✤ Once upon a time there was a king who had three sons. He loved all the sons dearly and wondered which one he should leave his throne to. He decided to send them off on a three-year journey of exploration and discovery, and each was to bring back a gift. From the three gifts he would choose the best one, and that son would be the next king. The three brothers agreed to the plan and decided to meet again in three years and share their gifts before going to see their father. Then each set out enthusiastically in search of the best gift for his father.

The eldest traveled north, to the land of strength. He saw mountains and faraway places and had great adventures that would stand him in good stead later as king. One day, toward the end of his travels, he was roaming through a marketplace and by chance his eye fell upon a carpet. There were stacks of them, every size and shape, color and texture, but he was sure that he saw this one move! Immediately he cornered the carpet seller and asked to buy that particular carpet. The shopkeeper admitted that it had moved; it was a flying carpet. Anyone who sat on it could go almost instantly anywhere he wanted. The prince handed over all the money he had brought with him and what he had earned in his travels. He just knew that he had the best gift of all!

The second son set off east, to the land of wisdom. He had studied all his life, and he was fascinated by the countries to the east of the kingdom. He knew that eventually he would find the perfect gift for his father and become king, so he studied with great teachers, learning what would help him to be a wise and good king in the future. He studied maps and books, and he sat at the feet of the best teachers. One day, while he was looking in a bookstall that was cluttered with all sorts of measuring devices, old tomes, and glasses, he picked up a spyglass, and in surprise and delight he looked into far places. He blinked and looked away and then back through the glass again. The picture had changed. He looked long and was utterly fascinated. This was the gift. He had to have it for his father. The bookseller smiled. His treasure had been found and appreciated by someone. A great deal of money changed hands and the second son had the gift that would surely make him king!

The third son, the youngest, set off south. It was a part of his father's kingdom that no one ever spoke about, and he was curious to see what was there. He roamed through villages and small towns, and out into the fields, working as he wandered. He saw much that delighted him and much that disturbed him. There were very rich and very poor people living side by side. There were those who worked hard and those who didn't work much at all, living off the back-breaking labor of those poorer than themselves. There were lush forests and fields and faces of people that fascinated and startled him. He listened to tales of hopes and dreams and lost loves and was amazed. So much existed outside his palace walls! He started lending money, then giving it away, contributing it to causes great and small. He helped to build a house and repair a bridge. He stayed with a farm family, watched a child being born, and took in the harvest of neighbors working together. He visited taverns and listened to the lore of the land and the rumors of the great and mighty. He learned of the generosity and anxiety of the poor. The time flew by. Suddenly he realized it was time to meet his brothers outside of town and compare their gifts before going to see their father, the king. It was time to head home. He hurried to get there on time, but just before dark, a few miles from home, he had to stop and sleep. He picked a tree and slept for hours. When he awoke and looked into the tree above him, he saw that it was in bloom with bright flowers and fruit. He reached up and picked a pomegranate, and as he did the blossoms and the other fruit disappeared. This was a most amazing tree. And he had his gift for his father.

The three brothers met and shared their stories and brought out their gifts. The first showed his carpet, the second his glass, and the youngest his fruit. They passed the gifts around, and one of the brothers, looking through the glass, saw into another kingdom where the king was frantic and worried. His only daughter was dying, and he was desperate to save her. Each brother looked, and then they looked at one another. The eldest brother suggested that they all climb on the carpet and arrive in the kingdom together. They'd think of something to save the king's daughter, for each had fallen in love with her. In an instant it was done, and they found themselves at the gate of a castle.

Once inside, they announced that they had come to save the princess. The king was willing to try anything. The eldest went in, showed the princess his gift, and came outside again. Then the second brother. Finally the youngest went in and sat beside the princess. He took out a knife and cut open his fruit. As he fed her pieces of the pomegranate, the color came back to her face. With half of the fruit gone she sat up, revived and bright, alive. There was much rejoicing in the kingdom that day and the king said that the three brothers should have their wishes fulfilled to show his gratitude. All three wanted the hand of the princess in marriage.

The princess replied that she would decide which one to marry. She looked to the eldest and thanked him for using the carpet on her behalf. She asked him if he had lost anything or been changed by the use of his gift. He answered no. Then she looked at the second brother and thanked him for the use of the glass, which had showed her to them, and asked if he had lost anything or been changed by the use of his gift. He answered that he had not. Then she looked at the youngest son and thanked him for the fruit that had restored her to health and asked him if he had lost anything or been changed by the use of his gift. He answered yes, that now he had only half the fruit left. His gift to her had changed what he could give his father. But he said he didn't mind because it had restored her to health. She smiled and announced that she would marry the youngest brother, because he had lost a piece of himself and what was precious to him in the giving. That was the best gift of all! And so they were married and in due time became king and queen of the kingdom.

The two older brothers returned to their kingdom and their father. He decided that they would both rule, for both gifts were remarkable. The king missed his youngest son, but he knew, like the princess, that he had found the best gift and given it away—a piece of himself given in compassion. There would always be justice and peace in that land because of that gift.[1]

This story introduces us to the choice for life with compassion and the sacrament of the anointing and pastoral care of the sick. "The Word became flesh and made his dwelling among us" (Jn 1:14, *NAB*). With these simple words we learn that God is like us. God has been born, lives, suffers, and dies with us. We don't often think of Jesus suffering except in his passion and death. But to be human is to suffer, and Jesus suffered a great deal throughout his life. He was born in poverty and in the midst of violent political intrigue. His parents were forced into exile. He returned to Nazareth to grow up, hidden from that violence.

Later, in his public life, there is much pain, rejection, and suffering. He is misunderstood, mocked, feared, and hated. He is the source of division among family and friends. His very initiation into public life is heralded by the gruesome death of his cousin John, beheaded at a dinner party. Jesus is steeped in the psalms and the prophecies of the Hebrew scriptures and describes himself as the Suffering Servant of Isaiah. He knows what Jerusalem does to her prophets. He tries realistically to warn his friends and disciples, "The Son of Man must suffer much, be rejected by the elders, the chief priests, and the scribes, be put to death, and rise three days later" (Mk 8:31, *NAB*). When they do not understand, he describes it in more detail: "We are on our way up to Jerusalem where the Son of Man will be handed over to the chief priests and the scribes. They will condemn him to death and hand him over to the Gentiles, who will mock him and spit at him, flog him and finally kill him" (Mk 10:33, *NAB*). He lives with the reality of brutal death always in the back of his mind, haunting him. He is afraid.

Jesus heals others of their sickness and infirmity. He gives sight to the blind, speech to the mute, and hearing to the deaf; he gives wholeness back to lepers and releases men and women from debilitating illnesses and exclusion by others. He heals in compassion.

There is a beautiful expression in the Gospels that appears only twelve times and is used exclusively in reference to Jesus or his Father. That expression is "to be moved with compassion." The Greek verb *splangchnizonai* reveals to us the deep and powerful meaning of this expression. The *splangchna* are the entrails of the body, or as we might say today, the guts. They are the place where our most intimate and intense emotions are located. They are the center from which both passionate love and passionate hate grow. When the Gospels speak about Jesus' compassion as his being moved in the entrails, they are expressing something very deep and mysterious. The compassion that Jesus felt was obviously quite different from superficial or passing feelings of sorrow or sympathy. Rather it extended to the most vulnerable part of his being. It is related to the Hebrew word for compassion *rachamin*, which refers to the womb of Yahweh. Indeed, compassion is such a deep, central, and powerful emotion in Jesus that it can only be described as a movement of the womb of God. There, all the divine tenderness and gentleness lie hidden. There, God is father and mother, brother and sister, son and daughter. There, all feelings, emotions and passions are one in divine love. When Jesus was moved to compassion, the source of all life trembled, the ground of all love burst open and the abyss of God's immense, inexhaustible, and unfathomable tenderness revealed itself.[2]

Jesus tells his disciples that they must "be compassionate as their heavenly Father is compassionate" (Mt 5:48, *NAB*).

Jesus being human suffered all the vagaries of human life. He lost his friends and family to death: his father, Joseph; his cousin, John; his friend Lazarus. We are told that upon hearing the news of Lazarus's sickness, he wept (Jn 11:35). The night before he died, he retreated with his friends to the Garden of Gethsemane and his heart was "filled with sorrow to the point of death." Even in this time of need, his friends fell asleep and left him to face his fears and distress alone. Then he was tried, condemned falsely, betrayed by his disciples, abandoned, tortured, humiliated, and finally crucified in public. He cried out in need to his God—"My God, my God, why have you forsaken me?" (Mt 27:46b)—a prayer, a plea, a cry of pain. He was buried in a borrowed tomb, hurriedly, because the Sabbath was drawing near.

There is a story in John's gospel that is endearing and tender in its telling and in Jesus' response to an act of kindness and compassion. Jesus is seated at table with his friends when Mary, the sister of Martha and Lazarus, anoints his feet with expensive oil and then dries them with her hair. Judas is incensed at her behavior and the "waste" of the ointment and rebukes her. But Jesus says: "Leave her alone. Was she not keeping it for the day of my burial?" (Jn 12:1-11). Her act of kindness and compassion does not go unnoticed and unappreciated. She does for him what he had done for so many others; touched him with gentleness and simple human care, with love and tender regard.

Jesus describes himself as the Suffering Servant of Isaiah:

Like a root out of dry ground
like a sapling he grew up before us,
with nothing attractive in his appearance,
no beauty, no majesty.

He was despised and rejected,
a man of sorrows familiar with grief,
a man from whom people hide their face,
spurned and considered of no account.
Yet ours were the sorrows he bore,
ours were the sufferings he endured,
although we considered him as one
punished by God, stricken and brought low. . . .

He was taken away to detention and judgment—
what an unthinkable destiny!
He was cut off from the land of the living,
stricken for his people's sin?
They made his tomb with the wicked,
they put him in the graveyard of the oppressors,
though he had done no violence nor spoken in deceit. . . .

For the anguish he suffered,
he will see the light and obtain perfect knowledge.
My just servant will justify the multitude;
he will bear and take away their sins.

Therefore I will give him his portion among the great,
and he will divide the spoils with the strong.
For he surrendered himself to death
and was even counted among the wicked
bearing the sins of the multitude
and interceding for sinners (Is 53:2-4, 8-9, 11-12).

Jesus suffered much because he did not turn aside from his understanding and knowledge of his Father's kingdom and his own mission. Much of what he suffered was for others, at others' hands, both those who loved him yet failed him and those who sought to destroy him and refused to believe his good news. He was open and vulnerable to others' pain and suffering and sought to alleviate it, transform it, to lift the burden of illness and exclusion from the community and guilt from those who suffered. He touched people who were sick and rejected by society, and let them touch him. He blessed those who would suffer for his sake and those who mourned and wept, telling them they would be given solace.

In the early church the disciples continued this healing, forgiving, and comforting mission of Jesus. Peter tells a crippled man who begs from him that he has nothing to give him—except health in the name of Jesus Christ (Acts 3:6ff.)! We read later in Acts that people sought to have Peter's shadow fall on them and carried their sick into the streets and laid them on cots and mattresses so that when he passed by he would heal them (Acts 5:12-16). Paul too heals, and sometimes it gets him into trouble (Acts 16:16). He is imprisoned for healing a slave girl who had been clairvoyant, for she can no longer make money for her masters. In James's letter we find the clearest indication of the practice in the early Christian communities regarding anointing and praying for the sick:

> If anyone among you is suffering hardship, he must pray. If a person is in good spirits, he should sing a hymn of praise. Is there anyone sick among you? He should ask for the presbyters of the church. They in turn are to pray over him, anointing him with oil in the Name. This prayer uttered in faith will reclaim the one who is ill, and the Lord will restore him to health. If he has committed any sins, forgiveness will be his. Hence, declare your sins to one another and pray for one another that you may find healing (Jas 5:13-16, *NAB*).

Mark's gospel refers to the use of oil in healing: "Jesus went about all the cities and villages, teaching in their synagogues and preaching the gospel of the kingdom, and healing every disease and every infirmity" (Mt 9:35). Jesus entrusts this healing ministry to his disciples: "And he called to him his twelve disciples and gave them authority over unclean spirits, to cast them out, and to heal every disease and infirmity" (Mt 10:1, *NAB*). "They drove out many demons and healed many sick people" (Mk 6:13). Anointing with oil has many references in the Hebrew scriptures. Oil was used for the coronation of a king, the ordination of a priest, the installation of a prophet, the consecration of cult objects, the care of wounds, healing the sick, and embalming the body. Olive oil was used as an all-purpose medium of exchange in the Mediterranean world. Charles Gusmer in *And You Visited Me* lists the uses of oil in the Eastern world:

Oil was used for cooking and eating . . . oil provided illumination
for lamps; today the Eastern Orthodox rite of unction is still sometimes referred to as the Rite of the Lamp, as the oil for anointing
may be taken from the oil lamps standing before icons. Oil served
as a cleansing substance in bathing similar to soap today; hence
the origin of the pre-baptismal oil of the catechumens with its
exorcistic and purgative meaning. Oil was also a cosmetic. Chrism
or the Greek *myron* is a kind of sacred perfume with a rich symbolism retained in the Greek language; through chrismation we
are conformed to Christ ("Anointed One") and become Christians
("anointed ones"). Oil was used as a healing medicine, as attested
to in the account of the Good Samaritan (Lk. 10:29-37). In short,
oil together with wheat and wine were the most important agricul-
tural products of the day, representing ancient civilization and indeed life itself.[3]

Oil was blessed in the community:

We invoke Thee, who hast all power and might, Savior of all men,
Father of our Lord and Savior Jesus Christ, and we pray Thee to
send down from the heavens of Thy Only-begotten a curative power
upon this oil, in order that to those who are anointed with these
Thy creatures or who receive them, it may become a means of
removing "every disease and every sickness," of warding off every demon, of putting to flight every unclean spirit, of keeping at a
distance every evil spirit, of banishing all fever, all chill, and all
weariness; a means of grace and goodness and the remission of
sins; a medicament of life and salvation, unto health and sound-
ness of soul and body and spirit, unto perfect well being.[4]

Gusmer continues with the explanation of what this sacrament is intended to effect:

Perfect well-being are the words that best summarize the purpose
of this anointing. Its comprehensiveness aims at a wholeness that
includes the removal of every disease and sickness, the exorcistic
casting out of demons and unclean spirits, and a means of grace
and remission of sins.[5]

Today, in the reformed rite, all Christians are urged to visit the sick,
remember them in prayer, and celebrate the sacraments with them, be-

cause the sick are the common responsibility of the church (no. 43).[6] The prayers of the ritual, through simple, are indicative of the sacrament's power and meaning.

> Through this holy anointing
> may the Lord in his love and mercy help you
> with the grace of the Holy Spirit. (Amen)
>
> May the Lord who frees you from sin
> save you and raise you up. (Amen) (no. 25)

But the foremost issue is the reality of *healing*, which is a rich and ambiguous word in meaning and fact, because healing can be considered a synonym for everything God has done for us in Jesus Christ: salvation, justification, liberation, and reconciliation. David Power writes:

> In the sacrament of the sick what is at stake is the sacramentality of sickness itself, or perhaps it would be better to say, the mystery which is revealed in the sick person who lives through this experience. In other words, the accent is not on healing, nor on forgiving, nor on preparing for death. It is on the sick person, who through this experience discovers God in a particular way and reveals this to the community.[7]

We are reminded that Jesus tells his hearers that he has come not for the healthy but for those who are sick, not the righteous but the sinners (Mk 2:17). The church is the gathering of the sick, sinners, those in need of the Physician. The *Apostolic Constitution* tells us what we are doing in the sacrament of the anointing and the pastoral care of the sick: "The whole church commends the sick to the suffering and glorified Lord so that he may raise them up and save them." In return, the sick are encouraged "to contribute to the welfare of the whole people of God by associating themselves willingly with the passion and death of Christ."[8] It is the sick who are the sign, power, and hope for the Christian community, the image of the Suffering Servant still with us, the reminder of death and of our faith, which looks at the face of suffering and death and rejoices in resurrection and hope for new life. The sacrament is a celebration of hope and solidarity with those who face the reality of life in their own flesh and blood and bone. It is the sacrament of doing for others, like Mary, what will be done for us in our own sickness and death. It is the church holding and easing pain, the church being a "Pietà," holding the suffering and dead Christ in her arms and weeping and mourning, comforting, being comforted, and living in faith through to the resurrection. The sacrament of anointing is the church attempting to be accepting, creative, sharing, prophetic, hopeful, respectful, and compassionate in the ever-present reality of pain and suffering in the world and in each person's life.

Pain is important. How we bear it reveals our deepest beliefs. Pain is fluid, it flows with us and through us; it is as much a part of life as our blood pressure or our emotions. We deal with it alone or with others, and we face our own hopelessness and helplessness in the pain of those we love and cherish and can do nothing to ease. Pain reveals a side of humanity that we often try to ignore. It comes to us, whether accepted and shouldered or fought against. There are phases in suffering just as there are in death. There is both active behavior and reactive behavior in relation to pain and suffering. It is the conquest of powerlessness or the submission to pessimism and despair. Jesus cried out in pain, prayed, fought against it, submitted to it, redeemed it, and conquered it. Our reaction to pain says much about our beliefs.

Listen to the pray-er in the Book of Lamentations:

> My eyes run with streams of water because of my
>   people's wound.
> My eyes stream with unceasing tears and refuse all
>   comfort, while
> the Lord in heaven looks down and watches my
>   affliction. . . .
>
> But I called on Thy name, O Lord, from the depths
>   of the pit;
> Thou hearest my voice; do not turn a deaf ear when
>   I cry,
> "Come to my relief." Thou wast near when I called
>   to Thee;
> Thou didst say, "Have no fear."
>   (Lam 3:48-50, 55-57, *NAB*)

Thomas Merton prays: "The world without storms and our lives without agony would give us nothing to grow on. Make us glad for stormy weather."

In *Leaves of Grass* Walt Whitman pens: "Agonies are one of my changes of garments. I do not ask the wounded person how he feels, I myself become the wounded person." And Shakespeare has Lear comforting his daughter:

> No, no, no, no! Come, let's away to prison;
> We two alone will sing like birds i' the cage.
> When thou dost ask me blessing, I'll kneel down
> And ask of thee forgiveness. So we'll live
> And pray and sing, and tell old tales, and laugh
> At gilded butterflies; and hear poor rogues
> Talk of court news; and we'll talk with them too—
> Who loses and who wins; who's in, who's out—
> And take upon us the mystery of things
> As if we were God's spies; and we'll wear out,
> In a wall'd prison, pacts and sects of great ones,
> That ebb and flow by the moon (*Lear*, V. iii. 6-19).

Louis Dupré talks about his understanding of suffering and what it teaches him:

> It means entering into the dark reality of my own suffering, loneliness and failure. Only in the brokenness and pain of life am I with Him where he continues to live His agony. . . . Christian piety teaches that every suffering of mine, however despicable and even sinful in its origins, is Jesus' agony in men. To him who suffers, suffering always means failure—not a clearly understood effective sacrifice— "My God, my God, why?". . . He is crucified in me, not in Jerusalem. . . . In this world there can be no grace but through redemptive suffering. To encounter God's agonizing grace I must walk into the bleak desert of my private pain and humiliation. . . . I must find Jesus' agony also in those private worlds of suffering around me, which I am so reluctant to explore and so unable to comprehend. Jesus' agony in the uncouth, the uncivilized, the unlovable. On Good Friday failure itself has become redemptive. That Jesus fails in me is the joyous mystery of the union between God and me.[9]

The Incarnation is a bond, a covenant between God and humans, the best gift that could have been given. Jesus is bound to us in our most intimate moments, our most despairing and difficult times, our humiliating and repetitive failures. He continues to love us, to strengthen us, to grace us and heal us. Redemption is particular, attentive to details, awesome in its terrible process, and shared in community for those who believe. The Christian's experience of suffering, pain, and sorrow is a call to participate in the passion of Christ, to be involved in the sufferings of the Lord, "to fill up what is lacking there in our flesh" (Col 1:24, *NAB),* and it continues in us, Christians, until the end of time. We are called to commiserate in and suffer along with the world in all its wretchedness, fallenness, and faith. Saints, like Francis of Assisi, known for their joy and exaltation and song, are also serious saints, steeped in the experience of physical illness and pain, psychological hurt and rejection and spiritual darkness. Still they sing. Francis sang because his suffering made him one with Christ, who knew so much pain in his own life. Francis loved passionately and wanted to stand in solidarity with his Master in his rejection, temptations, lonely nights on the mountain, night in Gethsemane, on the cross, in the tomb. For him, it was a chance to enter into and share the fate of Christ. Francis wanted to be as poor as Jesus himself, and we are all poor in the face of illness, old age, mental incapacitation, and death. We are all at a loss in the face of our mortality. Others too have sensed this "putting on Christ" and rejoiced in it, learning in faith to pick up not only their own cross but to shoulder another's.

This lesson of shared pain, compassion, acceptance of action with and for those who suffer is the concrete expression of the compassionate life and the final criterion of being a Christian, as attested to in Matthew's story of the sheep and the goats. Part of what makes us human as well as graceful is our ability to transcend the selfishness and individuality of our pain to help and encourage another. St. Gregory in one of his Lenten sermons preached:

> You who are fasting now in Lent. These are the men I bid you help. Clasp the afflicted man as if he were gold. Take the sufferer into your arms as if he were your own health, the welfare of your wife and children and all your house. Men shackled by illness, men cooped in some narrow lodging place or corner like Daniel in the den; these wait for you, the friend of the poor, to be another Habacuc to them.

There are contemporary witnesses to the Christian life, to "walking humbly with our God," who are probably little known. Kim Chi Ha, a Korean poet, struggles for justice and human rights in the tradition of the Old Testament prophets. He has been jailed repeatedly, tortured, and isolated. In his play "The Gold-Crowned Jesus," a leper, the most despised of social outcasts in Korea, even today, encounters Jesus imprisoned in concrete by the government, business, and church officials.

> The leper asks him: "What can be done to free you, Jesus, to make you live again so that you can come to us?" Jesus replies: "My power alone is not enough. People like you must help to liberate me. Those who seek only the comforts, wealth, honor, and power of this world, who wish entry to the kingdom of heaven for themselves only and ignore the poor . . . cannot give me life again. . . . Only those, though very poor and suffering like yourself, who are generous in spirit and seek to help the poor and the wretched can give me life again. You have helped to give me life again. You removed the gold crown from my head and so freed my lips to speak. People like you will be my liberators."[10]

Kim Chi Ha wants only to alleviate and diminish pain, because in his own person he has experienced its power and destructiveness. But he has also learned in his flesh that pain and suffering are a part of his vocation as a Christian and that, like all of life, they can be redeemed by sharing them in faith as a sharing in the sufferings of Christ.

All Christians are called to celebrate the hope that is found in Revelation 21:1-4, the vision of the new heavens and the new earth, the holy city, the New Jerusalem that will be proclaimed with a loud voice:

> Then I saw a new heaven and a new earth. The first heaven and the first earth had passed away and no longer was there any sea. I saw the New Jerusalem, the holy city coming down from God, out of heaven, adorned as a bride prepared for her husband. A loud voice came from the throne, "Here is the dwelling of God among men: *He will pitch his tent among them and they will be his people.* God will be with them and *wipe every tear from their eyes.* There shall be no more death or mourning, crying out or pain, for the world that was has passed away."

Our world is marked by pain, suffering, despair, and death. William Stringfellow writes:

> It has lately come to pass that America has entered upon a dark age. . . . It is, I believe, an authentic dark age; that is, a time in which the power of death is pervasive and militant and in which

people exist without hope or else in pursuit of transient, fraudulent, or delusive hopes. It is not merely an episode of passing mal-
aise, not only an interlude of economic or cultural or political depression, though it has some such aspects. It is an era of chaotic
activity, disoriented priorities, banal redundancy. Creativity is sup-
pressed; imagination has been lost; nostalgia is superficial and in-
dulgent. Society suffers massive tedium. There is very quick re-
sort to violence, usually of overkill dimensions. People become
frantic about their personal safety and concentrate solemnly on
their own survival. The infrastructures of great institutions crumble.
For those who consider that there is a God, there is widespread
suspicion of abandonment. It is a period marked by intense ani-
mosity toward human life and, indeed, intransigent hostility toward all of created life. It is a time within itself persuasive of the
truth of the biblical description of the fall. It is a prosperous period
for death. It is, in short, a dark age.[11]

But Stringfellow is not pessimistic or despairing. He sees his realism
as a threshold of hope, a place where vibrant biblical spirituality can be
a source of resistance, hope, vision, and conversion. He calls for

the solemn offering to Almighty God of all the cares and needs of
this world whatsoever represented in the offertory of certain particular necessities and issues implicating persons and communities known to those who intercede. In the tradition of intercession,
as I understand it, the one who intercedes for another is confessing
that his or her trust in the vitality of the Word of God is so serious
that he or she volunteers risks, sharing the burden of the one for
whom intercession is offered even to the extremity of taking the
place of the other person who is the subject of the prayer. Intercession takes its meaning from the politics of redemption. Intercession is a most audacious witness to the world.[12]

Stringfellow's words echo James's words to his community in the early
church: "The prayer of the upright man has great power, provided he
perseveres. . . . Brothers, if any one of you strays far away from the truth
and another person brings him back to it, be sure of this: he who brings
back a sinner from the wrong way will save his soul from death and *win
forgiveness for many sins*" (Jas 5:16b, 19-20). The demands made of a

Christian are for the community's health, strengthening, and healing as well as for our own.

The sacrament of anointing and pastoral care of the sick calls us to the works of mercy—mercy for those in this century and culture who are forgotten, outcast, lost, powerless. All of us must die, all of us must suffer, as humans who live fallen from grace in a world that groans waiting for its fulfillment and completion as the kingdom of God. But we do not have to die in certain ways, suffer in certain ways and we cannot be the cause of such pain to others. We have a responsibility for the suffering of all.

Daniel Berrigan, in a talk at the War Resisters League in New York over twenty years ago, told the group what Christians should do:

> We want to bury your dead.
> We want no one to die.
> We want to stand with your resisters.
> We want to bind the wounds of your victims.
> We want to challenge your premises.
> We want to weep with your widows.
> We want to suffer with your exiles and displaced
>   peoples.

The crux of the sacrament of anointing and pastoral care of the sick is that we suffer with, mourn with, and ease the pain of others. If we lay hands on those who come before us, anoint them with oil, and pray for their healing in body, mind, and soul, we are called to extend that prayer and action to all, especially to those who most need such love, care, and compassion. Pastoral care is ongoing, enduring, consistent, delicate, hard, and often repulsive. Physically caring for the sick, the dying, and the old is not easy, but it is being a "balm for all wounds" (Etty Hillesum). We all have a tendency to romanticize about such hands-on care until we are face to face with it. We imagine the great consolation and explain away the drudgery, mess, and smell.

In New York City there is a hospital unlike any other hospital in the city: St. Rose's Home. It is home to poor people dying of cancer. No one pays. There is no insurance, no grants from the state. St. Rose's doesn't even take gifts from the patients. Each person is treated individually, carefully, humanely. I worked there twenty-five years ago as a volunteer. It is a marvelous place, a place of hope, sorrow, and face-to-face

confrontation with death. It is a place of continual conversion, reconciliation, prayer, healing, and death. Daniel Berrigan also worked there and
has written about his experience in *We Die Before We Live*: "We resist
the death game (by way of radical understanding, resistance) in propor-
tion as we connect with the life game (by way of embrace, ecstasy)." He
writes of a child who dies, a child who never speaks. This child becomes
for him an image of God, "the fate of Jesus, which is to say, the fate of
humankind. That fate, as we may read in the gospels (and in the face of
this child), is ineluctably tragic; its highest form, the one furthest removed from the valid expectation of this world, from all cultural con
jobs and secular folderol—that fate is to be a victim."[13] A Christian who
looks on the face of one who suffers has to see God, has to believe in the
awful reality of God incarnate, suffering and loving us by sharing our
life and death and offering us companionship and resurrection.

Berrigan tells another story about an old Irishman dying:

> He said to me again and again, "Help me believe, help me in my
> despair." And I, "But you do believe, you took communion this
> morning." "But anyone can take communion," he cried. "Help me
> believe." And having led me to that deep, into that seam of dark-
> ness, he stalled there, and I beside him, a rock wall against our
> faces, nowhere to go.
>
> And I who confess to knowing little, and day by day lose ground
> on that little, at such moments I had nothing to say. And so said
> nothing, but held his hand in mine. He sensed it, he was savvy
> with that still insight of the near dead; were not he and I, after all,
> in a like predicament? . . .
>
> So we gained a bit; a fraternity of sorts, a human basis. That
> was what he wanted, not to go off alone. He had enough of being
> alone.[14]

We must, in the face of life, hold each other's hands, find some sense
of belonging together, of being in communion truly. What we celebrate
in the sacraments must be celebrated in the flesh first or else the ritual
will be shallow, full of the taste of ashes and death rather than the Spirit
and life. What we celebrate in community must find a home in our daily
life. If we anoint and strengthen life and lift up the sufferings of those in
our communities, we must resist death in all its forms and stand against
the forces of destructiveness and despair that each of us faces. We must
lay hands on people in the world with words of comfort if we lay hands

on them in church and expect healing and wholeness in our communities. Suffering is the way to God; it is the way of the cross. We must accept the passion of Christ, which continues to lift up to God the world and make it holy by embracing it with tenderness and love.

At the last supper, Jesus prays with and for his disciples, alerting them to the world and what it will do to them. He is facing the end of his work, his death, and he talks of joy that will one day be fulfilled (Jn 17:13). He is confident even as he faces pain and death. Faith gives us courage, hope, and strength to endure, to die humanly, and to suffer with Jesus. In suffering we come of age as the children of God. Childhood in God has nothing to do with age, but with sight, belief, and response in compassion. Jesus is always the Child of God, but he is crucified and believing, hanging on for dear life, for a dearer life. We hang on with him, rely on him, look to him, take heart from him, and look to the compassion of God who raised him up.

Jesus words are clear, simple: "A cup of cold water in my name to one of these lowly ones" (Mt 10:42, *NAB*) or "two or three gathered together in my name" (Mt 18:20, *NAB*). Simple things speak of the Spirit's presence in the world, of mercy, loving kindness, compassion, and being moved to pity, like Jesus. He has given us power and authority over demons and to cure diseases and spread the good news of freedom in the kingdom now. We who suffer are blessed, not because of our suffering, but because we will have cause to rejoice, to be comforted. "Christianity exists for the slaves. It is the religion of the oppressed, of those marked by affliction. It concerns itself with their needs. People are pronounced blessed not because of their achievements or their behavior, but with regard to their needs. Blessed are the poor, the suffering, the persecuted, the hungry."[15]

Nietzsche has remarked that "Christianity has sided with all that is weak and base, with all failures; it has made an ideal of whatever contradicts the instinct of the strong life to preserve itself. . . . Christianity arose among the lowest classes, the underworld of the ancient world . . . everything miserable that suffers from itself, that is afflicted with bad feelings, the whole ghetto-world of the soul."[16]

Suffering can embitter us, save us, or gentle us. It can instruct us in the wisdom of God, draw us into the embrace of communion and share with us the passion of Jesus Christ. Jesus goes to Gethsemane, and we follow. We can sleep or watch and pray, anoint and lay hands on the world that is broken and in torment. Rabbi Hanokh says of the Israelites: "The real exile of Israel in Egypt was that they had learned to endure it."[17] We too must take a hard look at suffering and see what it is that we endure, accept, or resist. The good news and our baptism call us to the power of life, of the children of God, of light, and commit us to stand against unnecessary pain, suffering, and agony. Our brothers and sisters teach us the difference. If it were ours what would we cry out for? Dorothee Soelle makes it clear:

> As long as Christ lives and is remembered his friends will be with those who suffer. Where no help is possible he appears not as the superior helper but only as the one who walks with those beyond help. That one bears the burden of the other is the simple and clear call that comes from all suffering. It is possible to help bear the burden, contrary to all talk about a person's final solitude. A society is conceivable in which no person is left totally alone, with no one to think of him and stay with him. Watching and praying are possible.
>
> Everyone who helps another is Gethsemane.
>
> Everyone who comforts another is the mouth of Christ. (from the Russian liturgy)
>
> That people suffer and can be disconsolate is taken for granted here. We should forbid ourselves the dream of a person who needs no consolation. There is a time for weeping and a time for laughing. To need consolation and to console are human, just as human as Christ was. We can change the social conditions under which people experience suffering. We can change ourselves and learn in suffering instead of becoming worse or insensitive. We can gradually beat back and abolish the suffering that still today is produced for the profit of a few. But on all these paths we come up against boundaries that cannot be crossed. Death is not the only such barrier. There are also brutalization and insensibility, mutilation and injury that no longer can be reversed. The only way these boundaries can be crossed is by sharing the pain of the sufferers with them, not leaving them alone and making their cry louder.[18]

As Christians we have much to learn. We can learn from those around us who suffer. We can laugh and take heart from someone like Katharine Hepburn, who says: "Life is very hard isn't it? It does kill you after all!" Or from Anna Magnani, who said: "Don't hide the lines in my face when you take my picture. I suffered too much to get them."

Pope John Paul II preached at a communal celebration of the anointing of the sick in St. George's Cathedral in Southwark, London, on May 28, 1982. In his homily he prayed and preached to the church:

Praised be Jesus Christ. Praised be Jesus Christ who invites us to share in his life through our baptism. Praised be Jesus Christ who calls us to unite our sufferings to his so that we may be one with him in giving glory to the Father in heaven.

Today I greet you in the name of Jesus. . . . I want you to know how I have looked forward to this meeting with you, especially those of you who are sick, disabled or infirm. I myself have had a share of suffering and I have known the physical weakness that comes with injury and sickness.

It is precisely because I have experienced suffering that I am able to affirm with ever greater conviction what St. Paul says: "Neither death, nor life, nor angels, nor principalities, nor things present, nor things to come, nor powers, nor height, nor depth, nor anything else in all creation, will be able to separate us from the love of God in Christ Jesus our Lord" (Rom. 8:38-39). . . .

By his dying on the cross, Christ shows us how to make sense of our suffering. In his passion we find the inspiration and strength to turn away from any temptation to resentment and grow through pain into new life. Suffering is an invitation to be more like the Son in doing the Father's will. It offers us an opportunity to imitate Christ who died to redeem humankind from sin. Thus, the Father has disposed that suffering can enrich the individual and the whole church. . . .

My dear brothers and sisters, as you live the passion of Christ, you strengthen the Church by the witness of your faith. You proclaim by your patience, your endurance and your joy the mystery of Christ's redeeming power. You will find the crucified Lord in the midst of your sickness and suffering. . . .

Today I make an urgent plea to this nation. Do not neglect your sick and elderly. Do not turn away from the handicapped and the dying. Do not push them to the margins of society. For if you do, you will fail to understand that they represent an important truth. The sick, the elderly, the handicapped and the dying teach us that weakness is a creative part of human living, and that suffering can be embraced with no loss of dignity. Without the presence of these people in your midst you might be tempted to think of health, strength, and power as the only important values to be pursued in life. But the wisdom of Christ and the power of Christ are to be seen in the weakness of those who share his sufferings.[19]

In Matthew's gospel Jesus is buried in Joseph of Arimathea's tomb. Then Joseph rolled a huge stone across the entrance and went away. "But Mary Magdalene and the other Mary remained sitting there, facing the tomb" (Mt 27:61, *NAB*). Mary Magdalene waits. And she who stood by and witnessed his death is the first to witness to the resurrection. Her compassion is rewarded with rejoicing and meeting that is beyond hope. To be compassionate opens us up for resurrection; to suffer and die in Christ is one day to rise with him and share his glory. This is our faith, this is our hope, this is to be our love for one another, especially those who suffer and die because of the world's indifference, insensitivity, and lack of compassion.

There is a simple and startling story told by the Quakers. In the years following World War II the Quakers worked in Poland distributing food and clothing. A woman worker who served a cluster of villages became ill with typhus and in twenty-four hours was dead. In the village there was only a Roman Catholic cemetery, and by canon law it was quite impossible to bury one not of that confession in its consecrated ground. So they laid their cherished friend out in a grave dug just outside the fence of the cemetery. The next morning they discovered that in the night the villagers had moved the fence so that it now embraced the grave.[20] There is a witness of unity and compassion that overrides the unique witness of particular confessions or beliefs in God. That witness is always mercy, charity, and compassion for others.

Let us pray with Jesus:

"Father, Lord of Heaven and earth, I praise you, because you have hidden these things from the wise and learned and revealed them to simple people. Yes, Father, this is what pleased you.

Everything has been entrusted to me by my Father. No one knows the Son except the Father, and no one knows the Father except the Son and those to whom the Son chooses to reveal him.

Come to me, all of you who work hard and who carry heavy burdens and I will refresh you. Take my yoke upon you and learn from me that I am gentle and humble of heart; and you will find rest. For my yoke is good and my burden is light" (Mt 11:25-30).

8

Marriage

The Choice for Life
with Friendship and Faithfulness

Some Background for the Sacraments
of Marriage (Chapter 8) and Orders (Chapter 9)

By the time Christians celebrate either marriage or orders they usually have been living in the church for a long time. But that doesn't mean they know the language or the basic principles of what it means to be a Christian, a baptized, confirmed, and eucharistic member of the community that follows in the footsteps of Jesus. They probably have been receiving the sacraments but not necessarily celebrating the reality in their lives. This lack is not necessarily their fault; the difficulty is to a large extent based in the approach the church takes to the sacraments.

There are at least four basic characteristics of the sacraments that we need to keep in mind as we look at marriage in this chapter and orders in the next:

1. the church's authority to celebrate the sacrament, which is found in the scriptures (the life of Jesus) and the tradition and practice of the church;
2. the context of the community that celebrates what it is already living and growing deeper into on a daily basis;
3. the education of the person participating in the sacrament; and
4. a conversion, that is, the change in ethical behavior and attitudes to which the sacrament calls believers, along with the desire of the individual to receive the sacrament.

Unfortunately, not all of these aspects are stressed fully in today's church. The church's authority to celebrate the sacrament, education, and the individual's desire to receive the sacrament receive attention, but there is little or no community involvement, certainly no calling forth from the community, and no accountability to the community in general for ethical behavior. Failure to live up to the ethical demands has serious consequences—sanctions such as exclusion from the sacraments, specifically eucharist—only for the married, where the church demands certain behavior with regard to birth control, abortion, adultery, and divorce/remarriage.

Although baptism initiates us into the church and gives us the opportunity if not the recourse to all the sacraments that belong to all the people of God, not all adults receive marriage or orders—and one usually precludes the other. A growing number of adults in the church are excluded from both at a time when adult Christians need the support, grace, and celebration of their lifestyles within the church and the world.

In order to deal with some of these theological inconsistencies I approach marriage and orders as sacraments of lifestyle within the Christian community. In the following chapters I will offer some suggestions for altering the celebration of these sacraments and how and who participates in them, as well as suggesting new sacraments. Sacraments are, after all, the heritage of Christians and can be claimed and re-created according to need. In these chapters I will deal with the reality of ministry, apart from the sacrament of orders, as charism, and with both single and religious commitments within the church that need to be sacramentalized. I deliberately avoid dealing with marriage primarily in regard to its more institutionalized demands as found in canon law and/or the issues of sexuality; I prefer the context of friendship, love, and faithfulness. I suggest further that all adult Christians be able to receive this sacrament in the context of friendship with one to whom they are faithful, no matter the choice of their vocation within the church. The sacrament of the friends of God includes *all* expressions of faithful love in the community of believers.

With the sacrament of orders in chapter 9 I will look at this sacrament as a lifestyle dedicated to obedience to the church, to the believing community, as a symbol of unity and public prayer. I will not deal with it as ministry, because all Christians are called to ministry by baptism and eucharist. Hopefully at the end of these two chapters it will become apparent that the reception of either of these sacraments does not necessarily rule out the celebration of the other.

None of this is meant purely as criticism of the church; it is intended to create a place where hope, conversion, and imagination can begin to reclaim the heritage of Christians for all Christians.

The Sacrament of Marriage

We begin at the beginning, in the garden! In the words of Dorothy Sayers in *Purgatory*, "Eden is, and was always meant to be, a starting-place and not a stopping-place." It does all begin in Eden, when God creates man and woman in his image and tells them to multiply and subdue the earth and that it is not good for man to be alone (Gn 1–2). A Jewish midrash or commentary on this story of creation is very enlightening.

> If husband and wife are deserving, God's presence dwells in their midst. If they are not deserving, fire devours them.
>
> "For," said Rabbi Akiba, "the Hebrew word for man is *ish*, spelled *aleph, yod, shin*. Remove the *yod* and you have *aleph* and *shin*, or *esh*, meaning fire. The Hebrew word for woman is *isah*, which is spelled *aleph, sin, heh*. Remove the letter *heh* and, once again, you have *esh*, meaning fire."
>
> From this we learn that there is a consuming fire in the heart of every man and woman. When they marry, two fires are brought together that are capable of destroying whole worlds, if not properly tended. To quench that fire is impossible—for it generates the life of the world. But to leave the fire as it is is also impossible, for it generates evil as well.
>
> What did God do? He placed one of the letters of His name, the first letter of the divine name, *yod*, between the *aleph* and the *sin* to make the Hebrew name for "man." And he took the second letter of His name, the *heh*, and placed it after the *aleph* and the *sin* to make the Hebrew name for "woman." In that way, both the man and the woman retain in their names the word "fire," but when they marry, the divine presence dwells in their midst, in the combination of their names. Wherever God's presence dwells, that fire gives warmth and heat, but it does not devour and consume. If husband and wife do not make the divine presence unwelcome, its blessing rests on the work of their hands and they become as partners in the act of divine creation. But if they make the presence unwelcome so that it does not dwell in their midst, they are left only with two consuming flames.[1]

Marriage is a social institution, an economic arrangement, and society's structure for perpetuating the race. It can also be a human relationship that is born of love, friendship, or accommodation. Marrying for love is a relatively new phenomenon. In the Hebrew scriptures only one woman was married for love: Rachel. Joseph worked seven years for her, only to find that he had married her sister, Leah, and had to work another seven years for his second and best-loved wife. In Jewish society marriage holds the social fabric of the nation together. Divorce is allowed, but primarily for men, only on rare occasions for women. The law in the Jewish community discriminates against women. It is this law that Jesus is questioned about in Matthew's gospel. He responds: "Moses knew your stubborn heart, so he allowed you to divorce your wives, but it was not so in the beginning. Therefore I say to you: whoever divorces his wife, unless it be for infidelity, and marries another, commits adultery" (Mt 19:3-9, *NAB*). In Luke's account the comments on divorce and marriage are given as ethical directives, but Jesus does not lay down laws: "The man who divorces his wife and marries another commits adultery; and the man who marries a woman divorced by her husband also commits adultery" (Lk 16:18).

Paul Hoffman explains what this means:

Jesus, then, designates as adultery (and therefore illegitimate) an action which in Jewish law was legitimate—the divorcing of a woman by her husband and his remarriage, or the marrying of a lawfully divorced woman. His provocative statement would have made two things clear to his listeners: 1) marriage unites man and wife in a way that cannot be dissolved by the Law; 2) a man can be answerable to his own wife as an adulterer and the obligations of a woman to her husband, formerly *one-sided*, are now *mutual*. Man and wife are shown to be equal partners with equal rights.

Should we, then, think of this saying of Jesus as a law? To understand it, we must compare it with other sayings in which he shows his attitude to the Law. If we do this, we see that his words here are no more a law than is his condemnation of anger (Mt. 5:21ff.), or of oath-taking (Mt. 5:33, 34a, 37; cf. James 5:12), or of committing adultery in one's heart (Mt. 5:27ff.). In these instances he does indeed use the language of the Law, but he does so in a way that alienates it from its customary legal use and breaks through the plane of law into that of reality. He reveals the reality of a human relationship in which God lays direct claim to man's response. And he frees this relationship from the strait-jacket of the Law. His statement on divorce must also be understood in this sense. Jesus criticizes the Law and lays bare the reality of marriage which, though subject to the Law, can never be adequately protected by it. His words contain a demand and a promise: he shows how great are the obligations human beings can assume with regard to each other, but also the chance of fulfillment which is offered to them. So his saying is the norm and the criterion for any Christian answer to the question of divorce. It is *not law*, for it goes to the heart of the *reality* of marriage.[2]

This question of divorce, let alone that of remarriage, has lain at the crux of the theology of marriage, perhaps wrongly so, but it must be dealt with, because it is Jesus' only allusion to marriage per se. An insight from C. S. Lewis provides perspective on the church's use—both the early church and the recent church—of this and Matthew's text on divorce in lieu of a solid theology of marriage. Lewis writes: "When you and I met, the meeting was over very shortly, it was nothing. Now it is growing into something as we remember it. What it will be when I remember it as I lie down to die, what it makes in me all my days till then—that is the real meaning. The other is only the beginning of it." The church takes these few words of Jesus about marriage and over the centuries makes meaning out of them.

Mark puts Jesus' saying on divorce and marriage in a catechetical presentation on divorce, children, and riches, following the announcement of the passion and death of Jesus and the demands of discipleship. Divorce in the Jewish community was taken for granted, which means the text is geared specifically toward Christians who are already dealing with the reality of marriage and its failure in different ways. Jesus quotes Genesis on the meaning of marriage: "At the beginning of creation God made them male and female; for this reason a man shall leave his father and mother and the two shall become as one. They are no longer two but one flesh. Therefore let no man separate what God has joined." His disciples find this teaching hard to take, yet Jesus continues by saying that the law holds not only for women but men also (Mk 10:2-12, *NAB*).

Matthew allows divorce in the case of adultery by the one partner (it is because of his Jewish background that he speaks only of unfaithfulness by the woman). But on the other hand he critically confronts the Jewish divorce "for any cause" with the irrevocable unity of marriage rooted in Genesis 1:2. He evidently knows cases where the unity of marriage can be so destroyed by the unfaithfulness of one partner that it *defacto* ceases to exist, with the result that remarriage is possible. It is true that rabbinical discussion may not have been without its influence on him here, but there is no doubt at all of the fact that he intends this solution of his to be understood as a commandment of the Lord. The irrevocable unity of marriage stands in Matthew as a *theological postulate* in tension with that unity which men have to realize *in their own history*, and often enough cannot realize it properly.[3]

History continues and

> Paul is confronted with the reality of marriage between pagans and Christians and its failure. He makes it clear that the Christian is bound to keep the Lord's "commandment" if the pagan party does not want the divorce. But if his partner does want it, the Christian is released from his obligation. Paul accepts the historical situation in which the Christian is put by the decision of his partner. . . . So in principle both of these factors must be given proper weight in any interpretation: the demand for irrevocable unity in marriage *and* the situation in which man finds himself. This . . . calls for development of the discussion not only in the field of theology but in that of canon law as well, so that we too in our present-day church practice may do justice to the demand made by Jesus and to its interpretation in the New Testament.[4]

Hoffman was published in 1970, and since then many exegesis accounts have further substantiated his basic premises.

Perhaps two more statements on the reality/sacramentality of marriage will serve as a basis for what follows. Denis O'Callaghan writes:

> The relationship of husband and wife is not that of one against the other, a tension characteristic of justice, but of both together, a union characteristic of love. When Vatican II defined marriage as a community of love it effectively endorsed the view of those theologians who claimed that love was not something to be forced in among the so-called secondary purposes of marriage. The community of love, the two-in-one-ness of the partners is not just a purpose of marriage, it is the very essence of the marriage institution. This is what marriage *is* in its own right before *being for* anything.[5]

O'Callaghan quotes the words of Cardinal Bellarmine, which Pius XI used in describing the sacrament:

> The sacrament of marriage may be considered in two ways; in the moment of its accomplishment and in its permanency afterwards. This sacrament, in fact, is similar to the Eucharist, which likewise is a sacrament not only in the moment of its accomplishment, but also as long as it remains. For as long as husband and wife live their association is always the sacrament of Christ and of the church. So "marriage is a permanent sacrament, not in the sense that the married relationship continues and perpetuates the sacramental force of consent, but in the sense that this relationship is the sacrament first and foremost in its own right."[6]

The church needs to learn how to preach the mystery of man and woman in marriage, monogamous and indissoluble, as a prophetic demand for Christians. At the same time it needs to realize the situation in particular marriages, as well as the call and announcement of forgiveness and repentance in the gospel. The church needs to work out an ethos that is faithful to the gospel, which upholds the dignity of individuals and encourages freedom and graceful existence, rather than rely on the law to gauge faithfulness in marriage.

Marriage is the Christian's choice for a life of friendship and faithfulness. Where does one begin? There is an ancient prayer in the Jewish community recited on a wedding day and every day afterward.

> Seven bindings on my forearm each morning remind
>   me
> that seven times the bride circles the groom:
>
> I bind myself to You forever.
> I bind myself to You in righteousness, in justice,
> in kindness, and in mercy,
> I bind myself to You in faithfulness,
> and You shall know the Lord.

Marriage allows one to draw so near as to absorb, without losing personal integrity, the other person's presence. This is the ritual and the reality of marriage. In *Letters on Love* Rainer Maria Rilke reminds us of the beginning and the process that unfolds:

Marriage is not a matter of creating a quick community of spirit by tearing down and destroying all boundaries, but rather a good marriage is one in which each appoints the other guardian of his solitude. . . . Once the realization is accepted that even between the closest human beings infinite distances continue to exist, a wonderful living side by side can grow up, if they succeed in loving the distance between them no less than one another.

I hold this to be the highest task of a bond between two people: that each should stand guard over the solitude of the other. For, if it lies in the nature of indifference and of the crowd to recognize no solitude, then love and friendship are there for the purpose of continually providing the opportunity for solitude. And only those are the true sharings which rhythmically interrupt periods of deep isolation.

This notion of friendship is not easy. For Christians it demands much more, just as the spirit extends the letter of the law. Teresa of Avila warned her sisters: "You will be immediately told that speaking with . . . [a friend] is unnecessary, that it is enough to have God. But a good means to God is to speak with His friends." "To be, rather than to seem to be, a friend of God" (Gregory of Nazianzus) is indeed the issue. Marriage for Christians is covenant bonding between the friends of God.

Aelred Squire quotes an old woman who lived in the Blaskets off the Atlantic coast of Ireland who speaks of friendship:

We helped each other and lived in the shelter of each other. Everything that was coming dark upon us, we would disclose to each other, and that would give us consolation of mind. Friendship was the fastest root in our hearts.[7]

This kind of friendship is a discipline, an art form, forged out of time, experience, and opposition to the world, as well as shared promises, hope, and freedom. It is the shared discipline of learning to become saints, friends of God.

We inevitably show ourselves to each other by reflecting, or failing to reflect, real possibilities which no one but we ourselves can realize. It can become a common task, valuable to both parties where friendship is real and intimate, to ground our dreams and canalize our energies into authentic, healthy growth. The best of many human lives runs to waste for want of a discipline informed by the insight of love.[8]

Friendship begins with simple human feeling, with need. This need, this sharing of human dignity, carves spaces in both friends. Thomas More struggled with his responsibilities to his family, his conscience, and his God, as well as to the Crown. In a scene depicted by Robert Bolt in "A Man for All Seasons," More is in prison and his wife, Alice, brings him lunch. He eats, complimenting her on the food and her dress. They are polite yet awkward as he tells her he must remain faithful to his convictions and that he needs for her to tell him that she understands. But she doesn't, and she wounds him by retorting that "his death is no good to her" and that she fears that after he dies she will hate him for what he has done. More breaks down and reveals his vulnerability, his struggle for honesty and the price it is exacting in his own heart and in his relationship with his wife: "You mustn't, you . . . " And then she holds him, "Shh . . . (like a mother and child). . . . As for understanding, I understand you're the best man that I ever met or am likely to." Then in anger she yells that she would tell the king and his council a thing or two if they wanted to know what she thinks. And he responds jubilantly: "Why it's a lion I married! A lion." Their friendship holds and human dignity is served even in the face of hardship and death. Squire points out that this connection among human dignity, politics, and friendship is intricate.

> For that each human being has a dignity which ought not to be publicly alienated is a presupposition for friendship, as we shall speak here, to exist at all. No political system can prevent people from choosing to fall below their human dignity in one way or another. And in a society in which the quality of life is not enriched by the practice of the virtues which friendship encourages, it is quite likely that human dignity *will* tend to fall low. But a relationship of warmth between a few, bought at the price of acquiescing in gross human injustice to the many, cannot be and does not deserve to be called friendship at all. . . . When it was suggested that situations *could* arise in which friendship might become the ultimate defense of human dignity, this was a remark based on the unhappy observation of political fact that situations already exist in many places in the world in which the right of friends to live and die for each other's good is the only political right which has not been, and cannot finally be, denied them.[9]

Many countries testify to this friendship. Friends can be used spuriously as well as in defense of human dignity. In "A Man for All Seasons" the Common Man addresses the audience as "friends," saying, "It isn't difficult to keep alive, friends . . . just don't make trouble—or if you must make trouble, make the sort of trouble that's expected."

Peter, unfortunately, uses the word *friend* in just this way on the night of Jesus' trial when he replies to the one who challenges him on being with Jesus: "My friend, I do not know what you are talking about" (Lk 22:60). In that moment Peter betrays his true friend. This is the friend who prayed for him to hold fast and give example to the disciples, the friend who took him to the mountain to share his glory with him. This is the friend he was too afraid to acknowledge. But this friend is also the one who forgives him as he dies and later questions him so that he can say over and over again: "I love you." This friend is true.

This friend, Jesus, calls his disciples, calls us, "friends" at the last supper in John's gospel:

> As the Father has loved me, so I have loved you: remain in my love. You will remain in my love if you keep my commandments, just as I have kept my Father's commandments and remain in his love. I have told you all this, that my own joy may be in you and your joy may be complete. This is my commandment: love one another as I have loved you. There is no greater love than this, to give one's life for his friends and you are my friends if you do what I command you. . . . I shall not call you servants any more, because a servant does not know what his master is about. Instead I call you friends, since I have made known to you everything I learned from my Father. . . . You did not choose me; it was I who chose you and sent you to go and bear much fruit, fruit that will last. And everything you ask the Father in my name, he will give you. . . . So I tell you to love one another (Jn 15:9-17) .

To be friends of Jesus is no easy task. To begin is to commit ourselves wholeheartedly to becoming Christians, followers of Jesus, intent on centering our life around God. But what is friendship? Cicero defined it as "an accord on things human and divine, accompanied by good will and love."[10] Such accord could hardly be more completely fulfilled than in those sentences on the life of the early church that appear in Acts and have been frequently cited as the basis of the common monastic life. But this sharing of life, love, goods, and worship is also the form of marriage. Aelred of Rievaulx writes, "The source and origin of friendship is love, that is to say, that love is presupposed to friendship, though they are not the same thing. For love can exist without friendship, though friendship can never exist without love." Aelred makes it clear how extensively we must understand the concept of love: "This must mean that a friend is the keeper of one's love or of one's very soul."[11]

The nature of this soul-keeping is rigorous and extensive. It entails trust, confidence, acceptance, and belief in the other. It requires time, forgiveness, sharing, respect, and tenderness. There is a touch of the everlasting about it. This kind of friendship is rare, priceless. It is "useless" in the sense of any other meaning to the friendship than the love and relationship itself, as in the sacrament of marriage, the sacrament of faithful friends. Love between friends, between husband and wife, is the end and purpose of the relationship, nothing more or less. Love and its expression in life are intimately bound together. Love not expressed dies. Our friendship with those we would commit to with all our heart, those for whom we would lay down our life, must bear fruit. Our love must be visible, expressed, shared, and passed on.

Squire encourages his readers to try such friendship:

> Not only does friendship help life along, so that by joining shoulders we bear each other's burdens; it is, in fact, only one step short of the knowledge and love of God. With its help, [Aelred of Rievaulx writes,] "from being the friend of man one becomes the friend of God, according to that word of the Lord in the gospel: No longer do I call you servants but friends." . . . True friendship can only arise between the good, grow between those who are growing and reach its fullness between those who are spiritually mature. . . . For it is not difficult to show from experience that friendship cannot survive between people who cannot depend on each other's uprightness. . . . That man has not yet learned what friendship is, who wants of it any other reward than itself.[12]

There are practices to consider in such a relationship if it is to be lasting and true. In order for such a friendship to be stable it requires careful and free choice, and "a sensible period of probation before the door can be opened to its fullest development." Squire names four things one must know about friends: 1) their capacity for fidelity, 2) what they expect from the relationship, 3) the integrity to be able to love another as you love yourself, and 4) patience and mutual help in growing. The element of integrity is possibly the most crucial. Only if we have personal integrity can we really love the other and care for his or her good first and foremost. To share another's soul is demanding and a discipline that does not come quickly. This kind of intimacy, this kind of sharing of souls, has to be kept alive and true by prayer, by God. Squire describes such a relationship:

> At the beginning, although Christ is, as it were, in principle present with the two who are talking, he is there perhaps most because they desire not to exclude him. Later, through the caring for each other throughout the mysteries of life and development, Christ becomes almost palpably present. [Aelred of Rievaulx writes:] "And so, praying to Christ for his friend, and longing to be heard by Christ for his friend's sake, he reaches out with devotion and desire to Christ himself. . . . As though touched by the gentleness of Christ close at hand, he begins to taste how sweet he is and to feel how lovely he is. Thus, from that holy love by which he embraces his friend, he rises to that by which he embraces Christ." Because of this utter openness created by true caring, the two can look forward to that condition of things where no one any longer needs to hide his secrets, and where that which one can share with only a few on earth can be shared by everyone and God be "all in all."
>
> To many in today's world this sounds impossible, unthinkable, very romantic, and idealistic, certainly unworkable in a marriage or committed public sacrament. But the tradition of the church is other: John Climacus, a Syrian monk in the sixth century has this to say about those who fail and yet still attempt to love.
>
> Those who have been humbled by their passions may take courage. For even if they fall into every pit and are trapped in all the snares and suffer all maladies, yet after their restoration to health they become physicians, beacons, lamps and pilots for all.[13]

What hope this offers to those in committed relationships and communities!

In the context of friendship like this the aspect of sexuality is seen to be a piece of the whole rather than the link that holds the relationship together. Intimacy on a physical and sexual basis is important but not overriding, and the ethical issues of birth control, separation, divorce, and remarriage are seen in the context of faithfulness. There is an old Chinese saying: I am interested in what remains after a pot is broken.

This is the context for looking at separation and divorce—as such a loss. If such a friendship did exist, then re-marriage is usually unthinkable. If one person betrayed such a relationship, it would be even more difficult to seek out such a sharing of soul again.

Perhaps this is where a pastoral response to the situation existing today is necessary—a period of probation where each person may ascertain whether he or she is capable of such a friendship, intent on such intimacy and fidelity, and willing to accept the consequences of failure—no remarriage. Or there is a variant on the pastoral response of the Eastern churches—to remarry again after a sufficient period of time, penance, reflection, and conversion, knowing that a second marriage is different from the first, not so clear in its symbolism of the relation between Christ and the church. It is more a symbol of the kingdom here, not in fullness yet, struggling for a foothold in the world, but a sacrament nonetheless because two Christians bind themselves together in Christ for the kingdom.

Such a friendship, such a sharing of souls, is recorded in the Book of Ruth. Although it is often used as one of the readings at a marriage celebration, it speaks of love and intimacy between a mother-in-law and her daughter-in-law rather than between a man and a woman. "Don't ask me to leave you. For I will go where you go and stay where you stay. Your people will be my people and your god my God. Where you die, there will I die and be buried. May Yahweh deal with me severely if anything except death separates us" (Ru 1:16:17). Such a friendship is also recorded in 1 and 2 Samuel, where "Jonathan's soul became closely bound to David's and Jonathan came to love him as his own soul. . . . Jonathan made a pact with David to love him as his own soul; he took off the cloak he was wearing and gave it to David, and his armor too, even his sword, his bow and his belt" (1 Sm 18:1, 3). These gifts are symbols of vulnerability, openness. They indicate a willingness to share all with his friend, his soul-keeper. The quality of such love is grace itself.

James Finley talks about love and what it does for us:

> Love is the epiphany of God in our poverty. By our love and our need for love we become for one another midwives of the true self. In our response to the outstretched hand we touch the infinite. Our real gurus, our real spiritual directors are those people in our life who place upon us unexpected, unexplainable burdens.[14]

Thomas Merton describes his own soul:

The true self is like a very shy wild animal that never appears at all whenever an alien presence is at hand, and comes out only when all is peaceful, in silence, when s/he is untroubled and alone. S/he cannot be lured by anyone or anything, because he responds to no lure except that of the divine freedom.

This is the soul that is shared in such a friendship, such a sacrament. This is the soul that is treasured, protected, and kept secretly as one's own soul though it belongs to another. One begins to see and hear more than words, or, as Emerson puts it, "A friend does not listen so much to what is said as to the silence." This kind of friendship is worthy of marriage, of faithfulness unto death in the Christian community, revealing in the two people the reality of the love of God. It is this kind of relationship that looks at the ethical demands of commitment in marriage, at children, and knows in its heart what is expected and commanded. In such a relationship there will be terrible pain, and equally terrible joy and delight. Such nakedness and openness will reveal over time both weaknesses and strengths and will form both partners into an image of friends of God that reveals marriage as the kingdom present here and now as well as struggling to survive in the world.

Again, as with all the other sacraments, we must see the sacrament of marriage in relation to the church and to baptism and eucharist. This kind of friendship is a sacrament because in it and through it the kingdom of God becomes a living experience. But any sacrament receives its true reality and meaning only if it leads to or expresses the corporate life of the church, the body of Christ, and the kingdom. For the first twelve centuries of the church marriage was celebrated between two Christians who participated in and celebrated eucharist and became the body of Christ. It is in the flesh of Christ that the flesh of two Christians can become flesh of each other. It is eucharist that binds the marriage of two believers, and in the eucharist they grow into the reality they proclaim. Like baptism and eucharist, marriage is ongoing, maturing, and transforming. It is marriage in the Lord rather than simply the social institution of marriage that contracts economic, sexual, and familial privileges within a legal system culturally defined. It is not just a blessing of a culturally acceptable ritual. Christians who marry, who bind themselves in this sort of friendship publicly, must always remain mindful of the vision their friendship announces and witnesses to for the church.

Perhaps the church should get out of the marriage "business" and allow the state to recognize that reality. Then Christians who wish to marry, to commit themselves to this friendship in Christ may, when their friendship and binding in Christ is a reality that is different from the world's understanding of marriage and friendship, celebrate the sacrament of friends as an alternative to the world's experience.

It is here, among adult Christians struggling to follow Christ, that the church needs to be converted herself, compassionately to recognize the dissolution of marriage and pastorally to respond to the sufferings of so many couples, children, and families. For it is the fault of the church itself that has not supported marriages but primarily legislated them; it has not prepared adult Christians for the unique demands of the sacrament but assumed that all would grow into the demands of the gospel without help, conversion, and constant care. We need to approach this sacrament and its preparation with at least as much tender care, hope, love, and serious attention as we provide catechumens. We can start by marveling at marriages within the church that are maturing and growing in spite of the lack of nurturing and unreasonable demands made upon the relationship.

There are so many stories for marriage, friendship, for faithfulness that call us to remember that Jesus calls us friends. This story is for friends, singular in their devotions to each other, and for all Christians called to faithfulness, man and woman, those in community, and those who remain single, all who would be the friends of God, women together, men with one another, the basis for all love in Christ.

✟ Once upon a time, long, long ago in China, there were two friends, one who played the harp skillfully and one who listened skillfully. When the one played about a mountain, the other would say, "I can see the mountain before me." When the instrument called forth a storm and the calm that followed, the one who listened would say, "Yes, I am battered and then released and breathed easily upon." When the notes rippled water, the one who listened would cry out, "Yes, I hear and see the stream, the waterfall, the wave." They grew so together. They were one mind, heart, flesh and hope. Inseparable.

Then the listener died. After a long period of mourning, the musician went back to playing. But the music was flat, dead and lifeless. The form and the skill remained, but the spirit had fled. He could not play no matter how much he practiced, no matter how often other listeners begged him to perform and suggested that he go on with his life.

The musician went back to his home and took down all his musical instruments—harps, violins, guitars, mandolins—and cut their strings. He never played again. Since that time the cutting of harp strings has always been a sign of intimate friendship.[15]

Here is a story for husbands and wives, again from the Eastern traditions:

✛ Once upon a time, long ago in the land of the rising sun, there lived a woman called Kyoko. Her name meant "shining one," for she was radiant from within, fair of face, and gentle toward all. She shone in wisdom and knowledge.

She troubled many, for she was married to a man who was fearsomely ugly and deformed. His hair was untamed, and nothing shone forth from his face that spoke of soul and spirit. People were repulsed.

But the couple were devoted to each other, tender in their regard, and obviously in love and happy. There were always whispers and wonderings about them.

This, they say, was how the marriage came to be. Kyoko had been a princess, the only daughter of a wise ruler who had taught her to read and write, to make music, to watch the stars, and to live compassionately. Because she was an only child, he prepared her to receive the kingdom. The man she would marry would be king, but she would choose, and so the ruler made sure that she knew the world and its wonders and knowledge.

One day a new teacher was needed, for the princess was maturing and had outgrown her old mentor. The king was distraught. He wanted to make sure that she kept learning and that there was no chance for her to fall in love with her teacher. He breathed a sigh of relief when Munakata applied for the position. He was ugly, deformed, and monstrous, but brilliant and possessed of wisdom and words. There would be no fear that Kyoko would fall in love! The tutoring began. Munakata lived in a house full of books, paintings, scrolls, art, and flowers, a house full of light open to the seasons and the stars. Kyoko was a willing student and immersed herself in such knowledge and beauty, awed by her teacher, but also feeling more and more sorry for him, pitying him. It was a shame that one so knowledgeable and so gracious was also so repulsive and horrible to look at. She wept for his curse and fate, because she had come to know the depth of his goodness and insight as well.

One day, while they were studying, Munakata spoke, "I know what you are thinking about me and we must speak. There is knowledge of experience, of things, knowledge of feelings and relationships and knowledge of spirit, of mystery. I want to tell you a story." Immediately Kyoko's face brightened. He told such good stories!

"Remember that before we are born, all of us keep company with the angels of heaven. It is a time of joy and awe. Then the time comes when we are to be born and the name of our beloved, the one we will search for and spend our lives with, is revealed to us. An angel speaks the name and then seals that desire and yearning within us with a finger pressed to our lips. It is a secret in our flesh, and in that instant we forget the name, for as human beings we must find the other through our feelings and our soul. That is why each of us is born with a slight depression in the skin above our mouths. It is where the angel touched us so fleetingly. So, since before we are born, we know.

"Of course, you know from looking at me that I have no depression above my lips. My face is deformed and twisted. You see, when I was with the angels before I was born, something strange happened. The time came for me to come to earth. The angel approached me to speak the name of my beloved and touch me, sealing the memory deep inside me. As the name was spoken by the Holy, the angel cried out in distress, gasping in horror. In fact, all the angels moaned and cried, looking at me with great pity. I could not bear it. I pulled away from the angel, demanding an explanation. There was none. There could not be. It was not allowed. But I would not obey. I would not be born until my questions were answered. I was in despair, angry and afraid. What was wrong with the one I was born to love? I demanded to see her. Finally, the angels agreed, for the Holy One allowed it. A vision was given to me and now it was I who was crying out in distress, for she was ugly, misshapen, horrible to look at, with warts and bruises. She was to be mine."

It was silent in the small house. The sun had left and dusk was slowly bathing the room with shadows and dark. He went on: "I knew instantly what I had to do. I demanded to see God. Unthinkable, but again they did not know how to resist my anger and cries. In an instance I stood in the presence of the Holy, overcome and mute. But then I spoke, garbled words, inchoate feelings, and a demand. My heart cried out: 'Make me that way, not her. Be kind to her, please.' So it was done. I was born, and the angel forgot to touch my lips or speak the name. I had become so terrible that even the angel didn't want to touch me."

It was quiet and dark now. After a long silence Munakata spoke again. "So you see, I am this way because of my own demand. I remember it all because the angel shrank from me, repulsed and pitying me."

Kyoko understood. Time passed and she grew in wisdom and knowledge and in love, for now she knew that she was lovely and fair because of his request. What was intended for her had been taken on by him. They became friends, inseparable, and they married. This was how it came to be, or so the story goes.

A friend of mine supplied a definition of such friendship: "A friend is someone that I would go to the cross with." I was stunned. The essence in a nutshell, the meat to be dug out with care, breaking open the shell and eating it, savoring it. The sacrament of friendship binds together those who would go to the cross with one another. It is a sacrament for all adult believers: those who marry, those who are single, those who live in a community. It is for all the friends who would be friends of God.

This kind of love, faithful devotion, and intimacy is the basis of a great and lasting Jewish tradition called the Shekhinah, the divine presence in exile, often referred to as the princess, the daughter of God who is King:

✢ It is said that once upon a time, in the beginning, the King ruled in heaven and his daughter was made entirely of light. The King had two thrones: one of justice and one of mercy. He could be demanding and just, but he could be tenderhearted and protective as well. The princess grew up, and the King sent her out into the world to breathe grace and blessings upon the earth and the people.

The princess, made of light, was usually invisible. She came and went in visions, dreams, sunrises and sunsets, sometimes in prayer and times of need. She came as light, a princess, a bride; sometimes as the divine presence hovering over a house, a person, a place of sanctuary; or was glimpsed flying over the Temple in Jerusalem. The sight of her gave heart and soul to the people, and they prayed in gratitude for her visitation, for they knew that the King was always aware of her and was close by them as well.

But one day the Temple in Jerusalem was destroyed and the people were forced into exile, weeping for all that was lost. The princess too was heartbroken and joined her people, dressed in rags and tatters. She had to go with them. Her father understood.

Time passed and a decree went forth from the King: "Anyone who can find my daughter in exile will wed her and exaltation will be proclaimed through all heaven and earth. The day of their wedding will be a time of rejoicing and coming home for all. But she will not be easy to find. She is a secret, hidden in and among the people, but she is always there with them."

Many princes tried to find her; they searched the earth, its wild reaches, back alleys, and courts of kings; the winding roads and hillside caves; in the inns and the homes of the poor. No one found her. But there was one prince who sat very still and dreamed and thought and prayed: where could she be? Hidden and yet present with the people? The prince knew a friend, a great and wise rabbi, and went to him saying: "How can this princess be so well hidden and yet so present with the people?"

The rabbi startled him with the answer. "There is only one thing that is well hidden among the Jewish people and yet present and powerful. That is the Torah, the words of the Holy One." The prince knew he was close, but he did not know the Torah and asked to learn, to be apprenticed to the rabbi. He became a student, a disciple of the Torah. Years passed, then decades, and the Torah seeped into him like air and moved through him like the blood in his veins. He was in love with the Torah! And he found her there, hidden in the words, and he came to understand the secrets therein. Often he would catch glimpses of the princess made of light and hope and his eyes would grow bright with wisdom and compassion.

The prince now knows where she is hidden. What remains is to set her free for all the world. He will, and he knows that the King, her beloved father, has promised to rebuild the Temple, bring the people back from exile and set up a light to the nations. The King will bring her home, and on the day of her wedding all the world will rejoice and all will be bound in *shalom* and wisdom. He knows the secret of freeing her is hidden in the Torah. He knows and searches for his beloved, his friend, the woman of light.[16]

When we remember that this story is not about a man or a woman but about the presence of God in exile with the people, about God's covenant of faithfulness and friendship with us, then we know that we dwell in a sacred place. The Shekhinah is this exiled presence of God with us but also the bride of God waiting for embrace and communion. The Shekhinah waits with us for God's embrace and fullness of love and unity. We are all friends of God.

The sacrament of friendship, of binding the friends of God, is more than marriage as it is celebrated in society. It is a qualitatively different relationship among those who are believers in God, bound in Jesus to the Father in the power of the Spirit. It is a sacrament for adult Christians, all adult Christians who wish to commit themselves to another in this kind of binding public friendship. The initial blessing for a rite of marriage after the civil ceremony would be one rite. The rite of marriage would be one rite, second marriage another; there would be a rite for those who remain single, for those in religious communities, and those who wish to dedicate their friendship with another to the honor of God and the coming of the kingdom in the community's presence, and a rite for widows and widowers (see chapter 10). Faithfulness is the essence of and the maturation of our baptisms. It is the lifestyle of love that enfleshes eucharist in our bodies. It is the sacrament of the friends of God.

9

Orders for the Sacrament of Foot Washing

The Choice for Life with Obedience

What is a priest? Perhaps this question has taken on more significance since Vatican II because of the enormous response of the laity to the Council and its subsequent involvement in the ministries of the church. Priests themselves are rethinking what it means to be a priest. Vincent Donovan comments in light of his own experience:

> What is a priest? Is he a sacramentalist? Or a prophet? Or a preacher? Or a blesser? Or a specialist of the world within? Or an expert and authority in some other specialized area? Or is he not simply a man taken from among men, to stand for them, to signify and focus for them the meaning of life of the people of God in community?
>
> There was a time when I thought priest meant missionary or evangelist, or at least an essential component of both. For a full year I was evangelizing pagan Masai. There was no Christian community at all. At the beginning of that year I faithfully got in my Mass early every morning in the privacy and secrecy of my tent— all by myself. Then the question occurred to me: What did a Mass mean with no Christians and no Christian community in existence? So for the rest of that year I realized I was not a priest, and I yearned for the end of the year, for the baptisms that would bring a new Christian community into existence, so that I could be a priest again, so that I could be their priest. It was only when that Christian community did come into existence that I realized numbly that I would never be the priest to that community. They would have to have their own focal point, their own animator, their own sign of unity. They would have to have a priest of their own.

I began to see that this pattern could be repeated over and over again in a missionary's life. It was only then I knew that a missionary did not have to be a priest at all.[1]

This is the feeling and belief of many in the church today, priest and lay person alike. The essence of priesthood is being the focus, the symbol of unity of a community. The priest is the gatherer, the animator, the shepherd, or, better yet, the sheep-gate, the open door into the community. The other ministries can and should be done by others. The confusion of functions and roles only serves to disrupt the community and to cause the power of the sacrament and the person to be blurred and ineffectual.

More than thirty years ago the Second Vatican Council signaled a shift in the church's understanding of itself and the way it lives in the world. Its documents called the laity to ministry within the church and to the transformation of the world at large, to work for justice and the coming of the good news to all. With the influx of lay ministries and roles, the priesthood began to experience an identity crisis and pangs of awareness. But still, thirty years later, though the experiences of priesthood have changed for many, the reality and the concept of a priest and his work have not. Donovan is clear in his examination of the state of priesthood.

A bigger change . . . is called for, a change in which the importance of priests would no longer be measured by their position alone, or by the fact that they occupy such a position, but rather by the way they fulfill the meaning of that position, by carrying out their function in the community—just as it is measured for every other Christian.

We have condensed all the hope and dignity and power and glory of Christianity into the narrow confines of a single individual. This is an obvious distortion. To remedy that distortion of Christianity we simply must move in a different direction, without abandoning the substance of Christianity in the process. All and everything we believed about the priest is true—as true of the Christian community as it is of him. It is not so much that priests must decrease, as that Christians must increase. . . . One wonders if that increase will ever be allowed to happen.[2]

What is a priest without a community? Can a person be a functioning symbol of community if he or she is appointed to a community rather than arising from within the body of believers? Does the power of the priesthood reside in the person or in the community that singles out that person to be its gatherer, pastor, its focus of unity? Do half a dozen priests gathering for liturgy in a religious community say anything about church? Does the priest—or should the priest—have other functions, or do other functions confuse the reality? Does being a high-school teacher, a college professor, a bishop without connection to a diocese, a social worker, a writer, a theologian have anything to do with priesthood if there is no community to hold together, to call together to worship, to gather together to initiate new Christians or to forgive and welcome people back to the community? Donovan says that "Christian witness in any field in which these people make contributions to the church is the proper arena of the priesthood of all believers, not of the ministerial priesthood. If the priesthood of all believers has no meaning here, it has no meaning at all."[3]

Scripturally there are many examples and suggestions for what priesthood consists in and the power and possibility of the priest as the one who pastors the community, who gathers and focuses the Spirit within the church. To begin with there is John the Baptizer. It is he who goes before the face of the Lord, to prepare his way; he points out to those who are seeking Jesus where to find him (Jn 1:35ff.). John's attitude is revelatory of priesthood: "I am not the Christ but I have been sent before him. Only the bridegroom has the bride; but the friend of the bridegroom stands by and listens, and rejoices to hear the bridegroom's voice. My joy is now full. It is necessary that he increase but that I decrease" (Jn 3:28b-30). Always it is the role of the one who unites to become invisible, decrease, not get in the way of the community.

Much of Jesus' teaching to his disciples, the leaders of his community-to-be, is about being small, about being like a child, a servant. He catches them out in their discussion about who is the most important in the group:

"What were you discussing on the way?" But they did not answer because they had been arguing about who was the greatest. Then he sat down, called the Twelve and said to them, "If anyone wants to be first, he must be the very last and make himself the servant of all." Then he took a little child, set him in the midst of them, and putting his arms around him said to them, "Whoever welcomes a child such as this in my name, welcomes me; and whoever welcomes me, welcomes not me but the One who sent me" (Mk 9:33-37).

Soon after he again speaks to his disciples, who are slow to understand what power or authority in his kingdom will look like:

> "As you know, the so-called rulers of the nations lord it over them and their great ones make their importance felt. But it shall not be so among you; whoever would be great among you must be your servant, and whoever would be first among you shall make himself slave of all. For the Son of Man has not come to be served but to serve and to give his life to redeem many" (Mk 10:42-45).

Jesus, we are told, is indignant that his disciples should be arguing over who gets the best places. The condition for power and authority in his kingdom is awful—it consists in "drinking the cup that he drinks and being baptized in the same bath of pain as he" (Mk 10:38, *NAB*).

In Luke's gospel the exhortation to such service, to such inconspicuousness, comes immediately after the celebration of the eucharist. Those who will "do this and remember" him must in their own persons reveal Jesus' way of power:

> "The kings of the pagan nations rule over them as lords, and the most hardhearted rulers claim the title, 'Gracious lord.' But not so with you, let the greatest among you become as the youngest, and the leader as the servant. For who is the greatest, he who sits at the table or he who serves? He who is seated. Yet I am among you as the one who serves" (Lk 22:25-27).

In John's gospel, instead of just repeating this commandment over and over again, Jesus takes up a towel and bends before his disciples, washing their feet. He tells them afterward that this is how they are to live and serve one another in community (Jn 13:1-17). Peter still is horrified that Jesus would kneel before him. He is slow to learn the power of God in Jesus Christ, power that bends, serves, and redeems by being lowly, washing the feet of betrayers, sinners, and those who remain faithful with equal care and regard.

To gather, to be pastor of the Christian community, is to model one's life and relationships on the Good Shepherd, the sheep-gate. The priest exists so that "others may have life and have it to the full," in imitation of Jesus who calls himself "the good shepherd; the good shepherd who lays down his life for the sheep" (Jn 10:11ff.). The work of the shepherd is unity, and the price of such unity is one's life, given freely. At the time of Jesus, the shepherd's body was the sheep-gate. The shepherd lay down between large stones so that the sheep would have to climb over him to leave and thieves and wild animals would have to go through his body to get to the sheep.

The prayer and work of the pastor is the prayer of Jesus at the last supper:

> I pray for them; I do not pray for the world but for those who belong to you and whom you have given to me—indeed all I have is yours and all you have is mine—and now they are my glory. I am no longer in the world, but they are in the world whereas I am going to you. Holy Father, keep them in your Name (that you have given me, so that they may be one, just as we are).
>
> When I was with them, I kept them safe in your Name. . . . But now I am coming to you and I leave my message in the world that my joy may be complete in them.
>
> I have given them your message and the world has hated them because they are not of the world; just as I am not of the world. I do not ask you to remove them from the world but to keep them from the evil one. They shall not be of the world, for I am not of the world.
>
> Consecrate them in the truth—your word is truth—for I have sent them into the world as you sent me into the world. For their sake, I go to the sacrifice by which I am consecrated, so that they too may be consecrated in truth.
>
> I pray not only for these but also for those who through their word will believe in me. May they all be one as you Father are in me and I am in you. May they be one in us, so the world may believe that you have sent me.
>
> I have given them the Glory you have given me, that they may be one as we are one: I in them and you in me. Thus they shall reach perfection in unity and the world shall know that you have sent me and that I have loved them just as you loved me (Jn 17:9-23).

The call to the priesthood is the call to give one's life for the unity of the church. It is an internal ministry, specifically directed toward the members of the believing community. It concentrates on prayer for the community, eucharist, reconciling members and drawing them back into the community, and the continuing revelation of the will of the Father and the work of unity. This unity is overwhelming in its vision—that the community of those who believe mirrors the unity of Jesus and his Father and Spirit. It is the work of communion, and the priest is its focus. Such an understanding is found in the ritual of ordination itself. As the newly ordained priest is given the gifts to celebrate eucharist, the bishop prays:

> Accept from the holy people of God the gifts to be
>   offered to him.
> Know what you are doing, and imitate the mystery
>   you celebrate;
> model your life on the mystery of the Lord's
>   cross (no. 26).[4]

In the prayer at the anointing of hands we hear:

> The Father anointed our Lord Jesus Christ
> through the power of the Holy Spirit.
> May Jesus preserve you to sanctify the Christian
> people and to offer sacrifice to God (no. 24).

The ritual of ordination helps us understand what is involved in the sacrament. It is the sharing of the Spirit (as in all the sacraments) by the church and singling out one person to offer sacrifice and become the reality of sacrifice that is proclaimed and celebrated in eucharist. It is a sacrament for ordering the way the church celebrates who and what it is.

The priest is described as a "co-worker with the bishops" (no. 22), and the priesthood is seen in relation to the office of bishops. The prayer of consecration of a bishop outlines the duties of this office:

> Father, you know all hearts,
> You have chosen your servant for the office of
>   bishop.
> May he be a shepherd to your holy flock,
> and a high priest blameless in your sight,
> ministering to you night and day;
> may he always gain the blessing of your favor and
> offer the gifts of your holy church.
> Through the Spirit who gives the grace of high-
> priesthood grant him the power

> to forgive sins as you have commanded,
> to assign ministries as you have decreed,
> and to loose every bond by the authority which you
>   gave
> to your apostles.
> May he be pleasing to you by his gentleness and
>   purity of heart,
> presenting a fragrant offering to you,
> through Jesus Christ, your Son,
> through whom glory and power and honor are yours
> with the Holy Spirit in your holy church
> now and forever. Amen (no. 26).

Priests are also compared in the ordination rite to the elders who accompanied Moses (Nm 11:16-17).

In the early church there were only dioceses and towns.

> As the church expanded, in smaller communities presbyters in fact took over the episcopal "leadership and priesthood" within their communities. From that stage on—differing from one area to another—presbyters too gradually came to be called sacerdotes. As a result, sacramentally the difference between bishop and presbyter really became problematical: a pastor is as it were bishop of a parish.[5]

The ordination of a deacon by the first half of the third century was even more a question of ordering church affairs, because at that time "a deacon was exclusively at the disposal of the bishop and not of the presbyters. . . . His charism remains 'open'; he receives his spiritual charism 'on the authority of the bishop'; thus he can and may do everything which the bishop specifically requires him to do."[6] Today the ordination of a deacon reveals some more specific duties and responsibilities. In the exhortation or teaching prior to the ordination rite itself the deacon's functions are laid out:

> He will help the bishop and his body of priests as a minister of the word, of the altar, and of charity. He will make himself a servant to all. As a minister of the altar he will proclaim the Gospel, prepare the sacrifice, and give the Lord's body and blood to the community of believers.

It will also be his duty, at the bishop's discretion, to bring God's word to believer and unbeliever alike, to preside over public prayer, to baptize, to assist at marriage and bless them, to give viaticum to the dying, and to lead the rites of burial. Once he is consecrated by the laying on of hands that comes to us from the apostles and is bound more closely to the altar, he will perform works of charity in the name of the bishop or the pastor. From the way he goes about these duties, may you recognize him as a disciple of Jesus, who came to serve, not to be served (no. 13).

In return, he commits himself to celibacy (a sign and motive of pastoral charity and special source of spiritual fruitfulness in the world). The emphasis in the rite is on personal transformation:

> Believe what you read
> teach what you believe,
> and practice what you teach (no. 24).

Specifically, the deacon is called to "love that is sincere, concern for the sick and the poor, unassuming authority and self-discipline and holiness of life" (no. 21). His conduct is to lead people to imitation. From the ritual of ordination we see that the duties of bishop, priest, and deacon are related to the altar, and because of the liturgy are extended outward to certain groups of people: the bishop to his diocese and as sign of unity to the larger, universal church; the priest to his parish, in communion with the bishop and other priests; and the deacon to the bishop and priests and in their name caregivers, especially to the poor and the sick. Schillebeeckx calls them a "specialized team" of leadership at an "official level." Leadership is tied to celebration or presiding at the eucharist as a sign of unity with the larger church. It is "the service of leading the community, and therefore as an ecclesial function within the community and accepted by the community."[7]

The sacrament of ordination reveals the history of the church over the last two thousand years—its development, side-trips, and creative innovations. Specifically it reveals two tracks: functions that define church-on-church relations, and functions that define those "chosen for the service of the offering."[8] The first is a hierarchical ordo that suggests that power comes through the bishop and directs the church members and ministries, especially those in regard to liturgy. At the beginning of development in the church there was a great deal of flexibility in organization and imaginative responses to new experiences. Ministerial forms shifted in response to the dual needs to fulfill the group's vocation and serve the group's needs. There were the apostles, prophets, teachers, presbyters, deacons, subdeacons, and so on. As the church operates now, all charisms given to believers, as well as all ministries, are bound into the structures of leadership tied to ordination and the ordering of functions of the church.

At Vatican II the church attempted to describe church ministries according to three ancient functions: the pastoral function—leadership in the community; the priestly function—liturgy in the community; and the prophetic function—proclaiming the word in the community.[9] But since Vatican II new forms of pastoral service and lay ministries have arisen, and ordained priests and deacons have shifted into other occupations and roles. With this historical phenomena crucial theological and structural questions have arisen regarding the sacrament of ordination, ministries and charisms. David Power poses some of these questions:

1. In what way is the episcopacy, as the primary form of church office, related to the apostolic church, and what other forms of office are consonant with Christian tradition and apostolic beginnings?

2. What is the link between community and ordination, and to what extent does ordination in and for, and with the recognition of, a community pertain to the legitimacy of church office?

3. What is the link between charism and office, or to what extent may charism be said to precede appointment to office, and what does this have to say to the question of power exercised by an office-holder?

4. Can there be offices which are directly related to baptism, rather than to the structures of leadership associated with ordination, and what are the appropriate forms of recognition for such offices?[10]

This last question is perhaps the most crucial but cannot be seriously dealt with until the others are clarified. Already many are looking at dynamic and creative ways to deal with the confusion and exclusion the existing structures can create. In December 1977 forty-seven members of the Roman Catholic Church in Chicago issued a brief document entitled "The Chicago Declaration of Christian Concern."

In brief the Declaration expressed regret that since the Second Vatican Council, the distinct and proper roles and responsibilities of the laity had ceased to be appreciated and promoted. Instead, the advancement of the laity in the church had taken the form of their "greater participation in work traditionally assigned to priests and sisters"; "lay ministry" had come to be seen as "involvement in some church related activity." Meanwhile, the "unique ministry of lay men and women" which is "essentially the service performed within one's professional and occupational milieu" not only had been neglected but had in many cases been taken over by the clergy and religious. . . . Priest and religious no longer saw their role as encouraging the laity to assume their proper responsibility "to transform the world of political, economic and social institutions." They often neglected the laity and undertook the task themselves. The result had been not only the decline of the laity in the world, but a depreciation of the role of the ordinary layperson in his worldly occupation and even, perhaps, "the loss of a generation of lay leadership."[11]

Pope John Paul II has also sought to look more closely at the separation of laity and clergy, though for very different reasons. In Puebla, Mexico, in 1979 he said:

It is necessary to avoid supplanting the laity, and to study seriously just when certain ways of substituting for them retain their *raison d'être*. Is it not the laity who are called, by virtue of their vocation in the church, to make their contribution in the political and economic areas, and to be effectively present in safeguarding and advancing of human rights?[12]

He has also spoken bluntly to priests:

You are not social directors, political leaders or functionaries of a temporal power. So I repeat to you: Let us not pretend to serve the gospel if we try to "dilute" our charism through an exaggerated interest in the broad field of temporal problems. . . . Do not forget that temporal leadership can easily become a source of division, while the priest should be a sign of factor of unity, of brotherhood. The secular functions are the proper field of action of the laity, who ought to perfect temporal matters with a Christian spirit.[13]

These statements reflect clearly the confusion of roles, ministries, and charisms within the church. In addition, the church at the Vatican Council extended more ministries to the laity, even in the understanding of sharing the office of the church:

> From now on [an ecclesiastical office] should be understood as any function which has been permanently assigned and is to be exercised for a spiritual purpose (PO 20). Not only clerics but also lay persons can participate in this official ministry: "Finally, the hierarchy entrusts to the laity some functions which are more closely connected with pastoral duties, such as the teaching of Christian doctrine, certain liturgical actions and the care of souls. By virtue of this mission, the laity are fully subject to higher ecclesiastical direction in the performance of such work" (AA 24).[14]

The church is struggling to define church-world relationships and clergy-lay relationships, and ministry is where the lack of distinctions is most acute. The reality is that church ministry is too "official"—limiting, exclusive, and not indicative of much ministry that is being done in the church. Neither does it reflect the reality that those ordained to a specific function do not necessarily fulfill that function adequately or in conjunction with a community, while those who obviously have the gift of the Spirit to preach, teach, forgive, care for souls, and care for the poor and the sick are not ordained. The problem is becoming more complicated because of issues of academics and the professionalization of ministries that are not ordained, in an attempt to make them more "official." This whole question will be dealt with more substantially in the next chapter, but it must be noted that accreditation and/or academic credentials as alternatives to ordination only complicate the issue.

There are a number of projects facing the church in the area of orders:

1. The encouragement, empowerment and recognition of "lay" ministries—what are they?—and their subsequent integration into the traditional ordained ministries;
2. A distinction between ministries performed solely for the internal church and those ordained by the church for the world as witness and evangelization;
3. The full participation of all adult believers, especially women, in ministries;
4. The recognition of legitimate ministries in other churches;

5. The distinction between professional ministries and service-oriented ministries, both recognized and confirmed by the community;
6. The recognition of the person ordained in the context or calling of the community;
7. The ethical demands that ordination to any of these ministries truly celebrates what is already a reality in the community;
8. The connection between baptism and ministry rather than the association of ministry with ordination.

These projects hold within them the ethical demands of the sacrament of orders in the church today. The challenges face not only the hierarchy, those aspiring to ordination, and those ministering in any number of capacities—education, theology, pastoral counseling, medicine; and pastoral associates, lectors, extraordinary ministers of the eucharist, preachers, spiritual directors—but to the majority of Christians, who do not think of themselves as ministers at all because of the vocabulary and structures of ministry in the church today. Yet the answers to today's issues lie in the ethic of Jesus, the person of Jesus, and not necessarily in the existing structures of organization in the church or organization as it is seen in more secular businesses such as schools, universities, hospitals, corporations or even some religious communities.

Following are some suggestions for the ethical demands inherent in orders both now and in the future. Please note that many are in opposition to the efforts of many in the church calling for change in specific ministries such as priesthood. Ordaining a new set of people to priesthood, bishoprics, or the diaconate will not adequately address the issues.

Jesus was not ordained; he was not a priest. His understanding of leadership was more bound to laying down one's life than to picking up authority. Those who image unity and communion for the Christian community must bear Jesus' mark of unbounded love and service; that is, be willing to give their life for the life of the community.

Jesus was seen most clearly as a prophet, calling the people to repentance and a return to God's kingdom of peace, justice, and mercy. This ability to proclaim the good news is assumed to be given along with ordination to the priesthood. Reality attests to the fact that often it is not. The charism must be apparent in a person *before* ordination if we are to be true to the process of the other sacraments. The prophet or preacher is usually easily recognizable, whether the person is ordained, educated, or not. This gift to the church entails honesty and courage more than an "official" designation. By its very nature this ministry is called to criticize the church both in its internal life and its life in the world, continually calling it to radical conversion and atonement.

Jesus' repeated warnings about how power and authority should be used in his community must be reexamined and accepted with a new heart. Anyone who is ordained to such power must be marked by the characteristics of Jesus himself: radical integrity, mercy, forgiveness, understanding, and tenderness, as well as firmness and the abilities to discern and call forth others. The power and authority to forgive must be a reality in the person's lifestyle, attitude, and demeanor; in other words, the one who leads must first be a follower and known as such to the community.

If ordering the community is a full-time ministry, then the community should support the person as a gift from the Spirit. Ministers can and should be encouraged to work at some other job, as did Paul with his tent-making. With more people recognized within the community there is less need for full-time ministers, as is now the case. But the support of the poor and the needy must come first, not the support of ministers.

This also touches the issue of professional or paid ministry. If professional ministry is to be truly service to the community, it cannot be dealt with on the level of competition and availability of services as if the church were a business corporation. The "laborer is worth his hire," but that does not mean that the church should adopt the system operating in American society as its norm in new ministries. Some ministries can be professions, but this is not the norm for baptismal ministries and should not be seen as normative.

Even today, ordination to either the priesthood or the diaconate is not a right of anyone, male or female. Current practice uses the individual's intention as the basic criterion for ordination. Instead, the person should be called from the community. Further, ordination to one community does not automatically allow a person to switch communities and move about at will. The issue of faithful service must be looked at not only in priesthood but in all the ministries.

The church must admit that one person does not receive all or even many of the gifts needed to build up the church community. At most two or perhaps three interrelated gifts will be found in one person, and usually only after a long apprenticeship within the community itself. To make young men and women the core of the ministerial structure of the church is to ignore the reality of life in Christ. People grow into ministry and move from one to another as they grow in their own lifestyle and following of Jesus. Ministries should not always be seen as permanent.

In all responses to the issues posed here the needs and hopes of the Christian community must come first. Those who consider themselves ministers—ordained, professional, or seeking such—must look upon themselves in service to the community, "washing its feet," like a servant, and not "lording it over them," proclaiming how the programs and liturgy will be run because they have been "hired to do this," "educated for it," and so on. Academic credentials do not make a minister except in selected circumstances, usually after the community has called the person forth. Paul tells his community at Corinth, if you have a gift the community doesn't need, pray for another. Those operating now within the structures of the church in ministry must be extremely careful not to take power and authority from the community without its first being offered or given in trust.

Those involved in and preparing for ministry must seriously look at two glaring realities and lacks apparent in groups today: First, if one does have a gift from the Spirit, is it ethically right to ask others to pay for the sharing of that gift as if it were a commodity to be bought and sold? Second, if a person has been given a gift of ministry for the community, what is the connection between lifestyle and the exercise of the gift? If we are going to begin looking at conversion and imitation of Christ as the norms in admitting that a person is ready for a sacrament, what are the criteria for ordination?

Closely connected to this issue is the question of how ministers become "worthy of their hire." If ministers are servants, then competition and salary ranges commensurate with those of the world are not normative. The gifts are given for the community, not to enhance the minister's lifestyle. The virtues of poverty, simplicity, and service are inherent in the gift's use in community.

That celibacy is not intimately connected to ministry must be acknowledged and dealt with honestly and constructively, even with some repentance and forgiveness extended and penance done for expecting the impossible. On the other hand, the community must recognize the ministry and gift of celibacy as a specific and necessary gift that enhances certain forms of service and ministry within the community, just as it recognizes marriage and supports and confirms it publicly in a sacrament.

Last, the ministry of holiness must be put forward as the most needed and desired aspect of service and ministry. Christ is our high priest and all who minister to his community must conform to his image and likeness. In Hebrews we see what that image entails:

> Christ, in the days of his mortal life, offered his sacrifice with tears and cries. He prayed to him who could save him from death, and he was heard because of his humble submission. Although he was Son, he learned through suffering what obedience was, and once made perfect, he became the source of eternal salvation for those who obey him (Heb 5:7-9).

The core and essence of all orders, of all publicly recognized ministry, must be reverence and obedience: obedience to the gospels, to the Spirit in the community and the world, to the cross and suffering that forms us in the image of children of God, and to the needs of the suffering community.

We must begin individually—lay, cleric, or religious—and examine why we minister, how we minister, and whether our ministry is truly at the service of the community and its desperate needs for justice, food, clothing, shelter, human rights, the dignity of the person, education, employment, health care, freedom, and solidarity, or whether we are taking something for ourselves, for our own life and work. Are we waiting to be called and willing to live with the fact that we might not be chosen by our brothers and sisters to be "ordained," but instead anonymously serve by bending to the washing of feet?

Perhaps it is only the prophet who is called by God, not the community, and no one in his or her right mind wants to be a prophet, knowing how prophets are still treated. But prophecy is needed within the church to call us to conversion and to pay the price for such change and gifting of the Spirit as well as atoning for the past and repairing the world now. Perhaps more than any ministry, it is the one the church most needs and yet fights against. In our criticism of the church we must be ruthless with ourselves and not base any change on what others do or do not do, or what we individually see as our "right."

Jesus' service was never appreciated or recognized. His ministry was never ordained, celebrated, or affirmed. He paid for his gifts with his life and was rejected by his own. If we are to follow and "walk humbly with our God," we must remember this as we begin to reform and renew the sacrament of ministry, seeing it as the sacrament of service and obedience even unto death—and belonging to all adult Christians as possibility. With marriage, the sacrament of faithful friends, orders holds in some measure the core of what it means to be Christians: faithful love and obedience to the will of God in the kingdom of mercy and justice. Above all, we need to believe that the Spirit is even more concerned and at work on these issues than we are and to hope that we might see the new creation as it unfolds in history.

Perhaps the last and hardest ethical demand as American Catholics will come with the acknowledgment that we are not the norm or even the best indication of the future of the church. We are being called to look for the signs of the Spirit in the Third World of Africa, Asia, and Latin America. For the reality of who we are—the first-world, most powerful and most educated, richest and dominant culture church—does not necessarily make us the most holy or the most open to the Spirit, the cross, and the word of God in history. Maybe the sacrament of orders and the problems of ministry will right themselves if we shift our energies to the plight and need of the majority of the church and the world in the areas of justice and peace. For the leaders of the church to be so concerned with internal issues such as orders is in itself a condemnation. For the ministers to be so concerned with ordination, recognition, and acceptance by those already ordained is in itself a condemnation. For such a minority group within the church to be so concerned with its own personal ethics of sexuality and freedom is in itself a condemnation.

The true shepherds are the ones who wait tables, unnoticed except when there is a need for more service. They are most easily forgotten, those who fill water jars at the request of a woman and those who wash the feet of those who don't want their feet washed. Perhaps we need to look for the ministers in our midst and in the world who are in fact gathering, welcoming, feeding the poor, visiting the sick, comforting the elderly, forgiving, giving hospitality, caring for the dying, laying down their life for others without recognition but with great love, and begin by ordaining them. Perhaps we should forget the seminaries, universities, M.A. programs, and whether we want to be ordained and be paid professional salaries, commensurate with power. Such a reversal would be the most powerful response to the problems of orders today.

Rainer Maria Rilke says it well:

> Be patient toward all that is unresolved in your heart
> and try to love the questions themselves.

> Do not seek the answers that cannot be given you
> because you would not be able to live and the
> point is to live everything.
>
> Live the questions now: perhaps you will gradually
> without noticing it live along some distant day
> into the answers.

Perhaps we even need to play some "children of God games" regarding what we want to be when we grow up. Try it in a group. Gather those who want to be bishops, priests, or deacons on one side and the "laity" on the other. Let the ones who want to be ordained talk first. Then have the ones who don't want to be ordained talk. Compare the differences in emphasis and insight. Then together come up with some "new" criteria for a good bishop, priest, deacon.

Then try a second game, asking for responses to "If I were a prophet . . . ." "If I were a theologian. . . . " "If I were a confessor (one who atones for the sin of the sinner and the church). . . . " "If I were a preacher. . . . " Ask the group members to choose the individuals they think really have some of the gifts needed for these ministries. After they present their choices, try to decide how the group would "ordain" them. Discuss the marks or characteristics of such a gift or ministry in a person. Sometimes we need to remind ourselves that practically no one is exactly what he or she wants to be. It seems to be God's peculiar sense of humor!

There is an old English story that is insightful here. The book and movie *The Man in the Iron Mask* are variations of the tale.

✟   Once upon a time there was a man who was terribly deformed and ugly. But he was left a rather large sum of money and had a mask-maker make him a perfectly fitted mask to cover his face. The mask followed his form but changed his features. When he first put it on he could not believe the alteration. He could hardly recognize himself! He paid the mask-maker his exorbitant price gladly and left with the mask on his face. He wore the mask always and never removed it. He had a life quite different from the one he had had before, with friends and opportunities unheard of previously.

And then one day he fell in love. As time went on he wanted more and more to take the mask off so that the woman he loved could see who he really was. His lack of integrity and his dishonesty were eating him alive. Finally she broached the subject, forcing the issue, by asking him to marry her! He broke down and said he couldn't because she did not know who he truly was. She gave him a week to decide. He could tell her what he had not been honest about and marry her, or he would never see her again.

It was a terrible week. He fluctuated back and forth, torn. First he would decide to tell her no and go off miserably to a life alone and in torment, and then he would decide to take off the mask and let her see what he was really like. But he couldn't bear the possibility of her rejection once she saw him as he truly was.

The day came and he began with the no—but she wore him down. She truly did love him and couldn't imagine anything that could alter her impression of him. At last he gave in. He told her that she would be horrified at what she saw, that he wore a mask to hide his face not just from her but from all others. Then he slowly began to peel the tight-fitting mask from his face, in pain, grimacing, and pulling at the skin of his face. Finally, he had removed it, and he looked at her, trembling, knowing that he would lose her love. Her face changed dramatically.

"You see how ugly I am?" he said with anger and weeping. "I knew you would be repulsed." He turned to rush out the door to escape into his own misery and loss.

But to his surprise she stopped him: "No, no. But why do you wear the mask? Your face is exactly the same as the mask!"

The man had become the mask he never removed.

Often we have operated as if this is what would inevitably happen to every man who was ordained or everyone who wanted to be a minister. But it doesn't. Wearing many masks has confused us and disoriented us while robbing the church of gifts that are not connected to beauty, academics, strengths, and power, but to weakness, the giving of the Spirit, and the tears and sin of the one who bears the gift in common with the rest of the community.

Here is a story for preachers and prophets from the Sufi tradition:

✞ Once upon a time Nasruddin (both a trickster and wise sage) was eating his usual diet, the diet of a poor man: chickpeas and hard bread. His neighbor, who also claimed to be wise, lived in a grand house and ate out often, dining in the houses of the rich and powerful. Even when he ate at home, it was more like a feast than a daily meal. He approached Nasruddin one day with pity and a bit of disdain, saying: "Nasruddin, if only you would learn to flatter the king and be subservient, as I do, carefully and without being sharp and vicious, you would not have to live on that diet of chickpeas and stale bread."

Nasruddin was silent a long time, chewing his peas and bread. Finally he spoke in a measured tone, using the man's own words: "If only you would learn to live on this kind of food, chickpeas and moldy bread, then you wouldn't have to flatter and bend to a king who needs to hear the truth, from anyone."

Finally, here is a story for all of us, made in the image of the Holy One, called to reveal that image to others in service, obedience, and gifts galore. From the tradition of India, it is called "The Image-Maker."

✠ Once upon a time, long ago, there was an artist. He made only one image, the god Shiva, and he made it over and over again, each unique, each more radiant and lifelike than the one before. His images were always in demand, but the image-maker never sold them. He was supported by a monastery and believed, along with the monks, that his gift came from the gods and that to sell such a gift would be blasphemy.

One day the king was passing though the village. The image-maker joined the long line of people waiting to catch a glimpse of the king. He wasn't impressive. In fact the king looked bored.

But the next day a messenger arrived at the image-maker's house. The king wanted an image of the god Shiva. The artist was delighted, but his delight fled when the messenger offered him a sack of gold coins in payment for the image. He began patiently to explain that the images were not for sale. He couldn't betray the gift that the gods had given him, but he would be delighted to make an image for the king. The image-maker put the image in the saddlebags of the messenger, and the messenger threw the sack of coins at the feet of the artist. The image-maker was furious. No one could buy one of his images, not even the king. He went back to his work, and in his anger began to break the clay from the mold that he had been casting around the bronze image—the work he had been engrossed in before the messenger arrived.

The image-maker used a lengthy process to make the images, called lost wax casting. First he carved the image out of wax, then covered it with clay. He put vents in it so that the wax could run out of the mold when it was baked or fired in the kiln. After the firing the mold was filled with bronze. Once it had hardened and cooled, the mold was chipped away. He worked at it furiously and as he worked he calmed down, for the image began to appear beneath his fingers—an image of serenity, peace, and passionate devotion. Shiva was seated on a lotus blossom, his six arms outstretched in teaching, accepting, and holding objects of worship and service—a flute, a cup, prayer beads, and a flower. It seemed that the image smiled, and the image-maker smiled at last too.

He polished the image, and as he did the image changed. Instead of Shiva, there was the king's face looking back at him! How could this be? What could this mean? He destroyed the image and made another. At the stage of polishing, the king's image appeared again. Again he destroyed the image and started fresh. Again the king's face appeared, displacing Shiva. What was especially chilling was that the face had that same bored look as when the image-maker saw him in the street. He stopped and started praying, reflecting, and meditating. He was an image-maker. What was happening to him? He now had no control over the image he was creating. He had lost the gift, the meaning of his life.

He thought long, and finally he knew what he had to do. He left home again, and this time went to the king, taking only the clothes on his back and his begging bowl. It was a long, hard journey into a place unknown to him. He begged and often was hungry, for there were many beggars and not much food to spare in the land.

Finally he arrived in the city and made his way to a door in the palace, knocked, but no one answered. All day he tried to get in, but then others began to tell him that the door only opened for official business. They would never answer the door for him. The image-maker refused to be turned away and became loud and noisy and insistent. Finally the door opened. He told the guard that he had come to do business with the king. The door was slammed shut. He stayed there, fasting, praying, and whenever the door opened he repeated the line: "I have come to do business with the king." Finally his presence and fasting was reported to the king, who said, "Let him in—I don't want him dying on my doorstep."

The image-maker approached the king, who realized almost immediately that this was no usual beggar. He walked with dignity and power. "Who are you and what do you want," the king asked?

The image-maker told the king who he was and that the king's messenger had come to him for an image of Shiva. The king remembered and was profuse in his praise of the image. The image-maker replied: "I'm honored that you appreciate the image, but those images are given to me, they come to me as gift. I cannot sell them. Your messenger left behind a sack of coins by mistake." And he returned the purse to the king.

The king was flustered. A mistake? They looked at each other for a long time. No further words were spoken, but in looking the king finally began to see and understand. The image-maker's gift from the gods, perhaps from Shiva himself, was not for sale. Finally the king spoke again: "Yes, a mistake was made. My apologies, please."

The king sent the image-maker home, and after meditating and praying again his heart rested and peace returned. He fasted and went back to work. He began the mold, carving the face of Shiva. Then the clay, the baking in the kiln, the melted bronze, cooling and hardening, and breaking through the mold, setting the image free. The image-maker polished the statue and the form of Shiva appeared, six arms, a smile on his lips, that familiar and beloved face. And the face radiated power once again.

Now many say that the king became a patron of the image-maker and that the image-maker made a number of images for the king's household. However, none of these images is to be found anywhere today. Were they hidden away, lost, destroyed in time's passage, melted down for other images, more popular ones? No one really knows. It doesn't matter. The gift was given. What is left is the story and the life of the image-maker, his integrity, his gift that could not be bought or sold, only given away again and again.

Some things never change. Our ministries, gifts, and charisms are given for the community, for our time and history, our place in the world. Nothing will remain except our life, our memories, and our stories of how we gave, without payment, only giving and obeying the gift. All of us are gifted by God, called to give, obey, and fill up the needs of those in our communities and world. The only thing that really matters is that the gift is used, cherished, kept with integrity, and given over and over so that we indeed become the gift.

10

Rites: What If . . . ?

Theological Options for the Near Future

There is an old Jewish story that I'd like to use to introduce some options regarding the sacraments of marriage and orders specifically, but for other sacraments as well, and the ethical decision-making that the church must face in the near future. It is the story of a journey with an unexpected end.

✝ Once upon a time there was a clay digger who lived in Russia. He was desperately poor and alone in the world. One day as he dug in the clay he found a stone, shining, sparkling, bright. He took it into town to see what he could get for it. It was a diamond, bigger than any the shopkeeper had ever seen. So he told the poor man to take it to the great city of Odessa, for only there could he find someone who would know its true worth and give him what was just. Off the man went.

Upon arriving in Odessa, he went to the largest shop that dealt in rare gems and showed his find to the owner. The man was amazed but told him that only in London would there be someone to pay him for such a stone—if he really wanted what it was worth.

The man worried. How could a poor clay digger get all the way to London with his treasure? He went down to the docks. There he heard that there was a ship captain who would probably take him, but only if he could pay his way. He waited for the man and asked for accommodations to London. Then he drew out his stone from his bag and promised the captain that once he got to England he would give him half of what it was worth there. Greedily the captain agreed and even decided to give him his own quarters, three meals a day, and a manservant for the duration of the journey.

They set sail, and the poor man could hardly believe his good fortune. Never had he lived so well. He ate all he needed and more.

His servant looked after him, so he had absolutely nothing to do for the whole journey. He praised God for his great goodness and enjoyed himself immensely. Time wore on. Days and nights passed, for the journey was long and uneventful.

One night after finishing supper, he took out his diamond, as he did every night, to marvel at its size and beauty and to wonder what he could get for it and what his life would be like as a rich man. The wine caught up with him and his head fell forward on his arms. The candle burned low and eventually went out. Hours later the servant came in quietly in the dark, cleared the table, and left the clay digger to sleep. Without realizing what he was doing, he took the dirty dishes, the leftovers—and the stone. He threw the garbage overboard—and the stone.

The clay digger awoke in the morning and frantically searched for the stone. It was nowhere to be found. Then he went looking for the servant and learned what had happened. He was at his wits' end. What would the captain do to him when he learned the stone was gone? Would he throw him overboard? He swore the servant to secrecy and vowed not to let the captain of the ship find out. For the remainder of the journey he lived in fear, prayed unceasingly, and tried to figure out what he would do when he got to London.

Day after day the captain would clap him on the shoulder, loudly call him friend, laugh knowingly, and tell him to take good care of their treasure. Then, the day before they were to arrive in England, the clay digger was summoned to the captain's room. He went, trembling and panic-stricken. Now it would come out.

But to his surprise the captain gave him a drink and asked him for a favor. The man was a smuggler and had been in trouble with the port officials in London before. Since they were such good friends and business partners already, could he help him out? He had a plan. In order to get past the customs officials without any problems, he would sign over the vessel and cargo to his friend—the clay digger. Then, when they got through customs and the clay digger sold his diamond and returned, they would split the money, the clay digger would give back the documents, and both would be free to go his own way—the clay digger to make his new life and the sea captain to his next destination.

In a daze, the clay digger signed the papers and went back to his quarters, still frantic about what would happen the next morning when they docked. All night he prayed. Should he jump ship and try to swim to safety? But what would he do in London? He knew no one, didn't speak the language; he couldn't even dig clay in England. Exhausted, he finally fell asleep.

The night passed and in the morning he was awakened by shouts and screams. Someone began pounding on his door, yelling for him to get up and come quickly. They were in port and the officials were looking for him. He quickly got up, and a man met him courteously, welcomed him to England, and passed him through the port. Then the man spoke his condolences on the unfortunate happenings of the night before and asked if he could be of service in burying his first mate. Stunned, the clay digger put together what had happened. All the time he had worried and prayed, life was moving quickly around him. The captain had died in his sleep, and now the clay digger was a ship's captain, wealthy, in possession of the ship's cargo, and recognized as a merchant.

When things calmed down he thought to himself: I could have jumped overboard so often. Even last night I could have left, and what would it have done for me? Now I am a rich man with a ship and its goods, though I don't have the diamond. God's ways are strange. He was meant to leave all he knew and to keep going on. He was not meant to have the diamond. He was meant to have the ship and its cargo. He would never have known if he had given up. He knew now that no matter what, he was to keep on in hope, no matter what he lost or what happened to him.

There is something meant for us on our journey, but it is not necessarily what we have in our hand.

In many ways this is the predicament of the church today. The church has a diamond, seven of them, and it is on a journey. But we don't know really the meaning of these "stones." We are in a process of searching out their worth and value and learning to live in the process. But we have a long way to go. Teilhard de Chardin tells us that "the church is like a crustacean; periodically, she must throw off her shell in order to grow." Surprisingly enough, we may have to lose a stone or two in the ocean in order to gain a ship and its cargo. We may have to change. "To live is to change and to be perfect is to have changed often," wrote John Henry Cardinal Newman. Since the Second Vatican Council we have experienced only thirty years of shifts and changes in language, rituals, and the sacraments. The changes resulting from the Council are still taking place.

The ways of the American church tend to be direct and pragmatic. But God's ways can be rather different, as C. S. Lewis has written,

> Everyone can consider the ordinary and open ways of God's providence, but there is this other way, full of meanders and labyrinths, the more particular and obscure method of his providence, a serpentine and crooked line whereby he draws those actions his wisdom intends.

Perhaps the long history of development of the sacraments has brought us to this day and place not for what we intend but for wisdom's ways. The gift of the Spirit could be calling us to a ship and its cargo that are necessary for another journey altogether than the one we envision. This chapter will look at some options pastorally and theologically on this future from two perspectives. First, what if the church had the sacrament of . . .? This will deal with some crucial areas and people who need some portion of their life experience sacramentalized publicly within the church.

The second part of the "what if . . .?" will deal with how the church makes ethical choices and will look at a process that involves scripture, Jesus as the Christian ethic, the sacraments, the community, education, and Christian conscience together with the element of prophecy and the Christian's unique call to continual conversion. The suggestions for sacraments are culled from the previous chapters and are given in order of need based on numbers in the church and obvious lacks within the structure of the church's life and celebration.

What If the Church Had a Sacrament for Children?

In light of the ethical demands of the sacraments and the need for aware and deliberative conversion that is inherent in all the rituals of our belief, it seems imperative for the church to devise and call forth from its tradition a sacrament for children, one that would hold them within the church's protective and nurturing arms but would not treat them as mini-adults or as persons capable of choosing the life of discipleship. It would respect them as children in need of an environment that prays with them, holds them, plays with them, accepts them, learns from them, and draws them slowly into the protective net of belief and fellowship where they will want to be as adult members of the community.

There are only two references to children in the Christian scriptures. The first is in Mark's gospel, where Jesus lets the children come to him. It is noteworthy because it reveals what children could be for the community as well as what the community should be doing for the children.

> People were bringing their little children to him to have him touch them, and the disciples argued with them for this.
>
> When Jesus noticed it, he was very angry and said: "Let the children come to me and *don't stop them*, for the kingdom of God *belongs* to such as these. Truly, I say to you, whoever does not receive the kingdom of God like a child will not enter it." Then he *took the children in his arms and laying his hands on them, blessed them* (Mk 10:13-16).

I've italicized certain phrases to emphasize how we can best treat our children. First, we must touch them by embracing them, blessing them, and placing our hands on them, which is the scripture's usual description of praying for someone. We are not to hinder them by demanding that they understand things that are impossible to understand, even as adults. We are not to hinder them by our lack of faith, our criteria, our perceptions. We are to learn from them, for the kingdom of heaven already belongs to them; it is we who have lost sight of it or chosen other things in its place. They are to teach us how to act, how to be children of God. We are to teach them by our love, our touch, and our prayer, and by our lives in the world.

The other place in Mark's gospel where a child is present is in Jesus' exhortation to his disciples against ambition and envy. He catches them in a private discussion:

> They came to Capernaum and, once inside the house, Jesus asked them: "What were you discussing on the way?" But they did not answer because they had been arguing about who was the greatest.
>
> Then he sat down, called the Twelve and said to them: "If anyone wants to be first, he must be the very last and make himself the servant of all." Then he took a little child, set him in the midst of them, and putting his arms around him, said to them, "Whoever welcomes a child such as this in my name, welcomes me, and whoever welcomes me, welcomes not me but the One who sent me" (Mk 9:33-37).

"*Putting his arms around him,*" Jesus takes the child as the model for living as a follower of the Way. We are told to welcome children as they are, to make them feel at home. What we have done, however, is cheated them of growing into belief, of choosing and valuing. We have given them things they cannot appreciate before they even want them. Then, when they do need and want ways to celebrate who they are in the community, we have nothing left to give them.

Augustine was enrolled in Bishop Ambrose's classes and catechumenate. He stayed there for almost thirteen years, because that's how long it took for him to decide to commit himself to Christianity. Perhaps we hinder our children from becoming mature Christians most by the way we treat them; we make demands of them, bribe them on occasion to go to church and receive the sacraments, and belittle their own experience of God, which could be perceived, acknowledged, and appreciated on its own merits without connecting it to the sacramental life of the adult church. Gandhi has this to say about children: "I would develop in the child their hands, their brains, their soul. The hands have almost atrophied. The soul has been altogether ignored." We cannot continue to use education as the sole criterion for our sacraments. We must find ways to nurture and protect their souls and move their hands and hearts to play, praise, and become familiar with the ways of God in the community.

The United Nations Declaration of the Rights of the Child provides a focus for our work and relationships with our children:

THE RIGHT TO:
affection, love and understanding.
to adequate nutrition and medical care.
to free education.
to full opportunity for play and recreation.
to a name and nationality.
to special care, if handicapped.
to be among the first to receive relief in times of disaster.
to learn to be a useful member of society and to develop individual
     abilities.
to be brought up in a spirit of peace and universal brotherhood.
to enjoy these rights, regardless of race, color, sex, religion, na-
     tional or social origin.

These rights appear so basic that we may presume they are being taken care of, when in reality they are being sorely neglected. Perhaps the most important thing we can do for our children as Christians is to *be* Christians, recognizable as such in the world. We can provide an atmosphere of peace with justice and mercy in a world where these virtues and values are often lacking. We can touch our children with care, love, and gentleness, as God touches us; then they will grow up believing in God's love because they have experienced it and grown up on it rather than merely hearing about it in class. And we can learn from them, for children are the teachers.

There is a Jewish tale that tells us what we need to hear.

✝ Once upon a time the young grandson of a Hasidic master came weeping to his grandfather.

"Why are you crying, child?" the rabbi asked.

"I was playing hide and seek, but when I hid no one looked for me."

The teacher took the child in his arms and held him. And he thought to himself: So it is with the Lord. He hides, but we do not go looking for him.

If we seek to nourish our children, as Paul says, on milk rather than beginning with solid food, then we will have children who in their innocence and enthusiasm will teach us. We need to enroll our children in the catechumenate before baptism (or after baptism, if they are already baptized), bless them as gifts to our community, welcome them into our midst, and keep our arms around them, rather than give them the sacraments before they have anything to celebrate. The day will come soon enough, for, as Graham Greene says, "there is always one moment in childhood when the door opens and lets the future in." It is then that our children need to know the sacraments in their own lives and can truly rejoice in having them to celebrate and experience in community.

If we continue to baptize children, then we must change drastically the way we as adults celebrate the sacraments and call ourselves community. Community does not happen automatically just because we baptize, confirm, or give eucharist (or any other action of the sacraments with children or adults).

We do not encourage children to drive or vote or take on other adult responsibilities. Why then do we insist on having them study their religion more than we adults do, conform to criteria that we ourselves often do not try to meet, and frequently lump them in age categories to do so? The norm for sacraments and the norm for ethical decisions and responses to life is that of the adult. We must quickly devise, with the power and the grace of the Spirit, ways to nurture our children that are more consonant with their experience and abilities. And we must look to our own lives to see what we are teaching our children by our example, apart from our words and classes.

What If the Church Had a Sacrament of Faithful Friends with Multiple Rites?

We are all friends of God in the family of church. We need to offer this sacrament to all adults who seek to sacramentalize their relationship with another publicly. One rite would be for first marriages that called adult believers to friendship and faithfulness on the way of the cross together, to being soul-keepers for each other. This rite would be celebrated long after the legal ceremony of marriage.

Another rite would be for those who have failed at marriage but wish to try again to live faithfully in the calling of the gospel, having acknowledged within the community that they still have much to learn as Christians. This rite would only be celebrated after a period of penance and discernment with a religious confessor or counselor. It would echo the rites of marriage in the Eastern churches, where the first marriage is symbolized with the couple crowning each other as they will live forever in the kingdom, with great rejoicing and pageantry, while the second marriage is celebrated simply, quietly, without the crowns and external symbols, acknowledging that this marriage is not a full sign of the kingdom's presence but is struggling to be born in this couple. In between there is a period of penance and prayer, oftentimes lasting for years, at the discretion of the spiritual advisor.

Yet another rite would be for couples who wish their union to be blessed by the church—but not sacramentalized—immediately after their legal union.

If our sacraments are in part celebrating the reality of the love of the friends of Christ in God, then people should be free to struggle together and encouraged to grow into their commitments. A time of dedication and searching with others in the arms of the community could be shared together as preparation for the celebration of a sacramental marriage, which would be binding forever in its faithfulness and friendship. The specifically Christian character of this marriage in the community would be its faithfulness. If a couple failed in this endeavor, then they would be exhorted to remain unmarried but would not be forced to stay unmarried.

Of course, all of this only makes sense if the other sacraments are experienced more as conversions rather than magic rituals that make something happen. Marriage for Christians must come to be a state of life, a lifestyle wherein adults experience the friendship and faithfulness of the love of God and the support, affirmation, and challenge of the community in their relationship; where they can know mercy and forgiveness and recognize that a Christian marriage is a drastically different calling than civil marriage. The values it upholds can then be seen as part of the vibrant structure of the community, the base of the church, and the usual way of love for Christians.

Another rite would be celebrated for individuals who freely choose to live alone while bringing the kingdom into their professions and lives. There would also be a rite for those who wish to commit themselves to a religious community within the tradition of the church. A last rite would be for widows and widowers who choose not to remarry. All Christians are called to this friendship with God. It is a primary value for adult believers and it can be expressed in various ways and gifts, and all these ways need sacramentalizing and public blessing in the church.

As it stands now there is no sacrament for those who remain unmarried by choice in the church, though there is a blessing of persons who choose to align themselves with a religious order. With such a sacrament the gift of celibacy would be recognized as the unique gift it is, not connected to any particular form of ministry or service to the community. The gift of aloneness, of single-heartedness, could then become valued for itself. We need this reality to remind us that no matter how close we draw to another human being there is always a part of us that remains unshared, that belongs only to God. There is a tale that brings this home beautifully.

✣ Once upon a time a Hasidic rebbe was asked why it was that God, blessed be His Name, who owns all things, felt the need to create the world. The rebbe answered: "Because God was lonely." And then he reflected further: "Therefore we read, 'Hear, O Israel, the Lord, Our God, the Lord is alone.' We may dare to be alone without panic. It is good sometimes to be alone, like God."

This paradox of being alone in community, of attending first to God and the kingdom and the community, enriches the communion of the church. Especially in a world that decries being unmarried, such a sacrament has much to offer to the community as well as support and affirmation for the one who chooses to live like Jesus, Mary of Magdala, John, Martha, Mary, and Lazarus, all friends of Jesus who were unmarried. Jesus' words to his disciples regarding this style of life are these: "Not everybody understands what you have just said, but only those who have received this gift. Some are born incapable of marriage. Others have been made that way by men. But there are others who have given up the possibility of marriage for the sake of the kingdom of Heaven. He who can accept this, let him accept it" (Mt 19:11-12). We need to acknowledge those who live for the kingdom, reminders to the community of the single-heartedness of our love.

What If the Church Extended the Sacrament of Orders?

What if the church extended this sacrament to include two more rites: for those who are gifted as theologians, preachers, teachers, and catechists; and for those with the gifts of counseling and spiritual direction, as well as confessors and those who work in the healing and health-care professions? These rites could be celebrated in conjunction with the rites of bishops, priests, and deacons.

To connect the tasks of the bishop to those of the theologian and the preacher is not as strange as it might sound, and it has deep roots in the tradition of the church. The International Theological Commission (ITC) was established "for the purpose of offering effective assistance to the Congregation of the Doctrine of the Faith, especially in doctrinal questions of greater moment" by the First Synod of Bishops, October 27, 1967. Francis Sullivan, S.J., quotes Paul VI's words to the ITC to explain the relationship between theologians and bishops:

> The element that is common to the tasks of the magisterium and of theologians, though to be realized in ways that are analogous and proper to each, is "to safeguard the deposit of revelation, to seek ever deeper insight into it, to explain, teach and defend it" for the service of the people of God and for the whole world's salvation.[1]

The ITC went on to explain further the bonds bishops and theologians share:

1. They are both bound by the Word of God. For "the magisterium is not above the Word of God, but serves it, teaching only what has been handed on, listening to it devoutly, guarding it conscientiously, and explaining it faithfully. From this one deposit of faith it draws everything which it presents for belief as divinely revealed" (DV 10). Likewise, "sacred theology relies on the written Word of God, along with sacred Tradition, as on a permanent foundation. By this Word, it is most firmly strengthened and constantly rejuvenated, as it searches out, under the light of faith, the full truth stored up in the mystery of Christ" (DV 24).

2. Both are bound by the "sense of faith" of the church, both of past ages and of our own day. For the Word of God in a living manner pervades all ages in that "common sense of the faith" of the whole people of God, by which "the whole body of the faithful, anointed by the Holy One, cannot err in believing" (LG 12), in such a way that "in maintaining, practicing and confessing the faith that has been handed down, there results a unanimity of bishops and the faithful" (DV 10).

3. They are both bound by the documents of Tradition, in which the common faith of a people of God is set forth. Although the magisterium and theologians have different tasks with respect to these documents, neither can neglect such records of the faith which are stored in the history of salvation of God's people.

4. In performing their ministries, both are bound by the pastoral and missionary care they must have towards the world. While the magisterium of the Supreme Pontiff and the bishops is specifically called "pastoral," still the scientific character of the theologians' work does not free them from pastoral and missionary responsibility, especially in view of how quickly even scientific matters are given publicity by modern means of communication. Moreover theology, as vital function to be exercised within and on behalf of the people of God, must have a pastoral and missionary purpose and effect.[2]

The theologian is seen as a mediator between the bishops and the community, listening to both and culling from the peoples' experience and knowledge and from the church's tradition and belief what is necessary for deepening the experience of life for Christians. This listening function of theologians is becoming more and more critical as the people of God grow in awareness and understanding of their own role in the church and their specific call to transform the world. In addition, the theologian interprets, teaches, translates into contemporary thought-forms, and integrates the doctrine and admonitions of the magisterium into a broader synthesis. Recent testimony to this process is the pastorals of the American bishops on peace and economics. At present, bishops derive their authority from the sacrament of orders and theologians derive their authority from their qualifications as scholars in their particular disciplines and the individual gifts of the Spirit.

Perhaps the person who best symbolizes the charism of the theologian is Catherine of Siena, who often made her way from the poor areas of the city to the steps of the Vatican. She spent her time going back and forth—from caring for the victims of disease and poverty to exhorting the pope to reform his own life and the life of the church. She came from the heart of the people, from the streets of the poor, and that gave her insight, passion, and the determination to tell the truth in the chambers and cathedrals of the larger church. The poor didn't know that she was headed to the pope after leaving them, but they were her support, the wind at her back, the underlying force of her words.

According to the new Code of Canon Law lay people may preach with the permission of the bishop. The United States bishops have decided to certify and license lay preachers. So far this process has not been set up, but practically speaking, they are using the criteria of advanced studies and expertise in scripture and allied fields and offering programs on the diocesan levels for this training. The connections among bishops, theologians, and preachers are becoming clearer, but more is needed in order to make available the depth and extent of the wisdom that the church retains in its heritage. Sacramentalizing the function of theology would serve to extend the power of the word studied, preached, and explained. This could be one way to proceed, while still being open to the gift of preaching not based only on academic credentials.

The role of catechist is closely aligned with the function of the pastor, especially on the parish and diocesan levels in the United States church. In the words of Edward Schillebeeckx, ministry and ministers have "always been pioneers in the community, and those who inspired it served as models by which the community could identify the gospel." Schillebeeckx writes:

> Throughout the development of ministry in the New Testament one striking fact is that the ministry did not develop from and around the eucharist or the liturgy, but from the apostolic building up of

the community through preaching, admonition and leadership. . . . According to the New Testament understanding, ministry is a constituent part of the church (apart from the question of whether it is originally charismatic and then becomes institutionalized, and apart from the way in which it takes on different structures depending on the different needs of the church in changing circumstance). Ministry is necessary for building up the church along apostolic lines, viz., as the community of God, the apostolic discipleship of Jesus. Here, the apostolic community with its apostolic heritage, viz. the gospel, takes a central place. . . . Therefore the minister is not merely a mouthpiece of the community, but occasionally can also reprimand its ministers to order. Precisely because the ministers are leaders and pioneers in the community, the "greatest," they must in fact be the least in the community: the principal servant of all (Mark 10:43f). . . . The ministry of the church above all requires of its ministers leadership in the true discipleship of Jesus, with all the spirituality which this "disciple of Jesus" involves in New Testament terms.[3]

The pastor, as we have seen before, orders the parish community, builds it up as the body of Christ, and connects it to the larger church. The teacher or catechist as minister (not in a university setting) primarily attends to a particular community whether in the capacity of a paid professional or as a member of the parish who volunteers or who is called forth from the community. The pastor and the catechists share devotion to the same people, are bound to them in celebration of the sacraments and in preparation for them and share Christian life on a day-to-day basis. They are responsible for the same people, though in different ways. The pastor gathers, leads, walks with, and holds the community together. The catechist forms the mind and life of the community, especially, as it stands today, the soul and life of the young people in the community.

There is another Jewish vignette that throws light on this relationship.

✟ In a dream, a devout disciple of the master was permitted to approach the temple in Paradise where all the great old sages who had studied the Talmud all their lives were now spending eternity. He gazed in at them and to his amazement they were all sitting around tables, just as they had done on earth, studying the Talmud still! The disciple watched them passionately exclaiming and arguing and reverently fingering the text. He wondered: Is this really Paradise? It seems like earth. But then his thoughts were interrupted with warm laughter. "You are mistaken. This is not Paradise. The sages are not in Paradise. Paradise is in the sages."

Catechists are faced with the task of sharing wisdom, knowledge, and information with the community, of carrying and attending to the Paradise that is within them because of their love for the scriptures and their interpretation of the message for and with others. John's gospel tells of Nicodemus, a religious teacher who comes to Jesus by night to question, to study him, and to delve deeper into Jesus' words. Nicodemus sits in the dark with the Light of the world. His questions are so basic we wonder if he has been studying with others through the years. He tries to persuade his own structures and systems to honor its rules and protect Jesus, but backs down very quickly when there is opposition to his words and the depth of his association with Jesus is thrown at him. Jesus is gentle and patient with him but tells him to begin again, to be born again, to start over as a novice. He studies and is tutored by Jesus all night, and then he goes away. He will feebly attempt to stand up for him and then disappear quickly. Only when Jesus is dead will he come again. He steals in and out of Jesus' life, slowly coming to belief. This is the situation today for many adult believers without strong catechists on a parish level. Continual study, discussion, and learning are crucial to the belief of an adult and the formation of an adult community.

While the climate of the catechetical ministries in the United States is becoming more and more professional, it is also, unfortunately, picking up competition and a need for accreditation, not necessarily based on being held accountable for living out what one teaches publicly. In a document entitled "Lay Catholics in Schools: Witnesses to Faith" by the Vatican Congregation for Catholic Education we read:

> Conduct is always much more important than speech; this fact becomes especially important in the formation period of students. The more completely an educator can give concrete witness to the model of the ideal person that is being presented to the students, the more this ideal will be believed and imitated. For it will then be seen as something reasonable and worthy of being lived, something concrete and realizable. It is in this context that the faith witness of the lay teacher becomes especially important.[4]

What kind of teachers and catechists do we need? What kind of religious education do we need? Benedictine sister Joan Chittister is clear and precise:

> More than ever in our day we need religious education:
> - that leads rather than certifies;
> - that contributes to a just future rather than simply to an economically satisfying present;
> - that is willing to question whether or not what is scientifically, organizationally and economically possible is also humanly appropriate;
> - that is built on curriculums of conscience not just curriculums of content;
> - that knows that peace is based on justice and bends itself to build it;
> - that realizes that freedom is based on the sacraments of creation and restructures itself to reflect the equality given by God.
> . . . May Paradise live in us wherever we teach.[5]

The way is not easy.

In the United States people like to think of themselves as professionals, including most who call themselves ministers. But if we are to be true to the ethical demands of the sacraments, we must only celebrate and confirm the lifestyle of those who truly are seen to be what they teach. If we ordain them, we must ordain them for their own communities and not indiscriminately for all groups and times, and not based on academic degrees.

Last, we should recognize the service that counselors, doctors, nurses, and lay persons in health-care facilities offer to the people of God in their care for the sick, the poor, and the elderly. Ministry is not just a profession, it is also part of the mission and belief of the community and those who visit the sick and the elderly, bring them eucharist, pray with them, and give them comfort. It is also the work of those who work with families that are experiencing the power and devastation of a death or illness that reveals at a crucial time in the life of Christians the compassion and tenderness of God. These people, who have chosen to dedicate their lives to the service of others in need, deserve recognition and blessing for their work. More important, those to whom they minister deserve to know that the Christian community extends its power and compassion through them.

"Legislation is helpless against the wild-prayer of longing" writes W. H. Auden. The Spirit is at work in our parishes and communities, ordaining and ordering for the church to see and acknowledge and heed. Whether we recognize such services to the community in sacramental rite or blessing form, we must seek always to connect life and liturgy, liturgy and theology, witness and need in the person, the community, and the sacrament. We need to keep in mind, though, that recognition does not necessarily help to deepen appreciation for a gift or ministry. As baptized Christians we are all called to service and ministry within our communities and in our lifestyles in the world. Whatever recognition is given must be given in honor of the community, not the person, and in obedience to our baptismal promises. We are always apprentices in being followers of Jesus and always tempted to do things in the way of the world rather than in the way of the cross.

It is here that the function of the prophet is best understood. In the person of the prophet, the message, its style, and its effect are all tightly bound together. The church would never think to ordain a prophet. Certain gifts are best left to the power of the Spirit, the creativity and imagination of the individual, and the discipline of the tension involved in sharing the gift with the community. A prophet is always one-sided. His or her "thus sayeth the Lord" arises out of an intense personal vision of the truth as it bears upon a particular historical situation. But truth is always larger than any one person's ability to grasp or express it. The clearer a prophet's vision, the more partial it is. Prophets are more often the focus of controversy than unity, the prelude to conversion. Rarely in history has the prophetic utterance come from the official levels of society or church. The Spirit gifts individuals whose clarity of vision places them far in advance of their times and makes them a sign of contradiction. Personally they are often faulted for needing to learn to temper their demand for total commitment by tenderness and trust for those who "aren't there yet"; nonetheless, their gift lies primarily in their stark denunciations of injustice and threats of what will happen if their warnings aren't heeded.

The church is made up of sinners and those who are lukewarm. The gift of the prophet inevitably sets up tension within the church community, within the institution, and between the institution and the world. Philippians 2:15 tells us to

do everything without grumbling, so that without fault or blame, you will be children of God without reproach among a crooked

and perverse generation. You are a light among them, like stars in
the universe, holding to the Word of life. I shall feel proud of you
on the day of Christ on seeing that my effort and labor have not
been in vain.

The prophetic gift goes beyond the institutional sacramental system
itself, especially when it is not true to its core. It denounces any form of
holiness without justice. It is manifested as intimately personal, judg-
mental, confrontational, demanding, punishing, and promising. Prophets obey a deep need within their own soul that others cannot or will not
see. They struggle in a world and often in a church that refuses to look
and recognize evil for what it is. They speak in images, gestures, rituals,
and sacramentals, with poetry, prose, story, drama, and autobiography.
Simone Weil says: "Imaginary evil is romantic and varied; real evil is
gloomy, monotonous, barren, boring. Imaginary good is boring; real good
is always new, marvelous, intoxicating." We seem able to respond forcibly with a pure yes or pure no to a prophet and his or her message. There
is no middle ground. Daniel Berrigan, considered a prophet by some,
describes himself and some of what he does:

> Gratitude is a kind of mystifying and constant angel of mine. I
> write poetry, because this is a way of submitting my anger to a
> strict discipline. . . . It's a way of surviving. It tells you your soul is
> kicking, that it is your own. Indeed that it is inalienable property,
> not to be trespassed on by the mad tinkers and triflers, whether of
> the pentagonal or the charismatic variety.

And he describes his role more specifically:

> In the transept window in Chartres Cathedral there are four evan-
> gelists perched on the shoulders of four prophets, breathtaking and
> stark, a balancing act. The one below must take the weight of the
> future, the one above must see further, must tell what he sees, must
> use all that borrowed strength and height to deal a further pro-
> phetic word.[6]

However we respond to the present-day confusion and need within
the church in regards to ministry, orders, and the other sacraments, we
must be careful to leave unordained and untouched those people and
services to the church that operate best without recognition and affirma-

tion while acknowledging those that give further credence and service to most members of the church. We must be careful not to undermine the Spirit's way of making holy, doing justice, loving tenderly, and asking us to walk humbly with our God. Ordination for in-house ministries is limited to needs within a church, while all believers are called to sanctify, transform, and repair the world. This is the primary vocation or call to ministry and all orders should be seen in light of this larger and more demanding call to make holy the world and to wash the world's feet in service to others.

What If the Word of God Were a Sacrament?

Much of our reflection has been rooted in the words of Jesus: "Do this and remember me." It is in this process of remembering that the scriptures reveal what we as Christians are to do and who we are to become. The scriptures provide a framework of meaning, a progression of the acts of God in history, a narrative of saving grace, a tradition of our ancestors in faith, and an account of the presence of the Spirit weaving through the lives of all. The scriptures testify to the covenants and give us perspective on being believers in a community that belongs to God.

Our unity, our life, and the quality of our relationships together are based on our telling the story of Jesus and living it with our own words and acts in this portion of history. Our identities as believers and as church are derived from the word of God that we celebrate in the sacraments and liturgy, in our ethical decisions, in our communities, and in our personal lives. We differ from the world around us by rendering our memories in the choices we make in our communities. The scriptures tell us who we are: sinners, forgiven and forgiving. We are the children of God, intimate with the Holy, nonviolently resisting evil while bringing the kingdom of justice, lasting peace, and the possibility of mercy to the world. We are commanded to go forth with this news, to tell the stories of hope that are already true because of the incarnation, crucifixion, death, and resurrection of Jesus. We conspire with the Spirit of God to draw the world into the arms of the Father. We remember what sin and evil have done and can do, and stand under the word, intent on repairing the world and atoning for all sin. The scriptures make us people who continue to believe and to make the story come true in our own lives.

The community tells the story and becomes the story just as Jesus became the message. Ethics are prior to actions and serve as the basis for answering practical questions. What shall we do? is the core of the church's response to the message and life of Jesus as well as the individual's response to baptism. In relation to the world, Paul VI wrote in 1971:

> In the face of such widely varying situations it is difficult for us to utter a unified message and to put forward a solution which has universal validity. Such is not our ambition, nor is it our mission. It is up to the Christian communities to analyze with objectivity the situation which is proper to their own country, to shed on it the light of the Gospel's unalterable words, and to draw principles of reflection, norms of judgment and directives for action from the social teaching of the church.[7]

Ethical decision-making entails the community, scripture, history, tradition, and the magisterium of the church, the witness and testimony of the prophets, and the personal conscience of the believers. We are called to be disciples, to change our hearts, and to live alternatives of hope in history, in our communities. This is fundamental to our identities. We are followers of the Way, the way of life rather than the way of death, the way of the Spirit in the world. This is what we celebrate in liturgy and in the sacraments, because this is what we practice in our lives. Without living the Way, the rites of justice, and the life of the Spirit, our liturgy and sacraments are hollow or, worse, hypocritical.

Jesus' own words vividly describe who we are and how we are to live: "I solemnly assure you, the one who has faith in me will do the works that I do, and greater far than these" (Jn 14:12, *NAB*). Our times call for a response of Spirit and grace to the crying needs of individuals and the world. We must begin with ourselves, our parishes, and our communities with the words of Jesus: Repent, reform, change your lives, bend your hearts. There is a story told of a German woman who hid Jews during the Second World War. When her friends found out what she was doing, they said: "Don't you realize that if you are discovered you yourself will be imprisoned, perhaps even executed?" The woman said evenly: "Yes, I know that." "Then why in heaven's name," they asked, "are you doing it?" And she replied simply: "Because the time is now and I am here."

The time is now and we are here—the future of the church depends on each of us, each of our communities, responding in the power of the Spirit, under the challenge of the scripture, with the support of other communities, to the realities of our times. No less is asked of us, and no more. Our liturgy and our sacraments have within them the power and possibility for mystery, holiness, and righteousness. What we do or do not do in the immediate future will say a great deal to our children and to the earth. We must have something hopeful and freeing to say to them. We must offer ethical responses to the demands of our day. If we are to follow Jesus so that others can see and take heart, we must begin again at the beginning, as novices, new Christians, followers of the Way.

The scriptures describe us, teach us, exhort us, reform us, announce forgiveness and good news, and reveal to us the meaning of the sacraments and liturgy.

> It is not ourselves we preach, but Christ Jesus as Lord; and for Jesus' sake we became your servants. God who said: "Let the light shine out of darkness," has also made the light shine in our hearts to radiate and to make known the Glory of God, as it shines in the face of Christ.
>
> However, we carry this treasure in vessels of clay, so that this all-surpassing power may not be seen as ours but as God's. Trials of every sort come to us, but we are not discouraged. We are left without answer, but do not despair; persecuted but not abandoned, knocked down but not crushed. We carry everywhere in our person the death of Jesus, so that the life of Jesus may also be manifested in us. For we, the living, are given up continually to death for the sake of Jesus, so that the life of Jesus may appear in our mortal existence. And as death is at work in us, life comes to you.
>
> We have received the same spirit of faith referred to in Scripture that says: "I believed and so I spoke." We also believe and so we speak: We know that He who raised the Lord Jesus will also raise us with Jesus and bring us, with you, into his presence. Finally, everything is for your good, so that grace will come more abundantly upon you and great will be the thanksgiving for the glory of God (2 Cor 4:5-15).

We are called to be no less than the glory of God shining on the face of Christ. We are called to celebrate in our sacraments, liturgy, behavior, persons, and communities the injunction of the prophet Micah: "Do justice, love tenderly and walk humbly with your God" (Mi 6:8). The only way we can do this is to approach the scriptures as reverently as the eucharist; to gather around the word in community, to search its meaning, and to allow it to resound in our minds and in our lives. The word is core to all the sacraments, to the celebration of the liturgy, and to our daily lives as believers.

The universal church over the last forty or more years has been drawn to the study of the word in small groups, listening to it for conversion of heart and conversion of life, both individually and as communities of justice and mercy. Such groups are called base Christian communities, ecclesial Christian communities, and their leaders are called delegates of the word. Perhaps the Spirit is urging the church to acknowledge the power of the word in these communities of believers, its strength as life-line and source of hope for Christians when it is proclaimed aloud and taken to heart together. The word of God to the poor is a sacrament that should be celebrated and honored not only in the context of the sacra-ments and liturgy, but as a sacrament as powerful and revelatory as the body of Christ. We break open the word and chew on it and we break the bread of eucharist and chew on it to become in word and flesh the body of Christ for the world.

✢ Once upon a time a sculptor was chipping away at a huge block of marble. Two young children, a boy and a girl, watched him work for many weeks. They stood silently and were amazed when finally a magnificent lion emerged from the stone and stood towering over them. They ran to him excitedly, their eyes wide with wonder and asked: "How did you know that there was a lion hidden in that rock?"

The sculptor laughed and thought to himself, How do I tell them that I had to know the lion before I knew the marble stone and what it hid? But he looked at the children and said: "I was very quiet when I first started and listened to the stone and I heard the lion roaring inside. Then I chipped away at everything that wasn't the lion and set him free!"

The scriptures tell us of the Lion of Judah, and that we are all the lion's children, but the word makes us remember who we are and re-minds us how to roar, sets us free, and shows us how we can bring wide-eyed wonder to the world we dwell in. We must know the word and be known by it. It must be in our mouths, in our communities, before it can be let loose in the world. It must chip away at all that is not of God and form us daily. It is the undergirding of all the sacraments and liturgy. The word of the Lord is the sacrament of the Word, Jesus; it is good news to the poor, the body of Christ. If we are to be this word enfleshed, if it is to shine radiantly on our faces and be the source of conversion in our communities, we must celebrate it and take it to heart as food for our minds, hearts, and souls. "Remember" sends us first back into the scriptures and then, after listening and being "re-membered," we are sent into the world to preach the word, to be good news, and to practice the ethic of Jesus that is now incarnated in our flesh. Then when others see us, they too can remember, catching an echo and a glimpse of the word, which is both a two-edged sword and as sweet as honey on the tongue of believers.

We end as we have begun, with the word of the Lord:

Listen to what Yahweh said to me, "Stand up, let the mountains hear your claim, and the hills listen to your plea."

Hear, O mountains, Yahweh's complaint! Foundations of the earth, pay attention! For Yahweh has a case against his people, and will argue it with Israel.

"O my people, what have I done to you? In what way have I been a burden to you? Answer me.

I brought you out of Egypt; I rescued you from the land of bondage; I sent Moses, Aaron and Miriam to lead you.

O my people, remember . . . remember your journey . . . and how you have come to know Yahweh's righteous paths."

"What shall I bring when I come to Yahweh and bow down before God the most high? Shall I come with burnt offerings, with sacrifices of yearling calves? Will Yahweh be pleased with thousands of rams, with an overabundance of oil libations? Should I offer my firstborn for my sins, the fruit of my body for my wrongdoing?"

You have been told, O children of the earth, what is good and what Yahweh requires of you: to do justice, to love mercy, and to walk humbly with your God (Mi 6:1-8).

11

The Liturgy

Do Justice in Word and Bread

There is a marvelous old Jewish story called "Joseph Who Loved The Sabbath" based on eight lines of Aramaic in the Babylonian Talmud, which ends with "He who lends to the Sabbath, the Sabbath repays him."[1]

✢ Once upon a time there was a poor man who worked hard all week. He waited all week for one day, the Sabbath. All week he slaved so that he could buy good things to celebrate the Sabbath. His name was Joseph. In fact, everyone called him Joseph who loves the Sabbath.

Joseph worked for a wealthy landowner, a mean-spirited, greedy man named Sorab. Joseph sweated in the fields, planted the seeds, harvested the crops, milked the animals, pressed the oil, picked the grapes, and took care of Sorab's household. For all that Sorab paid him a pittance.

After many years Joseph asked for more, saying it was necessary and just, because he worked so hard all week. But Sorab laughed and wouldn't hear of it. He would sit in the shade, sip his cool drink and say, "Oh, it's hot today," as he watched Joseph work in the sun.

Still Joseph worked all week to remember the Sabbath. As soon as he was done on Friday afternoon, he raced home to his small house, quickly putting it in order and cleaning it. He ran out to the market to buy what was needed to celebrate the Sabbath. He bought only the best, the freshest. He went from stall to stall, looking intently, choosing oil, flour, candles, wine. He would pick a plump fresh chicken or a freshly caught fish. He paid high. A merchant might ask others near him, "Is this a wealthy man?" And one of Joseph's old friends in the market would laugh and call back: "No, that's just Joseph. He loves the Sabbath!"

Then Joseph would go home, change out of his work clothes, and put on his best shirt and gather his tallit (prayer shawl). He set his house to welcome the Sabbath, fixing the bread and wine, cooking the fish or chicken, and, as the stars rose in the sky, he would light the candles and sing. That night he would sing the psalms, read the scriptures, and meditate. He would have a bit of wine, toast the Almighty, eat some bread, enjoy his meal, and sing the hymns of praise and adoration, thanking God, blessed be His Name. Then he would sleep. The next day he would share what was left of his meal with others: people from the market stalls, other families who worked as hard as he did all week, and strangers. Together they would sing the songs of freedom and read the stories of Exodus, eat, play with the children, and enjoy the Sabbath rest. And then, as the stars again rose in the sky, Joseph would reluctantly put away his candlesticks and tallit, sing a last song, and go to sleep to face the week ahead. The Sabbath was over for another week.

This was Joseph's life, week after week, year after year. Nothing changed. No matter how hard Joseph worked, Sorab only paid him his pittance. And Joseph waited for Sabbath and celebrated, reluctant to let go of the day of rest and *shalom*.

But then one night Sorab had a dream. An angel with bright wings, huge and awesome, came to him and sang: "Sorab! Sorab! All you have, your house and lands, have come to you from Joseph's hands. Before this month's full moon grows dim, all you have will belong to him!" The angel sang it over and over. Sorab woke up sweating and shaking. No! Never would that happen.

But as the hours passed he calmed down and forgot it; after all, it was just a dream. But the next night the angel came again and sang all night. Sorab was shaken and upset. He worried about it all day, wondering what to do. Again the third night the angel came and sang over and over: "Sorab! Sorab! All you have, your house and lands, have come to you from Joseph's hands. Before this month's full moon grows dim, all you have will belong to him!" Sorab awoke cursing and yelling, "No! Never!"

That morning Sorab set off into town and sold his house, lands, estates, animals, harvest, even his slaves, for a huge amount of money. He then bought a ticket to another land, where he had friends and business associates. He would be able to live in peace and not worry about singing angels and the specter of Joseph. Then, realizing he couldn't carry all this money with him, he went to a jeweler. He looked at all the great stones: diamonds, sapphires, emeralds, rubies, opals. They were stunning and exquisite. Finally he settled on a large bright red ruby and had it sewn into the folds of his turban. He was set. That very night on board ship, as the moon waned above him, he sailed out to find his new life. He shook his finger at the sky and cried out: "Never, never will Joseph get what I own, the moon can wane and dreams can sing, but I go now to better things." And the ship sailed.

The next morning Joseph came to work as he always did to find out that he had a new master and that life had changed. But he still worked hard for a small pittance and hungered for the Sabbath to come so that he could pray and rest and feast with his friends and neighbors. Out on the sea Sorab's ship ran into a storm, a terrible one, and those on board prayed for their lives. In the midst of the waves crashing and the wind furiously blowing Sorab went overboard, never to be seen again. But it would be years before word of his death came again to his homeland.

Joseph labored, and the Sabbath came again. He ran home as always, cleaned his house, went to the market, bought fresh oil and flour, long tapers, and a bit of herbs and seasonings. Then he rushed from stall to stall to find a succulent chicken or fish for his Sabbath meal. As he passed the fish stall, the vendor cried out: "Joseph! Joseph! Look what I have for you! A great fish, fresh. Your friend Judith told me to save it for you. It's perfect for this Sabbath." Joseph agreed and bought the fish. Home he went, to make his bread, cook his fish, and change his clothes. The stars rose in the sky and found Joseph praying, singing, and chanting the psalms and praise of God, nibbling on a bit of bread, blessing the wine cup, and reading the scriptures, remembering all that God, blessed be His Name, had done for all God's people. Then he ate his dinner, savoring the bread and fish and wine, and lo and behold! what should he find but a stone, a large, bright, shining ruby, inside the belly of his fish! He couldn't believe his eyes. He put the stone aside and continued with his prayers and psalms and slept well that night, full of dreams of angels and ships and all his friends and neighbors feasting.

The next morning he gathered with his friends, the people from the market stalls, strangers, and the children, and they prayed, studied the Torah together, played, and sang ancient melodies of thanksgiving and praise as the day slipped away. The stars rose in the sky and everyone went home. Joseph put away his tallit and prepared to go back to work again.

But the next morning he took his stone and went to the market place and sold it to the jeweler for just enough money to buy Sorab's lands, estates, animals, and servants. Then he worked hard all week. Sabbath came, and he went quickly to the market to buy candles, wine, flour, oil, herbs and spices, a white tablecloth, and many fish and chickens. He ran home and quickly cooked everything and made many loaves of bread. Then, as the stars rose, he sat quietly, wrapped in his prayer shawl and good clothes, and prayed, pouring over the Torah portions, singing the goodness of God, blessed be His Name, and went to sleep.

The next morning the word spread and all gathered at Joseph's house: his friends and neighbors, workers from the market stalls, the jeweler, strangers from the street, those passing through town. All feasted at Joseph's table. Joseph who loved the Sabbath told the story of the ruby in his Sabbath fish and how generous and good God is, blessed be His Name.

They say that everyone was welcome and treated justly at Joseph's house, and there was always something extra for the children and the beggars and the strangers from the street. Joseph still loved the Sabbath. He worked hard all week, but he couldn't wait to honor the Sabbath and tell the stories of what God had done for God's people. Joseph who loved the Sabbath was always grateful and always full of joy.

The story is grand and simple, filled with truth. It is a story about justice, about the worship of God, and about God's care for the poor, as well as care for the poor by the poor, which honors God. It is about giving thanks and a way of life that is daily gathered up and given to God on the Sabbath. The story is about rest, prayer, contemplation, reflection, word, thanksgiving, and eating both alone and with others as celebration. But it is also about remembering what God has done, is doing, and still wants to do for God's people and for putting the world back together again the way it's supposed to be, the way God created it to be. It reminds us that everything is connected: the fish, the sea, the ruby, dreams of angels and the spirit world, the moon, weather, neighbors, friends, the poor and the rich, work and rest, children, and food. They form intimate relationships, whether we are conscious of those ties or not, or, like Sorab, resistant to them and intent on severing them so that we can escape responsibility and community. The story sings of only the best for God and only the best for the poor, saying that the way we work, spend money, and worship, as well as do justice and charity, is all one piece. Fasting, feasting, praying, singing, celebrating, especially with others, are ways to share God with one another. Our Sabbath, our eucharist of word and food, is not so different from Joseph's.

There are, at root, five elements that are needed for liturgy. In the order of importance and meaning they are the people, the bread and wine, the word, a collection for the poor, and a priest. Liturgy, the worship of our God, is the work of the people, our primary work all week, which culminates on Sunday when we gather. We sign ourselves with the cross and welcome one another with peace and begin by telling the stories of the presence of Jesus the Christ with us, risen and glorious, and of the great acts the Spirit continues to do in those who believe. We break open the word and break open our lives, break open our communities in reflection, song, and exhortation. We ask for forgiveness and recommit ourselves to the word of hope, the good news, as the substance of our living alone and together. Then we stand on our words of belief in the creed and offer our words, lives, bodies and souls, hearts and dreams, communities, resources, and even our lacks and sins as gifts to be transformed and given back to us by God. Then we tell the story again, the story of what the Father has done for us in Jesus through the power of the Spirit, and we call down that Spirit on our gifts of bread and wine and our offering for the poor. We break our bread and share our wine, and we break open our lives so that God can rush in with forgiveness, peace, hope, and life. Then the doors are broken open and we rush out to be word to others, to tell the story and let it come true in us, to be the bread, to be the wine, to be the body of Christ for a hungry, yearning world—to do justice and walk humbly with our God. We "do this and remember." We remember God, who we are, what we promised in our baptism, and God's covenant with us. We remember and make Jesus present in the community that gathers, in the word proclaimed, in the offerings and gifts given for the needy, in the bread and wine and eucharist, which is the gift returned to us. The liturgy overflows with the presence of the risen Lord, and we seep out into the world like leaven in bread, like balm for all pain and sorrow, like abiding peace with justice, like glory's radiant reflection.

The liturgy reminds us that we are known by the stories we tell and the company we keep. The word *company* is that used to describe those who became disciples of Jesus, "going off in his company." It is a rich and dense word, with the root meaning "to break bread together," "to share and eat together." But in our society and culture it also is an economic term. We are known by those we eat with, what we do with our money, and the stories we tell that come true in our lives, relationships, and structures. This storytelling and sharing of a meal reconcile us and forgive us, heal us and strengthen us. Among those who pass the cup and the bread, and share the word, there can be no divisions, only communion, only walking together again. We grasp hold of hope in the word of God and in the bread handed to us. We eat it, become it, and take it outside to share. It is the bread of justice that makes restitution and restores the world and our own lives, broken by sin and evil and injustice.

There are many images of eucharist. One that recurs is that of the beggar. We are all beggars in the presence of God, and so beggars are to be treated with special care and tenderness. Charles Peguy says: "Oh, if only we'd remember that before God we are all equal—begging with empty bowls." Those who went home from Jesus' feeding of the four and five thousand went home filled. The disciples picked up the leftovers. What did they do with them? Who got them? Did children, the old, the sick, and people who had never met each other before take them? Leftovers—the food of the poor.

We are the leftovers of God's feasting. We are a meal shared, bread blessed and broken, and wine drunk together, passed around. We become what we eat, and others feed on us, just as we feed on God. Liturgy is a celebration of resurrection, of the presence of the risen Lord, and a hint of God's coming in glory again. It is service, another way of washing feet, of bending before one another, of committing ourselves to the practice of the corporal works of mercy, of suffering with and for one another. It is memory—"Do this." Like the woman in the gospel, we too will be remembered for what we do for the poor, for those facing suffering and death, for God. It is thanksgiving. Eucharist means gratitude poured out, given away, yet it always is returned to us, a lifestyle of bending before God and one another because of the Incarnation and all that God does for us. It makes the story come true. It is the telling of the truth that constitutes who we are and our relationships in the Trinity and in community; it reconstitutes us in forgiveness and mercy.

The liturgy is full of words and full of stories, invitations, petitions and prayers. But it is also silence, what is between the words. Its attitudes and gestures speak volumes. Just as in John's gospel, the word is presented most clearly by acting it out, by Jesus presenting himself as a slave before his disciples, kneeling before them and washing their feet. Liturgy is a "feet-first" way of life. It is anonymous service, with bent head and shoulders, concentrating on the feet of others. It is giving because of others' need and our own gratitude for what has been shared so fully with us. This is our worship: doing for and with others what we would like to do for God, because God keeps doing marvelous things for us. It is the place too where God hungers for us, where Jesus reminds us how to hunger and thirst for justice. The liturgy makes community. We need others to tell the stories, to listen with, to make dreams flesh, to pass the word on to. As Paul said, "I pass on to you exactly what I heard and was given" (1 Cor 11:23, *NAB*).

The words of Jesus, these words of our tradition, remake the world and refashion us in the image of the crucified and risen One, the compassionate One, son of God, our brother. This is our family, and we feed on dreams, eat together, and become what we proclaim, so that others may come to gather with us. There is always room at the table for more, and God comes in the guise of the stranger, the poor, the outcast, the forgotten, the beggar, the prophet. The way we eat at liturgy and the way we eat daily reveal who we are and how we worship. Our liturgical ritual only extends what is already happening. When we gather, God rests with us and listens to us tell God's stories and our own, and God remembers us and puts the world back together as it was in the beginning, is becoming now, and will be forever. This is what puts flesh and blood on our bones and breathes spirit and life into us, so we can get up from the table and go forth together, sent into the world by Jesus, as the Father sent him to us, spirited, fed, at peace, and in communion.

An old story from India tells it well:

✝   Once upon a time there was a good man. He was a hunter and good at it. He fed his family, his relations, and many poor and needy people, and sometimes he sold the leftovers in the market so that he could get other things for his family. One day when he was out hunting he saw something most unusual. He came upon a fox with only two legs. He had heard of foxes like this one, and he wondered how it had managed to survive. It could barely drag itself around. How could it hunt? Was it alone? The stories told of foxes that loved their freedom so dearly that if they were caught in a steel trap they would chew their leg off to get free. He stood and watched this fox, amazed. It had chewed itself free twice and was still alive.

As the hunter mused over the determination of the fox, he was startled to see a tiger come out of the forest into the clearing. It was dragging a half-eaten carcass of a deer. It had obviously eaten its fill and now left the carcass for the fox to eat. The hunter had never seen anything like this before in his life. Were the animals so careful of each other that they tended to the needs of the weaker and the lame? The fox ate its fill and dragged himself off, leaving the rest of the carcass for the smaller animals to finish. Nothing was wasted. The man thought about this for a long time.

Even when he went home, it weighed on his mind. He was a very religious man and was sure that God was trying to tell him something. He went back to the forest the next day and hid, looking for the fox and the tiger to see if it would happen once again. He learned over days and weeks that it did, but only as needed, only when the fox was hungry. He was sure now that God was teaching him a great wisdom and truth. He prayed and thought and finally decided that he must learn the ways of the animals, especially of the fox: how to trust a natural enemy; how to trust that God would take care of him; how to wait for another to give to him. It was very hard. It did not come easily to the man.

He stopped hunting. No longer did he bring food home to his family and relations, his neighbors and the poor. He became poorer, along with his family and others. His wife begged him to go hunting, and he looked at her sadly, knowing that he couldn't and thinking that he couldn't explain to her what he saw in the forest. She would never believe him, yet he knew from his reflection and prayer that God was teaching him. Eventually his wife and children left him so that they could find something to eat, a way to live without him. Others shied away from him, wondering what had happened to him.

He grew weaker and weaker without food and prayed earnestly to know what to do. He worked at trust and being open to what others might bring. He came close to death. At the very end an angel came to him. He was overjoyed and heartened to see this presence of light before him. The angel looked at him long and hard and said: "Why are you so stupid? Why aren't you hunting and taking care of others? You were given a vision of what you were doing and should do, that all should do. Get up and stop thinking of yourself as the fox. Remember: you are the tiger!"

The liturgy reminds us to stop thinking of ourselves as the needy ones but to see we are the tigers! It reminds us to feed the lame and lost, the suffering, those aching for freedom and a life lived with others. God provides for us with lavish gifts; the body and blood of Jesus. We, children of this God who remains with us as food, are to do the same and let others feed on us. We are all tigers for the foxes and the folk of the world. Remember! "Do this and remember me!"

Notes

1 Jesus, the Ethic of Christians

1. James Gaffney, *Newness of Life: A Modern Introduction to Catholic Ethics* (Ramsey, N.J.: Paulist Press, 1979), p. 66.
2. Richard M. Gula., S.S., *What Are They Saying about Moral Norms?* (Ramsey, N.J.: Paulist Press, 1981), p. 7.
3. Rudolf Schnackenberg, quoted in Gula, p. 7.
4. James Gustafson, *Christ and the Moral Life* (New York: Harper & Row, 1968), pp. 264-65.
5. Walter M. Abbott, S.J., ed., *Documents of Vatican II* (New York: The America Press, 1966), pp. 15, 23.
6. Jacques Maritain, quoted in Thomas Merton, *Conjectures of a Guilty Bystander* (New York: Doubleday, 1968), p. 244.
7. Ibid., pp. 174-75.
8. Ibid., pp. 109-11.
9. Annie Dillard, *Holy the Firm* (New York: HarperCollins, 1988), p. 59.
10. Ibid., pp. 56-57.

2 The Church, the World, and the Kingdom

1. Walter M. Abbott, S.J., ed., *Documents of Vatican II* (New York: The America Press, 1966).
2. John Paul II, homily in Santo Domingo in 1984.
3. Vincent J. Donovan, *Christianity Rediscovered* (Maryknoll, N.Y.: Orbis Books, 1978), pp. 81-83.
4. C. S. Song, *Tell Us Our Names: Story Theology from an Asian Perspective* (Maryknoll, N.Y.: Orbis Books, 1984), pp. 39-40.
5. C. Humphreys, ed., *The Wisdom of Buddhism* (London: Curson, 1979), p. 135.
6. "Open Secret," no. 686, in *Open Secret*, trans. John Moyne and Coleman Barks (Putney, Vermont: Threshold Books, 1984).
7. Excerpted from *Man Alive* by Roy Bonisteel, the interviewer (Toronto: Totem Books, 1982), pp. 52-53.
8. Ignazio Silone, quoted in the *Catholic Worker*, 1981.
9. John Paul II, *Redemptor Hominis* (no. 16.10), in *Proclaiming Justice and Peace: Documents from John XXIII and John Paul II*, ed. Michael Walsh and Brian Davies (Mystic, Conn.: Twenty-Third Publications, 1984), p. 254.
10. Leonardo Boff, author's notes from an interview.
11. See notes on the document in Abbott, pp. 309-18.

12. Thomas Merton, *Contemplation in a World of Action* (Garden City, N.Y.: Doubleday, 1971), pp. 143-56; this article originally appeared in *Commonwealth Magazine* in 1966.

13. Matthew Lamb, *Solidarity with Victims: Toward a Theology of Social Transformation* (New York: Crossroad, 1982), p. 3.

14. *Justice in the World*, in *The Gospel of Peace and Justice: Catholic Social Teaching since Pope John*, ed. Joseph Gremillion (Maryknoll, N.Y.: Orbis Books, 1976), p. 514.

15. Peter Henriot, "Social Sin and Conversion: A Theology of the Church's Social Involvement," in *Conversion: Perspectives on Personal and Social Transformation*, ed. Walter E. Conn (New York: Alba House, 1978), p. 319.

16. Lamb, p. 1.

17. Enid Dinnis, *The Anchorhold* (London and Edinburgh: Sands & Co., 1923), p. 45.

18. Stanley A. Hauerwas, *The Peaceable Kingdom: A Primer in Christian Ethics* (Notre Dame, Ind.: University of Notre Dame Press, 1983), pp. 99-100.

19. Ibid., p. 101.

20. Donovan, p. 125.

21. Pierre Teilhard de Chardin, "A Prayer Over the World," *Hymn of the Universe* (New York: Harper & Row, 1968), pp. 103-4.

3   Rites of Initiation

1. For general background reading, see Joseph Martos, *Doors to the Sacred: A Historical Introduction to the Sacraments in the Catholic Church* (New York: Doubleday and Co., 1981), pp. 161-203 (particularly useful for historical issues of development and some indication of pastoral problems); *Made, Not Born, New Perspectives on Christian Initiation and the Catechumenate* (Notre Dame, Ind.: University of Notre Dame, Murphy Center for Liturgical Research, 1975); Gunther Bornkamm, *Early Christian Experience* (New York: Harper & Row, 1966).

2. Stanley A. Hauerwas, *The Peaceable Kingdom: A Primer in Christian Ethics* (Notre Dame, Ind.: University of Notre Dame Press, 1983), pp. 107-8.

3. Ibid., p. 132.

4. For the Rite of Christian Initiation of Adults (RCIA), see *The Rites* (Collegeville, Minn.: Liturgical Press, 1976).

5. It is this last stage that we often in practice call the RCIA as it is celebrated today. It usually lasts about nine months, from September to Easter in a given year, with a great deal of the ritual, the teaching, and the connecting to the community taking place in Lent.

6. Nikos Kazantzakis, *Report to Greco* (New York: Touchstone, 1975), frontispiece.

7. Ibid., p. 234.

8. Ibid., p. 391.

9. Ibid., p. 480.

10. Joseph Bernardin, talk given at Fordham University, December 6, 1983.

11. Origen, *Contra Celsum*, quoted in Margaret Quigley and Michael Garvey, eds., *The Dorothy Day Book* (Springfield, Ill.: Templegate, 1982), p. 43.

12. Bernardin, talk at Fordham.

13. Kazantzakis, pp. 87-88.

14. Unless otherwise specified, all prayers are from the RCIA.

4 Confirmation

1. Bernardin Schellenberger, *Nomad of the Spirit: Reflections of a Young Monastic* (New York: Crossroad, 1981), p. 12.

2. Ibid., p. 23.

3. Ibid., pp. 34-35.

4. Ibid., p. 37.

5. Ibid., p. 40.

6. "For the Rites of Christian Initiation of Adults (RCIA)," *The Rites*, vol. 1 (Collegeville, Minn.: Liturgical Press, 1976), p. 307.

7. Madeleine L'Engle, *Walking on Water: Reflections on Faith and Art* (Wheaton, Ill.: Shaw Publishing, 1980), p. 96.

8. Dorothy Day, *Catholic Worker*, early 1962.

9. Thomas Merton, *Conjectures of a Guilty Bystander* (New York: Doubleday, 1968), p. 165.

10. Ibid., pp. 178, 184, 348.

11. Abraham Heschel, *The Prophets* (New York: Harper & Row; Philadelphia: The Jewish Publication Society of America, 1962), p. 4.

12. My notes from a talk given by Elie Wiesel.

13. Nadezhda Mandelstam, *Hope against Hope: A Memoir* (New York: Macmillan, 1976), pp. 42-43.

14. Dalai Lama and Tenzin Gyatso, *My Land and My People* (New York: Potala Corp., 1983).

15. Etty Hillesum, *An Interrupted Life: The Diaries of Etty Hillesum* (New York: Pantheon Books, 1991).

16. Ibid., pp. 113, 142, 151, 152, 165, 190, 195.

17. Schellenberger, pp. 82-83.

18. Jürgen Moltmann, *The Church in the Power of the Spirit: A Contribution to Messianic Ecclesiology*, trans. Margaret Kohl (Minneapolis: Fortress, 1993), p. 279.

19. John F. Skinner, *The Christian Disciple* (Lanham, Md.: University Press of America, 1984), pp. 39-44.

20. Ibid., pp. 45-52.

21. Ibid., p. 52.

22. Audre Lorde, *Sister Outsider: Essays and Speeches* (Trumansburg, N.Y.: Crossing Press, 1984), pp. 40-41.

23. Ibid., pp. 42-44.

24. Hermann Vinke, *The Short Life of Sophie Scholl* (New York: Harper & Row, 1980).

25. Sheila Cassidy, *Audacity to Believe: An Autobiography* (New York/London: HarperCollins, 1977).

26. Nikos Kazantzakis, *Report to Greco* (New York: Touchstone, 1975), pp. 508-12.

5   The Eucharist

1. C. S. Song, *Tell Us Our Names: Story Theology from an Asian Perspective* (Maryknoll, N.Y.: Orbis Books, 1984), pp. 41-42.

2. Kim Chi Ha, "Declaration of Conscience," *The Gold-Crowned Jesus and Other Writings* (Maryknoll, N.Y.: Orbis Books, 1978), p. 30.

3. I saw this poem on a poster in Black Oaks Books in Berkeley, California, many years ago.

4. Monika Hellwig, *The Eucharist and the Hunger of the World* (New York: Paulist, 1976), pp. 32-33.

5. Gustavo Gutiérrez, *A Theology of Liberation* (Maryknoll, N.Y.: Orbis Books, 1988), p. 150.

6. St. Augustine.

7. *Dorothy Day: Selected Writings*, ed. Robert Ellsberg (Maryknoll, N.Y.: Orbis Books, 1992), p. 330.

8. *Fun Unzer Alter Otzer*, II, p. 9.

9. *Darkai Chayim* (1962), p. 137.

10. Religious Society of Friends, *Book of Discipline* (Philadelphia, 1927).

11. *Connection Newsletter* 3 (January 1981), Canada.

12. Interview, *Ground Zero Newsletter* (November/December 1983), pp. 2-4.

13. Mark Fitzgerald, "Hunger in America," *America* (December 29, 1984), p. 444.

14. Jeannette Easley, correspondence with author in 1982-83.

15. Gutiérrez, p. 118.

16. Hellwig, p. 46.

17. Ibid., p. 47.

6   Reconciliation

1. I recommend the following books on reconciliation: Jim Douglass, *The Nonviolent Cross: A Theology of Revolution and Peace* (New York: Macmillan, 1966); Jim Douglass, *Lightning East to West* (Portland, Ore.: Sunburst Press, 1981; reprinted Mahwah, N.J.: Paulist Press, 1984); John Dear, *The God of Peace: Toward a Theology of Nonviolence* (Maryknoll, N.Y.: Orbis Books, 1994), esp. pp. 18-29.

2. Oscar Romero and Bishop Rivera y Damas, "The Church and Popular Political Organization," August 6, 1978.

3. Jonathan Jacoby and Daniel Hirsch, *Judaism and Non-violence* (Fellowship of Reconciliation).

4. Virgil Elizondo, in *Church and Peace*, ed. Virgil Elizondo and Norbert Greinacher, Concilium 164 (New York: Seabury Press, 1983).

5. "Address of His Holiness Paul VI to the General Assembly of the United Nations," in *The Gospel of Peace and Justice*, ed. Joseph Gremillion (Maryknoll, N.Y.: Orbis Books, 1976), p. 384.

6. From a card published by the Fellowship of the Reconciliation.

7. Elie Wiesel, *Beggar in Jerusalem* (New York: Schocken, 1989), p. 138.

8. Ibid., pp. 56-57.

9. John Howard Yoder, from *The Christian and Capital Punishment* (Newton, Kan.: Faith and Life Press, 1961).

10. Thich Nhat Hanh, from a talk published in *Agape* (Spring 1983). *Agape* is the newsletter of the Bethany House Catholic Worker in Rochester, New York.

11. Daniel Berrigan, "A Prayer for Repentance," from a prayer service (1970s).

7   Anointing and Pastoral Care of the Sick

1. I used a version of this story in *Lent: Stories and Reflections on the Sunday Readings* (Maryknoll, N.Y.: Orbis Books, 1997) to illustrate how we commit our lives to God.

2. Donald McNeill, Douglas Morrison, and Henri Nouwen, *Compassion: A Reflection on the Christian Life* (New York: Doubleday, 1982), pp. 16-17.

3. Charles Gusmer, *And You Visited Me: Sacramental Ministry to the Sick and Dying* (New York: Pueblo, 1984), p. 6.

4. Ibid., p. 13.

5. Ibid.

6. *Apostolic Constitution on the Sacrament of the Anointing of the Sick* (November 30, 1972), in *The Rites of the Catholic Church: The Roman Ritual revised by Decree of the Second Batican Ecumenical Council and Published by Authority of Pope Paul VI*, Vol. 1 (Collegeville, Minn.: Liturgical Press, 1990).

7. David Power, "Let the Sick Man Call," *Heythrop Journal* 19 (1978), p. 262.

8. *Apostolic Constitution on the Sacrament of the Anointing of the Sick*, p. 773.

9. Louis Dupré, *The Deeper Life, an Introduction to Christian Mysticism* (New York: Crossroad, 1981), pp. 63-66.

10. Kim Chi Ha, "The Gold-Crowned Jesus," reprinted in *Sojourners* (April 1979), p. 15.

11. William Stringfellow, *The Politics of Spirituality*, Philadelphia: Westminster, 1984), pp. 69-70.

12. Ibid., p. 84.

13. Daniel Berrigan, *We Die Before We Live: Talking with the Very Ill* (New York: Seabury, 1980), p. 61.

14. Ibid., pp. 75-76.

15. Dorothee Soelle, *Suffering*, trans. Everett R. Kalin (Minneapolis: Fortress, 1975), p. 159.

16. Friedrich Nietzsche, "The Antichrist," *The Portable Nietzsche* (New York: Viking Press, 1954), pp. 1, 571, 589, 651.

17. Martin Buber, *Tales of the Hasidim*, Vol. 2 (New York: Schocken Books, 1947), p. 315.

18. Soelle, *Suffering*, pp. 177-78.

19. Pope John Paul II, Bishops' Committee on the Liturgy, *Newsletter* 18 (1982), pp. 22-23.

20. Douglas V. Steere, *Friends Journal* (November 15, 1984), p. 8.

8 Marriage

1. A. E. Kitov, *The Jew and His Home* (New York: Shengold Pub., 1976).

2. Paul Hoffman, "Jesus' Saying about Divorce and Its Interpretation," *The Future of Marriage as Institution, Concilium* 5, 6 (1970), p. 53.

3. Ibid., p. 65.

4. Ibid., pp. 65-66.

5. Denis O'Callaghan, "Marriage as a Sacrament," *Concilium* 5, 6 (1970), p. 104.

6. Ibid., pp. 104-5.

7. Aelred Squire, *Summer in the Seed* (London: SPCK, 1980), p. 136.

8. Ibid., p. 139.

9. Ibid., p. 140.

10. Cicero, quoted in Squire, p. 146.

11. Aelred of Rievaulx, *On Spiritual Friendship*, quoted in Squire, p. 147.

12. Squire, p. 150.

13. Ibid., pp. 152-53.

14. James Finley, *Merton's Palace of Nowhere* (Notre Dame, Ind.: Ave Maria Press, 1978).

15. A version of this story is found in Paul Reps, *Zen Flesh, Zen Bones* (New York: Doubleday, 1961), pp. 70-71.

16. This version of the story is close to versions found in Spain in the thirteenth century and based on the myth of the exile on the Shekhinah in Zohar 1:202b-203a and "The Lost Princess" from *Sippure Ma'aysiot* by Rabbi Nachman of Bratslar, ed. Rabbi Nathan Sternhartz of Nemirov, Warsaw, 1881. I heard the oral version from Harold Schwartz.

9 Orders for the Sacrament of Foot Washing

1. Vincent J. Donovan, *Christianity Rediscovered* (Maryknoll, N.Y.: Orbis Books, 1978), pp. 151-52.

2. Ibid., pp. 152-53.

3. Ibid., p. 151.

4. "Rite of Ordination," in *The Rites of the Catholic Church: The Roman Ritual revised by Decree of the Second Vatican Ecumenical Council and Published by Authority of Pope Paul VI*, Vol. 2 (Collegeville, Minn.: Liturgical Press, 1990).

5. Edward Schillebeeckx, "A Creative Retrospect," in *Minister, Pastor, Prophet? Grassroots Leadership in the Churches*, ed. Grollenberg et al. (New York: Crossroad, 1981), p. 63.

6. Ibid.

7. Ibid., p. 74.

8. Mary Collins, "The Public Language of Ministry," *Official Ministry in a New Age*, ed. James Provost (Washington, D.C.: Canon Law Society of America, 1981), p. 36.

9. *Lumen Gentium*, nos. 31 and 36, see also nos. 23, 25 and 28, in Walter M. Abbott, S.J., ed., *Documents of Vatican II* (New York: The America Press, 1966).

10. David Power, "The Basis for Official Ministry in the Church," in Provost, p. 62.

11. Joseph Komonchak, "Clergy, Laity and the Church's Mission in the World," in Provost, p. 168.

12. "Pope John Paul II, Opening Address at the Puebla Conference (January 28, 1979)," *Puebla and Beyond*, ed. John Eagleson and Philip Scharper (Maryknoll, N.Y.: Orbis Books, 1979), p. 69.

13. John Paul II, "Address to Priests in Mexico City," *Origins* 8 (1979) pp. 548-49.

14. James Provost, "Toward a Renewed Canonical Understanding of Official Ministry," in Provost, pp. 198-99.

10 Rites: What If . . . ?

1. Francis Sullivan, S.J., *Magisterium: Teaching Authority in the Catholic Church* (New York: Paulist, 1983), p. 185.

2. Ibid., pp. 185-86. DV refers to *Verbum Dei* and LG refers to *Lumen Gentium*.

3. Edward Schillebeeckx, *Ministry: Leadership in the Community of Jesus Christ* (New York: Crossroad, 1981), pp. 30-32.

4. "Lay Catholics in Schools: Witnesses to Faith," *Origins* 12 (1982), pp. 457ff.

5. Joan Chittister, Address to Catholic School Educators, *Origins* 14/4 (1984), pp. 54-55.

6. Daniel Berrigan, *Katallagete* (Spring 1978).

7. Paul VI, *Octogesima Adveniens*, cited in Richard Gula, *What Are They Saying about Moral Norms?* (New York: Paulist, 1982), p. 43.

11 The Liturgy

1. *Tractate Shabbat*, 119A. The story is found in *A Thousand and One Nights* as "The Devout Israelite," and in Emanuel bin Gorion's *Mimekor Yisrl: Classical Jewish Folktales. Note*: I heard this story told once orally and remembered the initial rhyme sequence and outline. I was told that there is a children's book that has many elements of this version.